Teaching Science and Technology in the Early Years (3–7)

Teaching Science and Technology in the Early Years (3–7) celebrates young children's amazing capabilities as scientists, designers and technologists. Research-based yet practical and accessible, it demonstrates how scientific designing and making activities are natural to young children, and have the potential for contributing to all aspects of their learning.

By identifying the scientific and design-related concepts, skills and activities being developed, the book enables the reader to make more focused diagnostic observations of young children and plan for how they can help move them forward in their learning. This second edition has been thoroughly updated and features:

- six new chapters providing practical advice and examples for enhancing scientific and technological learning through thematic approaches;
- a new chapter focusing on the outdoor learning environment and how this can support science and technology;
- new case studies of successful Early Years practice, alongside examples of practical planning for learning, and advice on documenting children's learning stories;
- guidance on the role of talk, narrative, documentation and planning in relation to Early Years science and technology.

Based on the latest research and first-hand experience, this practical and accessible book is essential reading for Early Years and Primary students on undergraduate, PGCE and Masters-level courses.

Dan Davies is Head of Research and Graduate Affairs in the School of Education, Bath Spa University, UK. He is Professor of Science and Technology Education and leads the Centre for Research in Early Scientific Learning (CRESL), which is a Primary Science Teaching Trust Regional Hub.

Alan Howe is Acting Head of the Department of Education and Childhood Studies at Bath Spa University and a founding member of CRESL.

Christopher Collier is a senior lecturer in Primary Science at Bath Spa University and a member of CRESL.

Rebecca Digby is a senior lecturer in Primary and Early Years Education at Bath Spa University and a member of CRESL.

Sarah Earle spent 13 years teaching in primary schools in Bristol before moving to Bath Spa University as a senior lecturer on the Primary PGCE. She is also a member of CRESL.

Kendra McMahon spent 10 years as a primary school teacher in the South West of England before becoming a senior lecturer in Education at Bath Spa University and a founding member of CRESL.

Teaching Science and Technology in the Early Years (3–7)

Second edition

Dan Davies,
Alan Howe, Christopher Collier,
Rebecca Digby, Sarah Earle
and Kendra McMahon

 Routledge
Taylor & Francis Group

LONDON AND NEW YORK

Second edition published 2014
by Routledge
2 Park Square, Milton Park, Abingdon, Oxon OX14 4RN

and by Routledge
711 Third Avenue, New York, NY 10017

Routledge is an imprint of the Taylor & Francis Group, an informa business

First edition published by David Fulton Publishers 2003

British Library Cataloguing in Publication Data
A catalogue record for this book is available from the British Library

Library of Congress Cataloging in Publication Data
Teaching science and technology in the early years (3–7)/
    edited by Dan Davies [and five others]. – Second edition.
    pages cm
    Based on earlier publication: Teaching science, design and
    technology in the early years/Dan Davies & Alan Howe, 2003.
    1. Science – Study and teaching (Early childhood) – Great Britain.
    2. Technology – Study and teaching (Early childhood) – Great
    Britain. 3. Design – Study and teaching (Early childhood) –
    Great Britain. I. Davies, Dan (Daniel John), 1962– II. Davies, Dan
    (Daniel John), 1962– Teaching science, design and technology in
    the early years. Adaptation of (work):
    LB1139.5.S35D38 2014
    372.35—dc23
    2013043285

ISBN: 978-0-415-82558-0 (hbk)
ISBN: 978-0-415-82559-7 (pbk)
ISBN: 978-1-315-77777-1 (ebk)

Typeset in Palatino
by Florence Production Ltd, Stoodleigh, Devon

To all past members of the Bath Spa University Primary and
Early Years Science Team

Contents

Contents

List of figures, tables and learning stories

Figures

Tables

Learning stories and boxes

List of contributors

Pat Black is head of Primary and Early Years Initial Teacher Education at Bath Spa University. She has taught the 4 to 7 age range in a South Gloucestershire primary school and is co-author of a maths programme for Reception/P1 called *Platform One*.

Christopher Collier is a senior lecturer in Primary Science at Bath Spa University where he is joint coordinator of science on the PGCE Primary and Early Years course. He teaches on a number of courses and modules on the PGCE and undergraduate Education Studies programmes, including the university's Early Years part-time course. He is a founding member of the Centre for Research in Early Scientific Learning (CRESL), based at Bath Spa, and is heavily involved in the centre's research activity.

Dan Davies is head of Research and Graduate Affairs in the School of Education, Bath Spa University. He is Professor of Science and Technology Education and leads the CRESL, which is a Primary Science Teaching Trust Regional Hub. He taught in Primary and Early Years classrooms in London before lecturing in Primary science education at Goldsmiths College, University of London.

Rebecca Digby is a senior lecturer in Primary and Early Years Education at Bath Spa University and a member of CRESL. She teaches Early Years modules on the Education Studies undergraduate course and leads International Perspectives on Early Years Education. She has taught Early Years Science on the PGCE training programme and has experience across Primary and Early Years phases in schools in England and Scotland with roles including Advanced Skills Teacher specialising in Science and Creativity, and deputy head teacher.

Sarah Earle spent 13 years teaching in primary schools in Bristol before moving to Bath Spa University as a senior lecturer on the Primary PGCE and a member of CRESL. She has a Masters degree in Science Education and is now carrying out research into science assessment for her PhD. She is reviews editor for the Association for Science Education's (ASE) Primary Science journal and a Primary Science Quality Mark Hubleader.

Lone Hattingh is a senior lecturer in Early Years Education at Bath Spa University. She began her career as an Early Years teacher before lecturing on a range of Early Years courses, including EYPS. Her main research interests are in early childhood literacy, with a particular focus on children's multi-modal representations, including recognising and acknowledging the richness of children's meaning-making practices in the margins of classroom activity.

Alan Howe is acting head of the Department of Education and Childhood Studies at Bath Spa University and a founding member of CRESL. He has taught in a number of primary schools and published widely in the fields of primary science and technology education, including *Science 5–11: A Guide for Teachers* (Routledge, 2009). He has also contributed to a number of books on Early Years education, including *The Excellence of Play*, edited by Janet Moyles.

Sue Hughes is associate head of department, Primary and Early Years, at the University of the West of England. She has taught across the Primary age range in Bristol primary schools and has developed training and resource materials for literacy in both EYFS and Key Stage 1.

Kendra McMahon spent 10 years as a primary school teacher in the South West of England before becoming a senior lecturer in Education at Bath Spa University and a founding member of CRESL. Her research interests include dialogic teaching in science and assessment in science. She led the 'See the science' project about the place of science in Early Years thematic planning and investigated the 'sustained scientific dialogues' funded by the Primary Science Teaching Trust.

Janet Rose is a principal lecturer and award leader for the Early Childhood Education undergraduate and Masters degrees at Bath Spa University. She has over 20 years' experience of working in Early Years education both in England and internationally. She is the co-author of *The Role of the Adult in Early Years Settings* and is currently writing a book on health and well-being in Early Years education. Janet is also a co-opted governor of a Children's Centre in Bristol and a trained Ofsted inspector.

Acknowledgements

Children and staff – particularly Bridget Johnson, Sandy Sheppard and Tonie Scott – at Bishop Henderson C of E Primary School, Coleford, Somerset.

Children and staff at The Red Room Pre-school, Chewton Mendip, Somerset.

Children and staff at Bellefield Primary School, Trowbridge, Wiltshire.

Children and staff at Bath Opportunity Pre-School, Bath.

Children and staff at St Michael's Pre-school and toddler group, Winterbourne, Bristol.

Children and staff at Blagdon Pre-school, Blagdon, North Somerset.

Children and staff – particularly Sue Thorn – at Millbrook Primary School, Swindon.

Children and staff – particularly Nancy Low – at Victoria Park Primary, Bristol.

Children and staff – particularly Emma Oliver – at Puddleduck Hall Nursery, Gloucester.

Children and staff – particularly Julia Holder and Jae Munroe – at St Phillip's Primary School, Bath.

Children and staff at Trinity Primary School in Taunton.

Children and staff at Moorlands Infants School, Bath.

Children and staff – particularly Amy Skuse – at St Martin's Garden School, Bath.

Children and staff at Twerton Infant School, Bath.

Children and staff at Chandag Infants School, Keynsham.

Children and staff – particularly Di Rhodes and Margaret Harrison – at Newbridge Primary School, Bath.

Children and staff – particularly Emma Oliver – at Puddleduck Hall Nursery, Gloucester.

Children and staff – particularly Judy Cooper – at Broad Chalke C of E First School, Wiltshire.

Children and staff – particularly Sue Thorn – at Millbrook Primary, Swindon.

Children and staff – particularly Nicki McBeth – at Batheaston Primary School, Bath.

Children and staff – particularly Katherine Laing – at Lypiatt Primary School and Children's Centre, Wiltshire.

Children and staff – particularly Sue, Cathy, Andrea and Fleur– at Red Beach Primary School near Auckland, New Zealand.

Children and staff – particularly Joanne Hobson and Danieka Rivers – at Point Chevalier Primary School, Auckland.

Children and staff – particularly Heidi Wood and Liz Evans – at Bathampton Primary School.

Children and staff – particularly Angela Millar – at Oak Tree Day Nursery, Bath.

Children and staff at Ashley Down Infant School, Bristol.

Fen Marshall (formerly headteacher at Hawkesbury Upton Primary School, South Gloucestershire).

Trainee-teacher John Paul Sharman.

The Primary Science Teaching Trust, for funding the 'See the science' project, from which many of the learning stories are drawn.

The principles of teaching science and technology in Early Years settings

Introduction

Alan Howe and Dan Davies

Purpose of this chapter

Through reading this chapter, you should gain:

- an introduction to our philosophy of Early Years education;
- an understanding of the ways in which we see science and technology as relevant to the education of young children;
- an appreciation of the structure and contents of this book.

Introduction to the second edition

We first published *Teaching Science and Design and Technology in the Early Years* in 2003, the result of collaboration between Early Years practitioners and tutors at what was then Bath Spa University College. We wrote not out of a desire to see design and technology (D&T) and science 'taught' to young children, but from a concern for a holistic approach to Early Years provision, which includes the sometimes overlooked elements of scientific, design-related and technological development. Since 2003 there have been many changes in Early Years education – a new curriculum in England for the Early Years Foundation Stage (EYFS) (DfE 2012), a growing awareness of the importance of 'sustained shared thinking' (Siraj-Blatchford and Sylva 2004) and documentation of 'learning stories' (Carr and Lee 2012) – which this second edition has incorporated. We have also updated many of the case studies (learning stories) from our research in Early Years settings, including those undertaken as part of our recent 'See the science' project, funded by the Primary Science Teaching Trust. This project, undertaken in six Early Years settings during 2012–13, has helped practitioners to identify the scientific concepts, attitudes and skills that young children are developing through participating in everyday, play-based learning activities. It has also focused upon practitioners' use of talk when intervening to draw out children's scientific learning, by analysing transcripts of discussion to identify the types of questioning and other verbal cues that could be described as 'dialogic' (Alexander 2008) and lead towards sustained shared thinking (see Chapter 3). We have taken the same approach in this book: helping practitioners 'see the science' going on around the setting and providing some suggestions for sensitive interventions to encourage thinking together about our wonderful world!

We have made several other changes in this second edition, including the title. Not only does *Teaching Science and Technology in the Early Years* slip off the tongue a little more easily than the previous version, it reflects the change in status of D&T as a subject in the Primary curriculum over the last decade. Although D&T is mentioned in the latest versions of both the EYFS (DfE 2012) and the National Curriculum (DfE 2013) in England, it is clearly given much less emphasis than when introduced as a subject in 1990. The phrase 'technology education' – which we take to include D&T (see below) – is not only a more internationally recognised term than D&T; it is also broader, more holistic and recognises the increasingly technological lives lived by young children in the second decade of the twenty-first century. Although controversy rages over whether children in Early Years settings should be moving icons around on touchscreens rather than interacting directly with natural materials, we cannot avoid the observation that those growing up in Western affluence are part of the 'iPad generation' – displaying the natural affinity with advanced technology that led Prensky (2001) to describe them as 'digital natives'. Although we do not want our use of 'technology' in this book to be seen as synonymous with 'ICT' (information and communication technology) or 'hi-tech' – it must include children designing and making real things from real materials – we nevertheless feel that to include the phrase 'science and technology' in the title is more holistic and relevant to children's lives than 'science and design and technology', for the reasons we have outlined above.

We have also made changes to the structure of the book, dividing it into two parts. The first half of the book – as in the first edition – deals with the big questions about children's learning, the role of talk, narrative, documentation and planning in relation to Early Years science and technology. It also includes for the first time a chapter specifically devoted to outdoor learning, reflecting the influence of 'forest schools' (Knight 2011) and greater recognition of the importance of the outdoor environment in children's learning. The second half of the book is new, providing practical advice and examples for enhancing scientific and technological learning through thematic approaches. This makes it more of a companion volume to our primary text, *Science 5–11: A Guide for Teachers*, while increasing its usefulness to practitioners and teachers in Key Stage 1 in England, since this section is structured around the main science topics featured in the National Curriculum (DfE 2013). The inclusion of this new section in the book raises two questions: why are we including children aged five to seven in our definition of 'Early Years'? Doesn't the inclusion of specific science topics belie our commitment to holism in young children's learning? In answer to the first of these questions, we have sought to clarify the age-range of children for which the approaches suggested in the book are appropriate in the new title *Teaching Science and Technology in the Early Years (3–7)* for the reasons outlined in the next section. In answer to the second question, we suggest that the contents of Part Two are used flexibly. Certainly, a Year 1 topic on 'what things are made of' could be taught by looking at Chapter 9. However, a Nursery or Reception class practitioner could also use Chapter 9 as a resource of ideas for intervening in children's sand or water play. In other words, the presence of what might be seen as science-specific chapters in Part Two of this book does not imply that it should be taught as a subject in the Early Years.

What do we mean by the Early Years?

In this book we are using the phrase 'Early Years' to refer to children aged between three and seven (i.e. from the start of Nursery education to the end of Key Stage 1 in England). Although this is out of line with the curriculum structure in England – the EYFS covers the age-range zero to five – it does correspond exactly with the Foundation Phase in Wales (Welsh Assembly 2008). We have taken this decision for two main reasons:

1. At the age of three, many children in England and Wales have their first taste of an educational setting outside the home; it is at this point that we can begin to share our understandings and offer advice for enriching children's scientific and technological experiences. Some would argue that the Early Years start from birth, or even conception. We would certainly agree that children have experiences before the age of three that relate to science and technology, such as bathtime, exploring the tactile properties of toys or changing the shape of playdough, but the opportunities for adults to intervene in this process are more limited.

2. At the upper end of our age range we believe that children between the ages of five and seven need the kinds of exploratory, contextualised, meaningful activities characteristic of good practice in Nursery and Reception classes. They are, in our opinion, still in their early years. For some, the early years come to an end when children enter compulsory education; play is put behind them and the 'serious learning' begins. Indeed, there are signs that Key Stage 1 in England has become more formal in recent years, with increasing use of whole-class teaching; the introduction of compulsory teaching of systematic synthetic phonics (Rose 2006) and an associated 'phonics screening check' at the end of Y1 (DfE 2011). Yet in several countries – Sweden for example – children do not begin statutory schooling until they are seven (i.e. at the end of Key Stage 1), and in others (USA, Finland,

Australia) the years from five to seven are described as kindergarten – 'children's garden' – implying an educational ethos more akin to that of Nursery education in the UK. In Piagetian terms, children in these age groups are working within a 'pre-operational' phase of cognitive development and, even if we accept that they are capable of more abstract thinking within meaningful contexts (Donaldson 1978), it can be argued that a child of seven has more in common with a three-year-old than an 11-year-old.

We therefore strongly reject the equating of Early Years with the EYFS in England and support the Welsh definition. Excellent Early Years practice should continue throughout Key Stage 1 and beyond. Characteristics of such practice include a concern for the 'whole child'; the fostering of independence through self-directed activities; attention to issues of inclusion; and the primacy of narrative and verbal interaction in the interventions adults make in children's learning. While government directives on the teaching of reading may have had a formalising influence on many Year 1 classrooms in England, we do not believe that this need extend to the whole curriculum. Science and technology, by their very natures, require exploration, interaction and discussion to be learned effectively. As we argue in Chapter 2, children (and adults) need to retain their capacity for play to be good scientists and technologists!

Why science in Early Years practice?

Science begins with children's very first acts of exploration.

(de Boo 2000: 1)

Science is not a 'subject' in the EYFS curriculum for England. Indeed, until comparatively recently (the 1980s) the term did not feature in Primary education at all and is still absent from the elementary curricula of many countries. This is not to say that science was not, or is not, happening in nurseries, infant classes, playgroups and childminders' and children's homes. Many activities in which young children spontaneously engage are intrinsically scientific, or can be made to be so: blowing bubbles, playing with sand and water, looking at flowers or spiders' webs etc. There are, however, major problems of definition and recognition. As practitioners, our definitions of science are often too narrow, resulting in difficulties recognising where it is going on in our settings.

The images we have of science in the world beyond the classroom will inevitably affect our attitude towards children's scientific activity, and will in turn be transmitted to the children with whom we work (Harlen 2000). A multiplicity of meanings surround the word 'science' in general use:

Science . . . can mean organised knowledge about natural phenomena ('Einstein's theory of relativity was a major contribution to science'), or the thought processes which generate such knowledge ('Discovering the structure of DNA was a triumph of modern science') or as a rubric for a set of disciplines ('Psychology as a science is a century old'); it can also refer to social systems and fields of work and study.

(Gardner 1994: 2)

If, from our own educational experience, we see science as a factual body of knowledge about the world, concerned with laws and formulae and 'discovered' through complex experiments, we will find it difficult to recognise the scientific significance of four-year-olds pushing each other around on wheeled toys. If, on the other hand, we regard scientific knowledge as shifting and tentative – inherently rooted in the 'here and now' of everyday things and events – Early Years science will appear as a natural component of young children's learning and development. Fortunately, many practitioners in England tend to take the latter view; Johnston and Hayed's international study (1995: 8) found that English primary teachers were more likely to subscribe to a 'process-based' model than other nationalities:

> This emphasis may, in part, be due to the English teachers' interpretation of the question 'What do you think science involves?' as 'What do you think school/primary science involves?'

Scientific processes (exploration, observation, asking questions, trying things out) are certainly very important aspects of Early Years science. Indeed, we could argue that the younger the child, the greater the emphasis that needs to be placed on the procedural ('doing') aspect, in comparison with the conceptual ('understanding') components of scientific learning. Not that we would wish to separate these elements; for young children doing is intimately bound up with knowing, and both depend fundamentally upon the development of scientific attitudes. Children's emotional disposition towards learning, and their responses to natural phenomena, can serve as the starting points for developing the attitudes of curiosity, open-mindedness and respect for evidence.

Why technology in Early Years practice?

As we explained above, our definition of technology education reflects its widespread international usage to include both what was previously referred to as ICT in the National Curriculum (now 'computing') and activities in which children design and make things – still called D&T in England. D&T is an educational invention; it does not exist outside school settings, though it relates in some ways to the tasks performed by different types of professional designers, technologists and engineers. Although the term was in use before 1988, it was the National Curriculum Design and Technology Working Group who in their visionary Interim Report (1988: 2) gave it an educational rationale:

> Our use of design and technology as a unitary concept, to be spoken in one breath as it were . . . is intended to emphasise the intimate connection between the two activities as well as to imply a concept which is broader than either design or technology individually and the whole of which we believe is educationally important.

Design and technology – spoken as a singular rather than plural term – is a holistic activity, involving thinking and doing, action and reflection. In this respect it parallels many approaches to Early Years education, including 'HighScope' (Schweinhart et al. 1993) with its emphasis upon the 'plan–do–review' cycle to develop intentionality in children's play. We believe that purposeful making – giving new arrangements to materials, textures, colours, shapes – is central to young children's quests to bring pattern and order to their physical environments. From their earliest manipulations of blocks, food or soft toys, children show themselves to be born designers. They learn to talk about what they are doing – Piaget's 'egocentric' commentary – and to empathise with the needs and wants of others, real or imagined (e.g. 'I'm making a bag for teddy'). The problem for practitioners (as with science) is to unpick our own preconceptions about 'technology' and 'design' so we can begin to recognise the D&T happening under our noses.

Research into primary teachers' beliefs about technology (Jarvis and Rennie 1996) has noted – as in the case of science – the strong influence of models from the school curriculum. Teachers in the study typically cited modern mechanical and electrical products such as computers, telephones and vehicles as 'examples' of technology, with little mention of 'low-tech' examples such as pencils or cups. Food or textiles rarely featured. Design is in some ways even more problematic for non-specialist primary practitioners, who may regard it as a mysterious language couched in the jargon of 'form' and 'function' from which the general public is largely excluded (Davies 1996). Designers tend to be viewed as 'trendy', 'creative' people concerned with style rather than substance, adding labels to products that increase their value in the market place. The ability to draw well is assumed to be part of the activity, which may further alienate teachers who lack confidence in their own drawing skills. It is important that we expand these limited conceptions to embrace the creativity of children's experiences with materials. Young children 'think' with their hands; their learning is profoundly kinaesthetic and the abstraction of 'drawing before you make' may be irrelevant to Early Years practice. We want children to have a rich experience of handling designed artefacts from many cultures, and opportunities to fashion objects of beauty for themselves or others, discussing the decisions they are making as they do so.

Why science and technology together?

As noted above, the word 'science' does not appear in the Statutory Framework for the EYFS (DfE 2012), while 'technology' and 'design and technology' both make a single appearance; the former within the Specific Area of 'Understanding the world', the latter under 'Expressive arts and design'. Hence there is no implied relationship between science and technology in the EYFS, since there is no science! Nevertheless, as the educational disciplines of science and technology are currently constructed, they have certain common qualities and purposes – as well as those that are distinctive – which, as Early Years practitioners, we need to be aware of in order to successfully integrate them into our practice.

In previous writing (Howe et al. 2001) we have identified a number of ways in which the relationship between technology and science in the Primary curriculum might be conceptualised. One alternative – perhaps attractive in the context of Early Years education – is that we might view the two areas as indistinguishable. In a topic on 'ourselves', for example, choosing fabrics to keep us warm might draw upon science and technology as strands of learning within the broader realm of understanding, emotional and social skills being developed. In practice, however, this model can often imply a hierarchy in which science plays the dominant role (Ritchie 2001) and any designing or making activities can be seen as an opportunity for children to 'apply' scientific principles they have learned earlier. This is an approach that in our view can be developmentally inappropriate if it implies a progression from the abstract to the concrete, whereas we know from experience and research that young children need to begin with concrete experiences.

As currently represented in the National Curriculum in England (DfE 2013), the differences between science and technology are more clearly accentuated than their similarities. Indeed, D&T has arguably more in common with art and design than it does with science. This is an example of what Gardner (1994) called a demarcationist model, leading to the establishment of two distinct subjects, with only very limited links between them. This too seems to us an inappropriate approach for Early Years practice; by treating science and technology entirely separately practitioners risk missing out on opportunities for contextualising scientific learning through D&T activities. The development of specific know-ledge in particular contexts – so-called 'situated cognition' (McCormick et al. 1995) – is central to our understanding of young children's learning, and underpins what Gardner (1994) terms a materialist model of the interaction between science and technology. The materialist approach elevates technology to a leading role in the relationship, encouraging practitioners to 'scaffold' children's development of science concepts through the hands-on, familiar contexts provided by evaluating products and solving design problems during making.

While there are clear educational benefits to be gained by framing the Early Years science and technology curriculum in this way, we would favour an approach that maintains a more 'even' balance between the two disciplines, such as that implied by Gardner's interactionist model (1994) in which they are regarded as distinct yet mutually supportive: 'When the two sets of ideas are brought together they immediately begin to spark off imaginative approaches because they support and complement one another' (Baynes 1992: 35). However, this model begs the following question: 'Which elements do science and technology share, and how much of each should be left in a discrete form?' For young children, while a developing understanding of their surroundings and 'how the world works' transcends any subject boundaries, it is in the processes informing this understanding that similarities emerge. For example, children exploring fabrics in order to find out about their texture and structure may be said to be operating in a scientific mode, while a similar process of exploration undertaken in order to choose materials for a teddy's coat would involve more technological thinking. While appreciating the similarities and differences between processes used in science and technology it is important in an interactionist approach to seek ways in which they can 'feed into' one another. For example, the imaging and modelling skills that children develop during designing and making activities (Baynes 1992) can support them in developing scientific models and pictures to help understanding of areas such as simple electrical circuits.

But how do science and technology differ? One useful way of looking at the differences between them is to consider the purposes for which we engage in them as activities. As scientists, young children are seeking to understand the world (and beyond) as it exists. They are trying out new ideas (e.g. 'light objects float') to see how useful they are in explaining the phenomena they observe. The product of scientific enquiry is a body of 'tested' knowledge and understanding for the enquirer. By contrast, when acting as technologists, children are seeking to change the world (or elements of it) to serve a particular purpose. For example, they might be trying to make a boat that will sail across the water tray. Testing materials for their suitability may appear to be exactly the same as the scientific activity above. However, the purpose in the child's mind is different, since he or she is now working towards making something that hasn't existed before. The product of technological activity is therefore a 'thing' – a changed reality that may take many forms and may also include the development of understanding on the part of the technologist. Both disciplines are driven by human wants and needs: in the case of science it is the desire for understanding; whereas for technology it is some improvement in our physical environment. On most occasions, for both children and adults, the motivations may be somewhat mixed, but it is useful for us as educators to recognise the scientific and technological strands within human endeavour.

The contents of other chapters

This book is organised in two parts. Part One (Chapters 1 to 6) outlines the principles of teaching science and technology in Early Years settings, while Part Two (Chapters 7 to 12) provides specific guidance on thematic science and technology topics. Chapter 13 rounds off the book by looking forward to children's transition to science in the primary school and beyond.

In Chapter 2, Janet Rose and Lone Hattingh explore some of the theoretical underpinning for the inclusion of science and technology in Early Years practice. They review some of the recent research into the human brain that sheds light on the ways in which children's scientific and technological aptitudes might unfold. They explore the implications of cognitivist learning theories for these areas, including the importance of symbolic representation and play in the development of scientific and technological thinking. Finally they move on to considering appropriate multi-modal teaching and learning approaches informed by a symbolic representational model of young children's cognitive development.

In Chapter 3, Pat Black, Sue Hughes, Kendra McMahon and Janet Rose emphasise the importance of narrative; an essential feature in the education of young children and a mode of verbal interaction that is also fundamental to science and technology. They explore the fundamental role of narrative in human culture, including the 'explanatory' stories told to communicate scientific understanding and interpret people's needs and wants for technology. They go on to stress the importance of children's personal narratives in making sense of their environment and telling stories about what they have designed and made. The role of caregivers' narratives and sustained shared thinking in dialogue with children in helping them bridge the gap between home and school is also explored through several case studies.

In Chapter 4, Sarah Earle explores the use of the outdoors environment in young children's science and technology. She considers the role of scientific and technological learning in outdoor play (sand and water, wheeled vehicles, large-scale construction, building dens); gardening in the setting or further afield; 'welly walks'; activities and discussions associated with a forest school approach; exploring habitats and experiencing the built environment.

In Chapter 5, Rebecca Digby suggests how practitioners might go about documenting children's 'learning stories' in science and technology, which has emerged from the practices of Reggio Emilia. She covers appropriate elicitation activities such as mind-mapping, floor books and concept cartoons, together with reporting to parents. She considers how teachers and practitioners might make judgements in relation to the EYFS profile and Key Stage 1 of the National Curriculum, particularly in the light of the removal of 'levels' of attainment in the 2013 version.

Chapter 6 provides practical guidance for Early Years practitioners seeking to plan for science and technology in the Nursery or Reception class. Rebecca Digby and Sarah Earle draw upon their a range of practice to provide models of long-, medium- and short-term planning that make explicit the scientific and technological skills that children can develop through a range of activities both inside and outside the classroom. They focus on effective planning for adult intervention, including the role of additional adults in the setting, and upon making effective links between home and school.

In Chapter 7, Alan Howe outlines relevant concepts in relation to living processes, classification, plant biology, habitats and sustainability at both practitioner (adult) and appropriate child levels. He considers the scientific process skills needed to classify plants, undertake fieldwork and appropriate attitudes to be developed towards living things. He goes on to suggest learning activities within broad Early Years themes, such as 'the seaside', 'growing' and 'gardening', illustrated with case studies, children's story books, curriculum and ICT links.

In Chapter 8, Kendra McMahon proposes a thematic approach to humans and animals in Early Years practice. She starts by outlining relevant concepts in relation to living processes, classification, human and animal biology, habitats and sustainability at both practitioner and appropriate child levels. She considers the scientific process skills needed to classify animals, undertake fieldwork and develop appropriate attitudes towards living things. She suggests learning activities within broad Early Years themes, such as 'ourselves', 'minibeasts' and 'the seaside', illustrated with case studies, children's story books, curriculum and ICT links. Related technology activities such as designing a home for an animal are also included.

In Chapter 9, Christopher Collier proposes a thematic approach to everyday materials in Early Years education. He considers the scientific process skills needed to sort materials, test their properties and relate these to uses. He then goes on to suggest learning activities within broad Early Years themes, such as sand and water play, 'our world', 'buildings' 'air', 'water' and 'homes', illustrated with case studies, children's story books, curriculum and ICT links. Related technology activities such as selecting materials for making things on the basis of their strength, tactile or aesthetic properties are also included.

In Chapter 10, Sarah Earle begins by outlining relevant concepts in relation to physical and chemical changes to materials at both practitioner and appropriate child levels. She explores the scientific process skills needed to explore changes of state and goes on to suggest learning activities within broad Early Years themes, such as 'cooking', illustrated with case studies, children's story books, curriculum and ICT links. She includes technology activities such as designing biscuits.

In Chapter 11, Dan Davies advocates a thematic approach to forces, magnets and electricity; starting by explaining concepts in relation to static (e.g. floating) and moving forces, magnetism, simple circuits (voltage, current, resistance) and static electricity. He draws out the process skills children need to explore and investigate moving things and to explore and solve problems with simple circuits, such as prediction, hypothesis, testing, recording and interpreting data. He suggests learning activities within broad Early Years themes, such as 'magnets', 'floating and sinking', 'toys', 'things with wheels', 'the playground', 'push and pull', 'things that move', 'things we use' and 'lighting up', illustrated with case studies, children's story books, curriculum and ICT links.

In Chapter 12, Dan Davies explores a thematic approach to sound, light and space in Early Years practice. He starts by outlining relevant concepts in relation to sound (sources, vibrations, longitudinal waves, pitch, amplitude, hearing), light (sources, colours, transverse waves, frequency, wavelength, reflection, refraction, absorption, how we see) and the Earth and beyond (day and night, the seasons, the phases of the Moon). He suggests learning activities within broad Early Years themes such as, 'our ears', 'listening', 'sounds around us', 'animal ears', 'day and night', 'what can we see?', 'the seasons', 'the Sun and the Moon', 'colour' and 'shadows', illustrated with case studies, children's story books, curriculum and ICT links. Related technology activities such as designing musical instruments (shakers, drums, scrapers, elastic band guitars), ear trumpets, kaleidoscopes, sunglasses and sundials are also included.

In the final chapter, Alan Howe explores how children can be supported through transitions in Early Years science and technology. He argues that children may experience many transitions in the ages 3–7: from home to nursery, from nursery to Reception class, from EYFS to formal schooling. Widespread research evidence suggests that many young children might find the transition to primary school confusing as they move out of an environment of autonomy into one of conformity to the school norm, with perceived lack of choice and explanation regarding what is happening. This chapter looks at these several transitions in terms of children's experiences of science and technology learning, from the informal, play-based exploratory activities of home and nursery to the relatively structured experience of science investigations and D&T projects of Key Stage 1. Alan considers the nature of progression in science and technology through the 3 to 7 age range, and suggests ways of reducing the discontinuities for children and their carers.

Summary

In this chapter we have introduced this second edition and defined our terms; we see the early years as a distinct phase of education for children between the ages of three and seven (corresponding to the Foundation Phase in Wales), though we regard an 'Early Years approach' as relevant for children outside this age range. We have also explored the nature of learning in both science and technology for young children, indicated how practitioners might go about identifying this learning and provided a rationale for an 'interactionist' approach to these areas of the Early Years curriculum. Finally, we have outlined the ways in which this approach is underpinned theoretically and supported practically in the other chapters of this book.

Discussion points

- Can children as old as seven really be considered to be in the 'early years' of education? Is a thematic, play-based approach, which may be appropriate in the EYFS, still relevant for this age group?
- Does it matter whether children know that they're 'doing' science or technology (or both) in Early Years practice? How would you characterise the relationship between science and technology, and does it matter?

2

Young children as scientists, designers and technologists – theories of learning

Janet Rose and Lone Hattingh

Purpose of this chapter

Through reading this chapter you will gain an understanding of:

■ the process of symbolic representation and how young children develop conceptual understanding of scientific and technological concepts;

■ how various theories of learning, including research from neuroscience, help us to understand young children as scientists, designers and technologists;

■ the importance of how our theoretical understanding of children's learning affects our teaching.

Introduction

In this chapter we will consider the thought processes involved in developing scientific and technological understanding in young children. We will do this by outlining the process of symbolic representation and by reviewing key theories and research from neuroscience in order to extract the messages they have for children's development of specific design-related, technological or scientific capabilities. In doing so, we will explore how young children begin to acquire scientific and technological concepts, and how we can create the conditions that allow such understanding to flourish. Emphasis is placed on how teachers in Early Years practice can help to lay important foundations for young children to become scientists, designers and technologists.

Young children learning

How children learn and acquire conceptual understanding has been the subject of extensive research and theorising in a range of disciplines, from physiological explanations to metaphysical interpretations. An extensive range of literature exists on the topic of children's thinking, most notably from the field of cognitive psychology and, more recently, from the field of cognitive neuroscience, as theorists have attempted to address the questions raised about its meaning, its process and its quality. In reviewing the models of cognition that have been developed, it is clear that they arise out of implicit conceptions of children and are often based upon differing emphases being placed upon the role of nature or nurture in children's learning. For example, an early perception of the child as a 'blank slate' at birth led to a belief by a group called the behaviourists that children are reliant upon the external world for their development and learn through passive absorption of their environment, while a group of theorists known as constructivists view children more as investigative scientists, actively driven by nature to construct their own understanding of the world and make progress under their own self-regulating terms. In this chapter, we are mainly concerned with gaining an insight into the way in which our thinking develops in order to enable us to engage with scientific and technological ideas. The recognition that such understanding is influenced by interrelated social and emotional factors is implicit.

What is symbolic representation?

Although this term is not easily definable, it refers to the processes by which young children 'make sense of external reality by representing . . . experiences internally' (Rose and Rogers 2012b: 93). These experiences, which are internalised via a variety of sensory information, are actively organised and stored as mental or cognitive structures commonly known as 'schemas' (or 'schemata'). 'Schema' is a term developed by a leading theorist of developmental psychology, Jean Piaget. For Piaget (1978), schemas are essentially cognitive forms of organised thoughts that enable children to represent and code their perceptions and understanding in meaningful ways. Rumelhart (1980) referred to schemas as 'the building blocks of cognition', while recent neuroscientific research (Goswami 2011) suggests that they correspond to neural connections within our brains. Since the brain is the main organ of learning, increasing our understanding of how it works can shed light on how we can support children's thinking.

Insights from neuroscience

The connectome

Thinking can be viewed as essentially an electrical and chemical activity; a matter of nerve cells passing 'messages' to each other via connections between neurons in the brain (Matlin 1998). Information is relayed in the brain through neurons, which collectively form a dense neuronal network or 'connectome' (Seung 2012) and link all the areas of the brain together. The denser these networks are, the faster and more reliable the connections. The way in which our brain operates has led to the development of 'information processing' theories (Sternberg 1985). In their simplest forms, such theories see learning as merely connections between stimuli (what goes in through our senses) and responses (what comes out in our behaviour). This has been used in the past to justify educational practices such as rote learning and teaching through the transmission and testing of subject content. Some teaching of science, particularly at upper Primary level, is still based on this model. However, simplistic models of the mind do not do justice to the intricate web of the connectome and the diverse individuality of the brain, which produces 'subjective representations' (Gardner 1987). Recent studies of the brain have led to more dynamic and sophisticated 'network' models of learning such as 'parallel distributed processing' (Matlin 1998: 16), since 'many cognitive activities seem to involve parallel processing, with many signals handled at the same time, rather than serial processing'. Edelman's (1992) notion of 'neural Darwinism' also offers a more fluid and dynamic account of cognition. Although Edelman would acknowledge that the brain does behave 'in some ways' like a computer, he argues that it more resembles 'the sound and light patterns and the movement and growth patterns of a jungle' (1992: 29). Edelman's metaphor of a jungle ecosystem is not unlike that of children in a classroom with their highly individualistic neural systems, each interspersed with complex layers and loops that change continuously.

When we think, patterns of electrical activity move in complex ways around our cerebral cortex using the connections we have previously made through learning. This has clear relevance for children as scientists and technologists, since it is the ability to make links between apparently unrelated ideas (e.g. clockwork and radio, the motion of the planets and a falling apple) that lies at the heart of both creativity and understanding (Howe et al. 2001). As children explore materials and physical or biological phenomena, physical changes are literally occurring in their brain as new connections are made; this is known as 'synaptogenesis' (Dityatev and El Husseini 2006). Goswami (2011) notes that some neural structures are dependent on the particular environment in which a young baby or child finds themselves, while others are already formed at birth (such as vision or hearing). However, even those pre-programmed connections are still reliant on experience to further their development and become more specialised (for example, enabling babies to focus more accurately with their eyes). Thus all neural structures in the brain rely on external experiences to create fibre connections between neurons and create the interconnected networks that enable us to develop more abstract scientific concepts. The adage 'use it or lose it' is based upon the understanding that personal experience creates neuronal connections and repetition strengthens the efficiency of the connectome.

Plasticity and sensitive periods

This ability to respond to experiences and environments is known as brain 'plasticity', and it allows children to adapt and respond continuously, to 'learn' from experiences, particularly if they are new or repeated. If neuronal connections are not used or reinforced they become weakened and can be 'pruned' to reduce simpler associations and maximise more complex structures. As we age our brains' plasticity reduces, making it more difficult to learn new things and adapt behaviours. This understanding has led to what is known as the 'sensitive period' effect (Nicholas and Geers 2007; Thomas and Knowland 2009) and the apparent limitations of certain aspects of learning. For example, if we are not exposed to certain phonetic sounds within the first year of life, we are less likely to be able to learn certain languages at a later stage, without speaking with an accent.

The notion of 'sensitive periods' has particular resonance for Early Years education. There is growing evidence from a range of disciplines and reviews that emphasises the significance of early experiences and their long term impact (Sylva et al. 2004; Shonkoff 2010). This underlines the importance of ensuring that young learners are inducted appropriately into scientific and technological thinking during this sensitive period and that the underlying structures needed for particular conceptual understanding are optimally developed. Neuroscientific research suggests that:

> children possess and demonstrate all the main types of learning (statistical learning, learning by imitation, learning by analogy and causal learning) even as babies. This includes learning the relationships between the sounds that underpin language acquisition, or the visual features that specify natural categories or concepts such as bird, tree, car.
>
> (Goswami and Bryant 2007: 1)

Thus young children can think and learn in similar ways to adults, but lack experience. For practitioners, this highlights the importance of the nurturing environment in providing experiences at sensitive periods that will help children develop scientific and technological concepts.

Mirror neurons and multi-sensory learning

In relation to the adult role in developing children's thinking, two other key messages from the field of neuroscience are also worth noting. The first of these is the discovery of what have been named 'mirror neurons' (Lepage and Theoret 2007). These are specialised nerve cells distributed throughout the brain that are stimulated both when a child performs an action as well as when they observe someone else performing it, whether those actions are perceived through sight, sound or any other sensory pathway. Although much debate and further research has been generated about the function and implications of mirror neurons, they do provide a neuroscientific basis for what has been known for a long time – that children copy others (also known as social learning theory). During learning, information from the mirror neurons is combined with previous memories and understanding to inform actions. An awareness of the role of mirror neurons in both formal and informal learning highlights the vital importance of role-modelling by adults.

Another key message from neuroscience of relevance to Early Years practitioners is that:

> learning depends on the development of multi-sensory networks of neurons distributed across the entire brain. For example, a concept in science may depend on neurons being simultaneously active in visual, spatial, memory, deductive and kinaesthetic regions, in both brain hemispheres.
>
> (Goswami and Bryant 2007: 1)

This suggests that we should focus on creating diverse learning contexts that stimulate *all* areas of the brain and body. The ideas of left-brain and right-brain learners or VAK (visual, auditory or kinaesthetic) learning styles have largely been dispelled by the recognition that 'learning is strengthened not only in relation to how many neurons fire in a neural network, but also by how they are distributed across different domains, such as the motor and sensory cortices' (Alexander 2010: 96). These points are revisited later in the chapter when we discuss the role of play in young children's thinking and the significance of active learning.

Theories of symbolic representation

How the physiological phenomenon of the connectome ultimately is transformed into mental comprehension remains a mystery. We are left with essentially hypothetical constructs to explain the bridge between the level of the neuron and the level of the 'cognitive concept' (Gardner 1987). So while we now know that schemas are essentially neural connections, we are still reliant on theories to 'translate' the connectome. All these theories provide pieces in the puzzle and can 'help us to crack the riddle of intellectual development' (Berg 1992: 14), yet we need symbolic representational theories, such as Piaget's (1978) to help us to interpret how cumulative learning might manifest itself.

Piaget's schema theory

Piaget's work is arguably the most well-developed in terms of helping us to further our understanding of young children's conceptual development. For Piaget, thought is essentially 'internalized action' and children make sense of new experiences by assimilating them and fitting them into existing schemas. However, a state of 'cognitive conflict' or 'disequilibrium' can arise when the child encounters new experiences that cannot be assimilated. To restore cognitive harmony or 'equilibrium' the child has to adapt the existing schema to accommodate the new experience. A child who has had many enjoyable encounters with a familiar pet dog meets another dog and hugs it enthusiastically, assimilating this new experience to an existing 'friendly dog' action schema. If the new dog growls and bares its teeth, however, the child's expectations are thrown out of balance and the 'friendly dog' schema has to be revised to accommodate this new discovery that not all dogs can be treated in the same way. Thus the complementary processes of assimilation and accommodation and the drive to achieve a state of equilibrium enable a child to learn. As Sutherland (1992: 26) describes it, 'assimilation involves transforming experience within the mind, whereas accommodation involves adjusting the mind to new experience'.

As children's thinking develops, Piaget also identified four main stages in this development and associated the stages with particular ages, although he acknowledged that such stages might vary in their duration for different children and might overlap to some extent. A key theme of Piaget's stage theory is the development from concrete to abstract thought. This occurs as thought and symbolic representation become increasingly logical and systematic, gradually assuming priority over action. The first two stages are the most pertinent for Early Years practitioners – the *sensori-motor* and the *pre-operational* stage. Babies begin to construct schemas through their sensory and physical activities, which initially begin as 'chance behaviours' (Berk 2003) motivated by their basic needs and exploratory drive. For example, a 'dropping schema' develops as a baby grasps and releases an object by accident, which then evolves into a more sophisticated, self-controlled and deliberate schema through constant practice.

Athey (2007: 48) has applied Piaget's notion of schemas to Early Years practice, which she calls *schema theory*, redefining them as 'patterns of repeatable actions that lead to early categories and then to logical classifications'. Such patterns of behaviour reflect how young children's experiences are assimilated and gradually coordinated. For example, in babies the schemas of 'tracking and gazing' reflect one of the first great cognitive 'accommodations' as babies learn that objects can be stationary or they can move. Schemas have dynamic (moving) and configurative (still) aspects. They tend not to be isolated patterns of behaviour but develop in clusters and are part of whole networks of senses, actions and thinking. Schemas are thought to be important stages in the development of key concepts, many of which may have scientific or technological links, as in Table 2.1. If adults are alert to these schemas and can provide materials that help children to explore them fully, they can help to support this conceptual development.

Some challenges to Piagetian constructivism

Since Piaget's work, new research has led to less emphasis being placed on specific stages and an acceptance that cognitive development is a far more complex process than Piaget suggested. For example, it is now broadly accepted that:

> differences between age groups may be ones of degree rather than kind. Not only are young children more cognitively competent than they appear, but older children are less competent than we might think.

> (Siegler 1998: 22)

Donaldson (1978) also showed that Piaget's experimental approach to investigating children's intellectual development was affected by the context and the type of situations in which they found themselves. She found that where activities were introduced in a way that made sense to children in relation to their previous experience, they were capable of what she calls 'disembedded thinking' – a more abstract type of thought that children need in order to grasp scientific concepts and imagine future possibilities. This led her to conclude that: 'The paradoxical fact is that disembedded thinking, although by definition it calls for the ability to

TABLE 2.1 Possible connections between children's early schemas and later scientific and technological concepts or activities

Early schema	Later concept/activity
Transporting – a child may move an object or collection from one place to another	Designing vehicles, carriers, conservation of matter
Vertical – actions such as climbing, stepping up or down	Lifts, escalators, cranes, work with construction kits
Intersections – e.g. drawing many criss-cross lines	Joining materials, e.g. strips of wood
Circular – circles may appear in drawings, paintings and collages	Wheels and axles, electrical circuits
Core and radial – circles with radiating lines, e.g. 'tadpole' figures	Minibeasts in nature, flowers and plants

Source: adapted from Bruce (1997: 79)

stand back from life, yields its greatest riches when it is conjoined by doing' (Donaldson 1978: 83). This points again to the value of ' hands-on' experiences with objects and materials in helping to develop higher-order thinking skills in young children.

Perhaps the most serious criticism of Piaget's work has related to his relative neglect of the socio-cultural context of learning. We now know that all learning is 'socially mediated' (Goswami and Bryant 2007), in that it arises from the 'intrinsically social and communicative nature of human life' (Mercer and Littleton, cited in Alexander 2010: 91). More emphasis is now given to the impact of the socio-cultural context on children's learning, such as that originally proposed by Vygotsky (1978) and Bruner (1963). If Piaget has helped to highlight the way in which children are actively able to construct their own understanding, Vygotsky has helped to focus attention on the social dimensions of cognitive development. While he shares Piaget's constructivist views of children's learning, he emphasises the importance of social interactions and the way in which children's experiences are embedded in the social context. Hence the term *social constructivism* is applied to his work.

Vygotsky's social constructivism

For Vygotsky, 'human learning presupposes a specific social nature and a process by which children grow into the intellectual life of those around them' (1978: 88). The emphasis shifts from individual discovery to social interaction. While Piaget emphasises the role of biology in cognitive development, Vygotsky is more concerned with the process of cultural transmission. Vygotsky's model identifies two dimensions to learning, the interpersonal and the intrapersonal. Young babies and children internalise external experiences into mental structures via a 'series of transformations' such that an interpersonal activity is reconstructed as an intrapersonal one. Hence 'external social processes' become 'internal psychological ones' (Robson 2006: 17). Vygotsky sees this transformational process as a prolonged 'series of developmental events' in which 'higher mental processes evolve and a child's cognition becomes increasingly more abstract or symbolic' (1978: 56).

In addition to his emphasis on the cultural and social context of learning (as well as the role of play), one of the most significant aspects of Vygotsky's theory for adults working with young children is his notion of the 'zone of proximal development' (ZPD). He proposes that two levels of development exist: the actual level of development and the potential level. These two levels define the boundaries of the ZPD, which is defined as 'the distance between the actual developmental level as determined by independent problem-solving and the level of potential development as determined through problem-solving under adult guidance or in collaboration with more capable peers' (Vygotsky 1978: 86). He maintains that differences in perceived 'ability' lie in the children having different 'developmental dynamics' and that the extent of the ZPD is variable over time and in different contexts.

Roth et al. (2013) draw on Vygotsky in their contention that children's development and learning can be seen as social in the first instance, becoming individualised as they gain in understanding. They point to the reciprocal nature of learning where teacher and child are not considered in isolation, but as part of the context as a whole. These ideas link to the notion of 'sustained shared thinking' (Siraj-Blatchford et al. 2002), which we will return to in Chapter 3. Sustained shared thinking draws heavily on the Vygotskian tradition and also links closely with the work of Bruner and the notion of 'scaffolding'.

Bruner's theory of symbolic representation

Bruner's (1990) contribution to our understanding of symbolic representation moves away from a maturational, stage-dependent perception of cognitive development but retains firm roots in the constructionist perspective. His model of cognition could be considered as a synthesis of both Vygotsky and Piaget. Like Piaget, he places emphasis on a child-centred context that enables 'discovery learning' to occur. In this respect, he is a constructivist. However, as an educationalist, he finds Piaget's ideas 'too passive and deterministic for teaching purposes' (Sutherland 1992: 2) and draws upon Vygotsky's emphasis on culture and social instruction. He considers that children developed their thinking via a process of skill acquisition in which they learned to represent aspects of their experiences in three different modes – enactive, iconic and symbolic. In the *enactive mode*, knowledge can only be understood or expressed through actions. In the *iconic mode* we represent the world via images or pictures, while in the *symbolic mode*, we are able to represent the world symbolically in a variety of forms that are free from the immediate context and are not reliant on visual images, such as words, mathematical symbols or via other symbol systems. Children move between these different forms of representation, but will increasingly operate within the more abstract, symbolic mode. Bruner's work links to Donaldson's ideas of embedded and disembedded thinking and show how activities that demand representation – symbolic play, drawing, making – will be of the greatest value in creating links between different modes. These ideas also link to the evidence from neuroscience about the potential importance for multi-sensory learning in helping children to move from concrete to more abstract thinking.

Bruner envisages a 'spiral' effect where 'learning is both recursive, that is, repeated in different contexts, and incremental, embodying developing expertise' (Robson 2006: 32). Thus, while a child might not grasp an idea or concept as would an adult, Bruner felt that even very young children can understand some aspects. It is the adult's role to intervene at the appropriate level within the child's spiral learning process until the child achieves independent mastery or self-regulation.

Bruner suggests the notion of 'scaffolding' to describe the interactive, instructional relationship between practitioner and child (Wood et al. 1976). The idea of a (temporary) 'scaffold' rather than a 'zone' is one with which Early Years practitioners can more readily identify (Edwards and Rose 1994). His work also helps us to challenge our 'conventional' ways of representing experience in the western world such as via books or equations. Traditional school contexts do not sufficiently emphasise visual or spatial representations such as drawings, models and patterns, which could be powerful tools for helping to lay the foundations for scientific and technological thinking. We need to ensure that in our Early Years settings this imbalance is challenged.

Multi-modal representation

The world in which children live today requires a familiarity with technology and visual or graphic means of expression, so that language has become just one way in which to communicate meaning. Kress (1997, 2010) and Jewitt (2009b, 2009a, Jewitt et al. 2001) have explored and researched the multi-modality of children's meaning-making practices since the 1990s, and have had a wide-ranging influence on our understanding of the different ways in which children communicate their thinking. For example, Figures 2.1 and 2.2 illustrate how Dominic was preoccupied with all things physical, and enjoyed representing and exploring his ideas in multi-modal ways. He used scissors, sticky tape and coloured pens

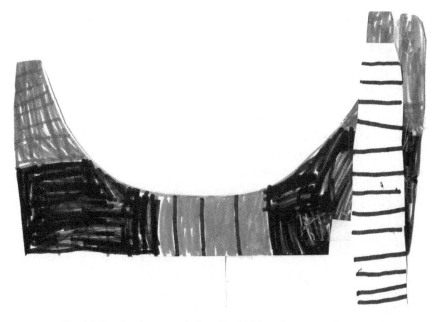

FIGURE 2.1 Dominic's cut-out representation of a skateboard ramp

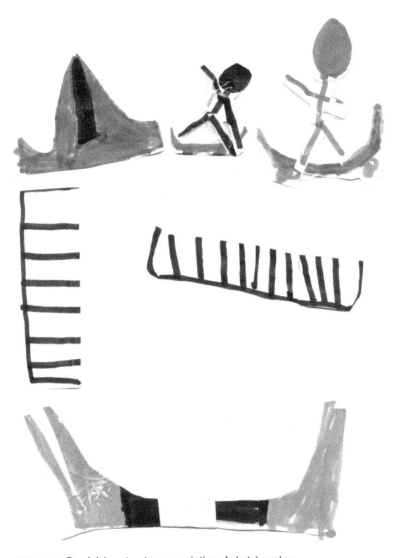

FIGURE 2.2 Dominic's cut-out representation of skateboarders

to represent his admiration for the children who were skateboarding in the park near his house. His cut-outs took on a three-dimensional appearance as he solved the problem of making his figures stand up while communicating the actions and speed with which the skateboarders were able to negotiate the ramps. Dominic explored concepts of balance, control and movement by arranging his cut-outs in different ways as part of his role play with his friends (Hattingh 2013).

Kress (2000) suggests that theories of learning based on the use of one mode of language are inadequate in providing children with the resources needed to make meaning. He suggests that multi-modality is a 'domain of enquiry' that recognises the representation of meaning in different modes as distinct, rather than merely as a replication or illustration of what is said verbally or in writing (Kress 2009: 54). There are many different modes within which children may choose to communicate their thinking, such as the use of visual images, speech, model-making, role play and drawing, among others (Kress 1997, 2010). It is important to recognise that modes used for representing meaning vary from culture to culture, as different cultures draw on different resources and materials to make meaning. Kress (2010: 8) maintains that there are 'no universals in communication', as we tend to only recognise and represent the cultures with which we are familiar and those we know reasonably well.

The rich potential of multi-modality can be seen in the ways in which children invent and design their own ways to make meaning using a variety of resources and materials, rather than using the ready-made signs of alphabetic writing or numbers. In the Nursery, a three-year-old boy used scrap paper to make a collar and lead for his toy dog so that he could take it for a walk – see Figure 2.3. His teacher scaffolded his learning with care, helping him to hold the paper together while using scissors and sticky tape to attach the lead. This enabled him to continue in his play, having solved the problem of attaching and securing the

FIGURE 2.3 Scrap paper collar and lead for a toy dog

paper. Children's use of their favourite and precious toys in their role play helps them to represent their thinking in a symbolic way that has real meaning for them.

Resources and materials need to be accessible and readily to hand so that children can make choices and decisions about how to represent and communicate their thinking. Kress (2010: 143) refers to 'ensembles of modes' to describe the ways in which children use several resources or modes simultaneously. For example, in Figure 2.4, we can see how Ellen was engaged in role play with her brother after watching the removal of a beehive in a neighbour's garden. The children learned about bees while talking to their mother and observing the bee catcher at work. Ellen made this mask for her brother, and they wrote books and messages about the bee catcher, exploring their new-found knowledge of bees. Role play provided a meaningful context within which to develop and explore their understanding, while the mask was made with found bits of string and card, requiring the children's problem-solving skills in working out how to make it fit to extend their play and exploration of the life of bees (Hattingh 2013).

A multi-modal approach to learning allows children to continually adjust their ideas according to the way in which they interpret their world. They use aspects of design in shaping their social world in their multi-modal representations: they might make use of different colours, shapes and materials to demonstrate meaning, for example, by the way they position aspects of their drawings in the foreground or background, or use colour to impart meaning. In this way, children can readily explore their own understanding of scientific concepts. For example, at three years of age, Sebastian was fascinated by the insides of the body, so that his drawings of people tended to show features of the internal workings of the

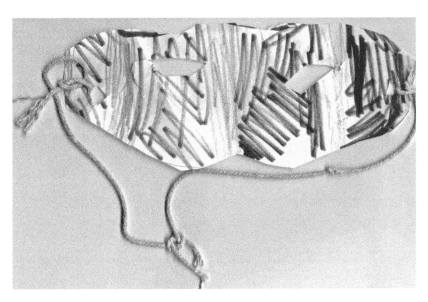

FIGURE 2.4 Ellen's bee mask for her brother

FIGURE 2.5 Sebastian's symbolic representation of his mother

body rather than its external physical appearance. Drawn spontaneously at home, he described his symbolic representation of his mother as her 'blood and bones'. In Figure 2.5 we can see how, at the lower edge of the drawing, Sebastian has drawn his mother's eyes and mouth, yet the way they are represented may seem surprising to adults as there is an expectation that children usually draw people with their features enclosed in circular shapes. In this case, taking the child's interest in the internal features of the human body as a starting point while acknowledging his meaning-making endeavours, enables the practitioner to make use of children's sometimes unexpected responses and creativity (Hattingh 2013).

The importance of play in young children's science and technology

Few Early Years practitioners will need convincing of the crucial role of play in young children's learning. All the research and theory discussed in this chapter endorse this; for Piaget, play is a manifestation of internal thought processes and is necessary for the development of symbolic representation, while for

Vygotsky, play enables the child's performance to be in advance of their actual developmental level, creating an intrapersonal zone of proximal development. Bruner considers that play ought to be the dominant activity in the pre-school years, while, Goswami and Bryant's (2007: 2) review of neuroscientific research suggests that:

> pretend play and the imagination are important for cognitive development in the early years of education, helping children to reflect upon and regulate their own cognitive behaviour, and to reflect upon and gain a deeper understanding of the mind.

Play, 'when in full-flow, helps us to function in advance of what we can actually do in our real lives' (Bruce 1994: 193). But what kinds of play lend themselves to developing learning in science and technology? Bruce (2011) offers the example of two-year-old Danny who plays with boats in the water tray – filling them with water, pushing them under the water and into every part of the water tray. He is experimenting with scientific concepts such as flow, motion, buoyancy and displacement. When he goes outside and has fun sliding down a slide, Danny is actively experiencing and learning about motion, gravity, forces, friction, velocity and momentum. As well as dealing with scientific principles, this kind of play is imaginative, enabling these children to conceive what they have never experienced in the actual world, and hence to start the process of designing. Bruner et al. (1976) have arrived at significant insights into children's play and its role in enabling them to negotiate, solve problems and imagine alternative futures – all crucial design capabilities. Bruner and his colleagues observed children playing with objects in different structured situations. In one such experiment, children were classified in terms of their attitude to a specially designed toy and the playfulness with which they interacted with it. The research showed that 'the more inventive and exploratory the children had been initially in playing with the super-toy, the higher their originality scores were four years later' (Bruner et al. 1976: 17). Significantly, Bruner's 'play' groups outperformed 'taught' groups consistently.

One of the fundamental characteristics of play is that it is low-risk; we cannot be wrong when playing. The security this gives to the player enables her to take risks – the experience gives her confidence to be inventive and make mistakes when the situation becomes more structured. Thus the ability to solve problems is linked closely with the freedom to play. Moyles (1989: 63) identifies 'specific exploration' as being the kind of play that looks at what the material is and what it can do, and 'diversive exploration' as leading a child to explore what they can personally do with the material. For example, a child might manipulate playdough for some time, exploring its properties (a scientific type of enquiry), then later start to make an animal out of it (beginning to engage in designing and making). Similarly, Hutt's taxonomy of children's play (1979) has close links with scientific and design-related exploration. She distinguishes between play that is *epistemic* (problem-solving, exploratory, concerned with skills and focused on objects and materials) and *ludic* (fantasy-based, creative, concerned with imagination and focused on symbolic play). Again, it is tempting to see these as scientific and design-related forms of play respectively, though this may be over-simplistic since science can be imaginative: 'Through epistemic behaviour the child acquires information, knowledge and skills. Ludic behaviour allows children to make the understandings their own' (Riley and Savage 1994: 136).

Another feature of ludic (imaginative) play that is of particular value to children's design-related development is the blurring between fantasy and reality in, for example, setting up a model town. The distinction between 'inside' and 'outside' the head is less clear-cut and more easily crossed during play, a situation analogous to the modelling activities of designers:

> In some ways, children are more adept at using models than adults. For infants, the division between model and reality is blurred and all children up to the age of 13 can get thoroughly lost in the world of imagination represented by role play, fantasy, toys, drawings and models. Many adult designers would give a lot to be able to enter the imagined future in such a wholehearted way.
>
> (Baynes 1992: 20)

What are the implications of learning theory for teaching science and technology in Early Years practice?

Explanations of children's learning are of little use unless they are applied by the adults whose role it is to promote such development. Any adult interacting with young children will draw upon a belief system about the best way to 'teach' or interact with a child, which may have profound consequences for the way in which that child will progress. We can take some key messages from the theories outlined above, such as creating a learning environment that is child-centred and play-based so that children can learn from active, concrete and multi-modal contexts. However, Rose and Rogers (2012a) have drawn attention to the dilemmas facing Early Years practitioners in terms of how much children should be 'left to themselves' and how much interaction or even acceleration an adult should provide. Although Piaget considers the adult's role to be that of a facilitator, his ideas about children's 'readiness' to learn raises questions about how proactive the practitioner should be. His emphasis on children as individual learners, independently exploring their environment through a process of discovery as they move biologically through various stages of development, implies a passive, enabling role for the adult in providing a suitable context for this exploration.

However, the work of Bruner, Vygotsky and other socio-cultural theorists, together with insights from cognitive neuroscience, emphasises the social and cultural context to providing children with access to scientific and technological concepts. Practitioners are also under pressure to raise levels of competency and diagnose appropriate intervention to move learning forwards (Rose and Rogers 2012b). Robson notes that Vygotsky's emphasis on instruction does not imply 'a simple transmission model of "teaching" whereby an adult instructs and a child listens' (2006: 26). Nonetheless, as practitioners we need to find 'that dynamic region of sensitivity in which cognitive development advances' (Rogoff and Wertsch 1984: 1). A Brunerian approach suggests a focus on 'the kind and quality of cognitive support which an adult can provide for a child's learning' (Mercer 1991: 64). Much of Bruner's work on play and child development has been translated into a *theory of instruction* – what we as adults can do to support and enhance learning, within his notion of a *spiral curriculum*:

> You begin with an 'intuitive' account that is well within the reach of a student, and then circle back to a more formal or highly structured account, until, with however many more recyclings are necessary, the learner has mastered the topic or subject in its full generative power.
>
> (Bruner 1996: 92)

Whitebread (1996: 6) interprets this model in an Early Years context as children encountering a set of ideas at a practical level when they are young, which will help them understand the same ideas at a more symbolic or abstract level later. For example, a child pushing a trolley who notices that it is harder to push when loaded with bricks will have the intuitive basis for understanding Newton's second law of motion (force equals mass times acceleration) some years later. This will be much more likely, however, if a knowledgeable adult has been with them in the early experience, encouraging them to talk about the 'heaviness' (inertia) they feel with the loaded trolley. The key knowledge this adult needs to possess is an 'understanding of the child's understandings' (von Glasersfeld 1989:14). Then, in order to 'scaffold' their understanding we need to stimulate initial engagement of the child's interest in the activity as well as maintenance of the child's motivation to perform the task, simplification of the task to suit the learner's capability and appropriate demonstration and assistance (Wood et al. 1976). Wood and Wood (1996) describe this adult support in terms of 'contingent instruction' since it involves constant assessment of the child's performance with accompanying changes in the level of assistance offered. However, following the 'contingency rule' is complex and challenging. Moreover, such intervention may prevent a child creatively pursuing a solution on their own terms (Robson 2006).

Assimilation of various models of learning and cognition may require us as practitioners to accommodate our thinking and adapt our practice according to the needs of each child. Sutherland (1992: 124) suggests that practitioners should 'use the appropriate cognitive-developmental model for the needs of particular [children]'. Similarly, Penn (2005: 39) believes that different theories of development should be seen as 'signposts to different routes to understanding young children'. Responsive practitioners will reflect upon the theories and choose what seems 'fit for purpose' as we accompany our children along their journey of discovery; sometimes pointing out new horizons, sometimes setting a challenge, sometimes gently guiding and sometimes leaving them well alone. Either way, a child's learning adventure will be enhanced by our sensitive integration of theoretical considerations on how best to light the way. As Rose and Rogers (2012b: 111–12) note:

> If we accept that all learning and knowledge development is an ongoing process of constructive inquiry for both ourselves and for children and we take into account the socio-cultural view of learning as a process of interpersonal relations and view the child as an active agent, it is possible to conceive how we can be co-constructors and co-collaborators with young children making meaning and knowledge together.

Summary

In this chapter we have reviewed some of the main research and theory from both neuroscience and the field of cognitive psychology that underpin our model of young children as scientists and technologists. We have seen how theories of brain development support a role for these kinds of learning in the curriculum, while symbolic representational models of young children's cognitive development emphasise the need for multi-modal activities and the role of play in the development of designing skills and scientific concepts. The next chapter takes this process forward as we explore some of the nuances involved in the socio-cultural process of learning and the role practitioners can play within this learning.

Discussion points

- How do you think young children 'learn' about science and technology?
- What are the key messages from neuroscience about how children learn and how do they link to theories of symbolic representation from Piaget, Vygotsky and Bruner?
- What can theories of symbolic representation tells us about the adult role in guiding young children's scientific and technological exploration?
- Think about your experiences of Early Years classroom contexts – what opportunities exist for learning science and technology through child-initiated play?

3

Talk, narrative and sustained shared thinking

Pat Black, Sue Hughes, Kendra McMahon and Janet Rose

Purpose of this chapter

Through reading this chapter you will gain an understanding of:

- the fundamental role of narrative – including scientific and technological 'stories' – in human culture;
- the importance of 'storying' as part of a spontaneous process of child–adult interaction from birth;
- techniques for developing narratives to support children's learning in science and technology;
- developing talk that supports learning in science and technology.

Introduction

In Chapter 2 we emphasised that children are motivated from birth to act upon the world (i.e. to engage in exploration, designing and making) in order to make sense of it. Through actions and experiences of the senses, including shared experiences and purposes with other human beings, their scientific under-standing of their environment – human, natural and made – will develop. In this chapter we will examine the role of talk between children and practitioners as an example of the socio-cultural view of learning, arguing that children's scientific and technological thinking is supported through using narratives – personal, cultural, traditional, contemporary, oral and printed.

Narratives are essential to human experience; scientific and technological concepts, skills and attitudes may be passed down through and exchanged within the stories that cultures share. Scientific accounts of the world – human, natural and made – can be expressed through 'explanatory stories' (Millar and Osborne 1998) and greater use of the narrative form can be used to present scientific responses to questions regularly asked by children. The construction of narratives is an early and spontaneous process in adult–child interactions; in these early exchanges children first encounter, make links and are inducted into methods of thinking relevant to science and technology. Narratives in rhymes, songs and stories, first shared in the home, can be developed in the classroom to provide meaningful starting points for scientific and technological activities. We shall explore the use of traditional and folk tales, myths and legends to develop cross-curricular work but will begin by first considering the concept of 'sustained shared thinking' (Sylva et al. 2004), which was first introduced in Chapter 2.

Sustained shared thinking

The concept of sustained shared thinking (SST) emerged from the large-scale and influential Effective Provision of Pre-school Education (EPPE) project (Sylva et al. 2004). The EPPE project (now known as EPPSE following its extension into Secondary education) is an ongoing, longitudinal study that is exploring the long-term impact of Pre-school education on children's learning and development. As part of this process, the project has identified quality indicators for effective Early Years provision. Sustained shared thinking is one of the key aspects of pedagogical excellence identified from the research and is now considered a pivotal part of Early Years pedagogy. Indeed, it has been included within the EYFS curriculum in England (DfE 2012), premised on the evidence that positive outcomes for children 'are closely associated with adult–child interactions . . . that involve some element of sustained shared thinking' (Siraj-Blatchford and Sylva 2004: 720). SST is defined as:

> An episode in which two or more individuals 'work together' in an intellectual way to solve a problem, clarify a concept, evaluate activities, extend a narrative etc. Both parties must contribute to the thinking and it must develop and extend.
>
> (Siraj-Blatchford et al. 2002: 8)

Within the current Statutory Framework for the EYFS (DfE 2012: 6–7) practitioners are required to consider the following three 'characteristics of effective learning and teaching' in their planning and support of children's learning: 'playing and exploring', 'active learning' and 'creating and thinking critically'.

This means creating an environment in which young children can, for example, investigate, develop their own ideas, notice patterns and make links and develop strategies for resolving problems. In the non-statutory guidance (Early Education 2012), sustained shared thinking is identified as a key strategy for enabling the characteristic of 'creating and thinking critically', helping children to explore ideas and make links, provided that adults follow children's lead in conversation, and think about things together. This description of SST disguises the enormous complexity of adult–child interactions and the high-level, intricate skills required to guide children's thinking. As Rose and Rogers (2012b: 79) note:

> Enacting sustained shared thinking in practice is challenging. Part of the skill of the adult is to make conceptual space for the child to contribute his or her ideas by listening carefully to what is said and endeavour to understand what the child or children mean and understand. This is challenging and requires that adults set aside their own ideas, beliefs and the 'teacherly' desire to give or to get the 'right' answer.

Since SST was first identified during the EPPE study, there has been surprisingly little research undertaken on this concept, but some attempts have been made to identify the particular 'interactional features and pedagogical strategies' (Wild 2011: 219) that might promote SST. Some of these include 'tuning in and showing genuine interest' in what the child is doing, sensitively 'offering suggestions' or 'clarifying ideas', perhaps 'speculating' or 'offering alternative viewpoints' (Siraj-Blatchford 2005: 10–11) . Part of this process might also include 'modeling ideas' or 'offering your own experience' to help demonstrate the thinking process or 'asking open questions' to stimulate the child's contribution (Siraj-Blatchford 2005: 11). Unfortunately, research suggests that most adult questions tend to be closed, requiring a simple yes/no response (Siraj-Blatchford and Manni 2008). This may limit the potential for further discussion and preclude a reciprocal exchange of ideas, since children may feel that the teacher is seeking a 'right' answer.

Perhaps the most significant aspect of SST is that it should involve 'co-construction' of ideas (Vygotsky 1978) through the adult acting as a 'knowledgable other' in supporting a child's learning. The concept also resonates with the work of other socio-cultural theorists, being associated with the well-known notion of 'scaffolding' (Wood et al. 1976) and related ideas such as 'guided participation' (Rogoff 1990). Some would argue that scaffolding and co-construction do not entail the same processes since scaffolding implies a more dominant role for the teacher, while co-construction envisages a more egalitarian exchange (Payler 2009, Rose and Rogers 2012b). However, Wild (2011: 230) notes that SST is not necessarily a linear exchange with equal levels of overt participation. She contends that the co-construction process is:

perhaps better characterised as a continuum of joint engagement with both participants potentially shifting position on that scale during an interaction. There is a time and place for silence, observation and consideration in the development of thinking.

In essence, SST involves responsive and contextualised attunement to the child's thinking and being alert to the appropriate 'timing' of an intervention. In other words, knowing just the right moment 'when a comment, question or suggestion might be useful' (MacNaughton and Williams 2004: 2) without disturbing the subtlety of the child's ownership over the thinking process. Read examples of sustained shared thinking in Learning story 3.1 and and see if you can identify the pedagogical strategies or interactional features in these exchanges between children and adults that reflect sustained shared thinking and the co-construction of ideas.

Learning story 3.1

Making puddles
This example is taken from Puddleduck Hall Nursery, Gloucester; it was provided by Emma Oliver, the head of Nursery.

Context
The children have been interested in materials, exploring smells, textures and sounds and mixing them together . . . sometimes to make magic potions or imaginary recipes! To enable children to continue this interest, a range of materials (as well as ones always available in a garden) were made accessible with sensitive staff ready to join the children's scientific discovery where appropriate.

During free play, a group of three pre-school children are making potions in the garden area using natural materials such as soil, bark, sand and water. Two of the children become fascinated by the way the soil changes consistency when water is added.

Child A: (*Pours a jug of water over a heap of soil.*) Look, it's gone all squidgy and wet. (*Prodding it with a stick and then mixing it with his fingers.*)
Child C: Ugh! Let me feel . . . it's squelchy like the bear book. (*Meaning the book, We're Going on a Bear Hunt.*)
Practitioner: What do you think might happen if you pour more water in?
Child C: Get a puddle! (*She pours a large jug of water in.*)

Child A and C watch what happens. The water sits on the top of some of the soil and does indeed form a puddle.

Child C: It can't go in any more . . . it's all full up.
Practitioner: Do you mean the soil cannot take in any more water?
Child C: Yeah, all full up.

Practitioner: Yes, I see what you mean. The soil cannot absorb any more water because it is so wet.

Child A: Yeah . . . can't 'apsorp' any more water . . . all full up!

At this point Child B momentarily looks up from what he is doing. He then looks back down at what he has been engrossed in for the last 10 minutes. Child B lies on the floor and is slowly trickling water from a small jug onto a mound of soil. With each drop he pours, he pauses and watches the water trickle down the sides of the mound.

Child B: Not all squidgy yet . . . need more water. (*He gradually pours more water onto the mound until it disintegrates completely and the water starts to puddle. He looks up.*)

Child C: Water can't go in any more 'cause it's all full up now . . . like his. (*Points to Child A.*)

Practitioner: That's right, the soil cannot absorb any more water for a bit because it's so wet.

Commentary

This interest led on to greater exploration of materials that absorb water in the water tray, with a particular favourite being sponges. It also gave opportunities to talk about materials that are waterproof and this is where the next observation stems from. Adult-initiated discussion on clothes (prompted by a book on what to wear in different weather) led onto thinking about how some are waterproof and some are not.

Child A: My coat stops all the rain.

Child B: And mine!

Practitioner: That means your coats are waterproof then.

Child A: Yeah, waterproof.

Practitioner: Can you think of any other clothes that stop the rain?

Child C: Wellies. I jump in puddles in my wellies and I don't get all wet 'foots'.

Practitioner: I see. Does that mean wellies are waterproof?

Child C: Yeah, waterproof.

Child A: My hat stops rain but only a little bit 'cause then I get wet on my hair.

Child B: And mine. I get all wet hair in my hat.

Practitioner: My hat does the same. That's because it isn't waterproof. Shall we see which of these clothes stop the water so are waterproof? (*The group nod excitedly.*)

The practitioner models putting the item of clothing over the clear washing up bowl and pouring some water from the jug onto the item of clothing. She encourages the children to watch what happens. Does the water soak through into the item of clothing and then the washing up bowl or does it sit on the top in a puddle? This prompts further discussion on which are waterproof and which are not.

Following this, the practitioner steps back and allows the children to explore the clothes and water.

Child A: Ah! It's all gone! (*As she pours the water over a T-shirt.*)

Child C: (*Pours water over a mac.*) It's a puddle! My coat stops the rain.

The children remain engrossed in pouring water over different clothes for a further 10 minutes, watching carefully to see what happens to the water.

Child C: I'm pouring lots on this, I am! (*She pours two jugs of water over a hooded top.*)

The children cheer when eventually the water starts to drip through into the bowl.

Practitioner: That's interesting. Some clothes take in lots of water and others none at all.

A range of materials was placed near the water tray (and hose pipe) to allow children to further their ideas and thinking in relation to these concepts.

Dialogic teaching

The concept of dialogic teaching (Alexander 2008) is also useful in helping us think about how to interact with children to support their learning in science and technology. Emerging from socio-cultural perspectives on learning that view language as a cultural tool through which children make sense of their first-hand experiences, it shares with SST the central importance of reciprocity. Harlen (2000: 34) gives the example of a child, who faced with an unfamiliar situation such as two wet wooden blocks sticking together, might suggest they are 'magnets sticking together – perhaps these blocks are magnetic'. This might be where the process ends, unless an interaction with a skilled adult who, producing a magnet and suggesting they 'Try this', moves the child forward in her understanding of magnets and forces, discovering that not everything that sticks together is magnetic.

Dialogic teaching helps us to both value children's ideas and introduce them to the established ideas of a discipline, so it has been particularly applied to science, which has a globally recognised body of knowledge that goes beyond an everyday understanding. What is important is that children have opportunities to appropriate the authoritative ideas of science – to make them their own – while maintaining their distinct voices as the group or class produces common language and shared understanding. This 'multivocality' (Wertsh 1998), involving interactions between different voices in the classroom, is central to dialogic practice.

Different authors use the term dialogic in slightly different ways. Alexander (2008) sees dialogic teaching as a collective and reciprocal process in which children and teachers address learning tasks together. According to Alexander, one characteristic of dialogic talk is that a series of interactions are chained together into coherent and deepening lines of enquiry: talk is 'cumulative' and it is also 'purposeful' with an educational aim in mind. In order to achieve this we need to go beyond responses to children's utterances that simply evaluate them – 'that's right', or 'good' – or the unhelpful 'almost' and 'well . . . sort of', to probe or challenge children's ideas, offering alternatives of our own. For dialogic talk to flourish is it essential that relationships between children and adults are trusting and mutually respectful so that challenges and questions are understood as a normal part of learning, not experienced as personal threats. Look at the transcript provided in Learning story 3.2 in which children examine a collection of materials to decide which would be make the best waterproof coat for Little Red Riding Hood. Would you judge it to be 'dialogic' using Alexander's criteria?

The culture of schools and settings can work against dialogic approaches. Alexander (2000) found that English schools are often so concerned with protecting children's self-esteem that they perpetuate environments in which challenging a child's ideas is seen as a criticism of the person, not the idea. This may have the consequence that many children will only offer ideas when they

Learning story 3.2

Soft or smooth?
The following short extract is from teacher Jae Munro, who works with a group of Reception children at St Phillips Primary School in Bath. In this extract the children were exploring and describing a collection of 'mystery objects', and Jae intervenes first to encourage the child to extend his description and then with a challenge to the vocabulary chosen.

Teacher: John?
John: Hard.
Teacher: Feels hard. Can you think of another word as well?
John: Soft.
Teacher: Soft. Hard and soft. Okay. I see what you mean, when you stroke it. I'm not sure soft is the word I would use, what word can we use instead of soft?
John: Smooth.
Teacher: You've got it in one, I think you're right actually John, I think it is smooth, so it's hard and smooth.

Commentary
When Jae intervenes he says, 'That's not the word I would use', offering a personal alternative viewpoint. John then realises the word 'smooth' expresses the shared idea he wants to convey better than 'soft'. Jae then moves into a more authoritative position in which he has the power to evaluate the idea: 'You've got it in one', before returning to being more tentative – 'I think you're right actually John', and handing back the ownership of the description to the child.

are sure they are 'right'. International comparisons suggest that different cultures develop different forms of interaction in educational settings, for example, a comparative study of the education of six-year-olds in England, Denmark and Finland found that in whole group situations:

> teaching in England was dominated by closed questions, brief answers and relatively little extended interaction. In Denmark and Finland, whole-class interaction was less tightly structured and more open and speculative. The English children were less confident speaking in whole-class settings, while in Denmark especially the strongly collective ethos encouraged rather than inhibited their contributions.
>
> (Ofsted 2003: 6)

Science is based on the rigorous examination of evidence and ideas, and so to 'do science' means to compare, debate and argue. According to Lemke (1990: 1) 'learning science means learning to talk science', which involves children gradually appropriating scientific ways of talking such as specific use of vocabulary and making causal connections. Learning story 3.3 provides an example of how a teacher intervened to develop children's use of descriptive vocabulary as they made observations of a 'mystery object'. The teacher was interested in using Mortimer and Scott's categories of 'communicative approach' to analyse his practice in terms of 'interactive/dialogic' and 'interactive/authoritative' categories (Mortimer and Scott 2003: 33; see Box 3.4 for more details) as he discussed children's ideas and compared them with scientific views.

Learning story 3.3

A waterproof coat

This transcript was provided by Julia Holder, teacher at St Phillips Primary School in Bath. The transcript illustrates a Reception teacher talking with a group of children about a collection of waterproof materials that they will select from to make a new coat for Little Red Riding Hood. Using Robin Alexander's characteristics of dialogic talk (Alexander 2008), to what extent do you think this episode is:

- collective;
- reciprocal;
- supportive;
- purposeful;
- cumulative?

Teacher: Let's talk one at a time. Let's go round the table. Suzy.
Suzy: This one feels the most waterproof.
Teacher: You think that one might be the most waterproof.
Jake: Yes, me too.

Teacher: Why do you think that one would be?

Child 3: No this one, this one is not.

Teacher: Are we listening to Suzy and Jake? Why do you think that one Suzy?

Suzy: Because umm, I think it's got no holes in.

Teacher: So there are no holes in that one. Is there one . . . Sarah, we're still listening to Suzy.

Suzy: Water is a little umm . . . umm . . . and you can go through liquid so it can umm . . . so if umm one of the . . . if this one had umm holes, umm, the water would go straight through and get you wet.

Teacher: What a good prediction there, so you're thinking about which one . . . no, we're going round one at a time. Thank you. Luke, which one do you think?

Luke: This one.

Teacher: Why do you think that one might be waterproof?

Luke: Uhh . . . because . . . uhh . . . because there's no holes in it.

Teacher: You think the same, so there's no holes, here, have a good look. Which one do you want?

Child : That one.

Teacher: Why do you think that one?

Child: I don't know.

Teacher: You're not quite sure. Any reason . . . does it remind you of anything, that material, where it might be used?

Child: No.

Teacher: Not quite sure. Don't worry. Well we'll see in a . . . Sam which one do you think is the most waterproof?

Sam: This one.

Teacher: Which one's that, in your hand? That one. Why do you think that one Sam?

Sam: Because . . . umm . . . it feels nice and . . . it . . . because it has just tiny holes, but umm the wind might not be able to get through the holes.

Teacher: Okay, so even though this has tiny holes, you think it won't be able to go through. Holly, we'll talk about that in a minute, okay, thank you Zak. Isla, which one do you think is the most waterproof? (*Isla points.*) Why do you think that one, Isla?

Isla: Because . . . umm . . . there's only tiny holes on it and the rain can't get through the tiny holes.

Teacher: Okay, so tiny holes, you think rain can't get through tiny holes.

Isla: And this is different because it goes . . . umm . . . in different directions.

Teacher: Oh okay.

Isla: And this one . . . if you wear this one, you can . . . you could . . . you would just get soaked because you can see through it.

Teacher: You can see through it, you can see those holes. Umm . . . Sarah . . . which one do you think?

Sarah: This one and it reminds . . . it really looks like an outside material of my thick coat.

Teacher: Ahh, so it reminds you of your coat. Okay, so how are we going to find out?

Commentary

In this transcript there is a sense of the development of a collective approach; the ideas of a wide range of children in the group are being sought and heard.

The teacher is also encouraging the children to listen to teach others' ideas carefully so they hear some alternative suggestions. She is probing the children's responses by asking the children to justify their ideas, but in this episode she is not yet challenging them. Although the discussion is purposeful it is not strongly cumulative: the ideas about the significance of 'holes' in the materials are collected rather than being evaluated. This seems appropriate as the evaluation and conclusion will come later, when the children have tested their choice of materials.

Box 3.4

Communicative approaches

Interactive/dialogic: the teacher and students explore ideas, generating new meanings, posing genuine questions and offering, listening to and working on different points of view.

Non-interactive/dialogic: the teacher considers various point of view, setting out, exploring and working on different perspectives.

Interactive/authoritative: the teacher leads the students through a sequence of questions and answers with the aim of reaching one specific point of view.

Non-interactive/authoritative: the teacher presents one specific point of view.

(Mortimer and Scott 2003: 35)

In the examples of practice discussed so far in this chapter, the contexts for talk have been meaningful for the children. Sustained shared thinking was developed from children's exploratory play with puddles, a teacher introducing exciting 'mystery objects' and the story of Little Red Riding Hood, which was used to engage children in designing and making her a waterproof coat. In Chapter 2 we noted that children's ability to blur the boundaries between fantasy and reality in their play can be maximised to support their designing and making. In the next part of this chapter we argue that when this fantasy element is introduced through a story we greatly enhance the imaginative possibilities.

Narrative and culture

Although much has been written about the pivotal role language plays in teaching and learning – including that of science and technology – the potential of narrative as a powerful vehicle or tool for learning is often overlooked and undervalued. Bruner (1990: 77) provides a detailed and compelling analysis of narrative's critical role in the development of meaning, arguing that it is 'one of the most ubiquitous and powerful discourse forms in human communication'. In the rest of this chapter we will discuss narrative as a vehicle or tool for supporting children's thinking and thus their potential as scientists, designers and technologists. We will include narratives that are cultural and personal, traditional and contemporary, oral as well as published.

Narrative is central to children's experiences at home, at school and in the wider community. This is not limited to language; children are surrounded by and exist in a world of settings, characters and events. From a very early age children hear all sorts of narratives involving themselves, their families and their community. The narratives told by parents or caregivers that involve the child as the principal character are perhaps most powerful in developing their understanding of the world. Whitehead (2010: 104) suggests that narratives are essential to human existence and that they are created by human beings as a means of making meaningful patterns in life and interpreting experiences that they or their ancestors, near or distant, may have had:

> At its most elemental, narrative begins with the urge to tell stories about an event, person or feeling. Narrating may even be the oldest and most basic human language activity . . . explaining, gossiping and speculating about human behaviour and the chances of life.

Narrative can therefore be viewed as a basic human language activity; a form of communicating meaning from individual to individual, community to community and from generation to generation. Mercer (2000) provides powerful illustrations of how culture and communication are inextricably linked: a community has a shared history, a collective identity, reciprocal obligations and a discourse. The function of narrative has been to act as a powerful means through which shared knowledge and understanding of self and the community, present, past and future, is developed. Rogoff (1990) argues that the cognitive activities of individuals are embedded within a cultural context. Values and skills thought to be worthy by the community constitute a 'cultural legacy' inherited from near and distant ancestors, with the assistance of caregivers and peers. She suggests that, through cultural institutions, technologies and traditions, problems of the present that may need solving are set; tools to assist problem-solving are provided and efforts to solve problems are channelled in ways valued by the culture.

However, even within the same culture, cognitive activities such as problem-solving may be influenced by values specific to the context. For example, learning about food production through designing and making a pizza may be thought of as worthwhile within both the cultural institutions of school and home. The language tool for this activity may consist of a recipe (a culturally organised procedural text) plus verbal instruction to support the text. Adults' values, relating to food either in the home or the school, may be influenced by past or present circumstances. In either of these institutions learning through making mistakes – for example, burning the pizza – may be thought acceptable and a valuable part of the learning experience, but the issue of wasted ingredients may be differently expressed through verbal disapproval. Whether acceptable or unacceptable, factual or embellished, between peers or family, it is likely that a 'narrative' of the experience will develop and will be a contributing factor to the child's learning process. Narratives, then, are essential to human existence and are used to communicate an understanding of our culture's past and present, as well as its predicted future:

> Narratives may be a crucial element in human evolution and intelligent adaptability, enabling the species to predict or make up stories about likely outcomes as well as remote possibilities.
>
> (Whitehead 2010: 105)

Some of the most powerful narratives about the past, present and future of western society are those presented by scientists, technologists and designers. Our current understanding of human evolution, the influence of biotechnology on us as a species, and the utopian or doomsday scenarios of our hi-tech or environmentally catastrophic futures, all emanate from these professions. So it should come as no surprise that narrative plays an important part in their work.

Stories used by designers, technologists and scientists

Designers sometimes use narrative to gain understandings of their clients' lifestyles and needs (Davies 1996). In the early stages of a project, a designer might envisage the type of person who is likely to use the product in question and invent simple narratives to describe the situations in which they might make use of it. This is known as 'human factors' research:

> We think about all the steps a person will go through as they use a product: how they will get started; what they have to do while they use it; and how they stop and put it away. Sometimes we write or draw these sequences to remember them. For each step we think about what the important human factors are.
>
> (Human factors designer, quoted in Davies 1996: 54)

Mercer (2000: 110–11) suggests that the use of narratives as a way of communicating key information is prevalent in industry. He suggests that those working in industry spend most of their time telling each other 'stories' . . . [for these] are a means for displaying experience and expertise, provide 'models' for doing the shared action in which the partners are engaged, and communicate technical knowledge in a memorable form.

Many of the stories technicians share are based on told or learned knowledge about how the world works and may include tales of work, family and community: 'In the community . . . telling relevant stories about dealing with past problems is a way of thinking together' (Mercer 2000: 111). For young children, giving a running commentary about what they are making in the construction area, or telling an adult about the teddy for whom they are designing a hat, may fulfil some of the same narrative functions.

Scientists too have their own narratives, which have been constructed to offer explanations of the world, its inhabitants and the environment, natural or made. These narratives change over time as knowledge and understanding increase. For example, most people once believed that the Earth was flat and was the centre of the universe. Through the work of scientists including Copernicus and Galileo in the sixteenth and seventeenth centuries these understandings changed to a view of the Sun as the centre of the universe with a spherical Earth orbiting it. Later scientists realised that the Sun itself was orbiting the Milky Way galaxy, and Einstein in the twentieth century introduced the idea that the universe has no centre, since all motion is relative. Recent work by cosmologists and physicists, including Stephen Hawking, suggests an expanding universe (or universes), complete with a Big Bang, black holes, dark matter and many other strange phenomena. The public has an insatiable appetite for popular science books and television documentaries propounding the latest competing stories about our place in the universe.

This form of narrative has implications for practitioners in all phases of education. Millar and Osborne (1998: 13) suggest that 'science education should make greater use of one of the world's most powerful and pervasive ways of communicating ideas – the narrative form'. They recommend that science education should present scientific knowledge as a number of key 'explanatory stories' (see also Harlen 2000: 25) and that children need to approach these stories 'not as "given" knowledge but as the product of sustained inquiry by individuals working in social and historical contexts'. The examples they give of such explanatory stories include the Earth and beyond (above) and the particle model of matter:

> Imagine being able to 'peek inside' matter. Then you would 'see' that matter is made of tiny particles of less than 100 different types. These particles, called atoms, move about, arranging or re-arranging themselves in patterns or sticking together to make new, more complex particles. Alternatively, complex particles can be broken up into their constituent atoms.
>
> (Millar and Osborne 1998: 14)

This important idea, from which many ways of understanding phenomena such as mixing, dissolving and burning derive, is really a story in that we don't know whether it is 'true' or not. Dalton's original hypothesis about atoms, made at the beginning of the nineteenth century, has found much support from experimental evidence and led to all sorts of other ideas such as quantum theory, but the fact remains that nobody has ever actually 'seen' an atom! This is an important characteristic of science that we believe it is important for children to grasp; namely that science tells us great stories to help us understand our surroundings, but they are not 'facts' and will almost certainly change.

Children could explore the stories of scientists' work and the evidence they have used – another example of using narrative in teaching and learning science – such as Edward Jenner's understanding of antibodies that led to early vaccination. For children in the Early Years context, most will have recent experience of 'having an injection'. We can use this experience to begin to tell the explanatory story about our bodies' defences against disease. What does it feel like to be ill? Why do we need to have injections? Have any children felt a 'little bit' ill after having an injection and why do they think this is? Setting up the role-play area as a doctor's surgery where children can go and 'have an injection' will spark numerous recollections and acted-out stories related to vaccination.

Personal narratives or 'storying'

We will now turn our attention to personal narratives and their function in developing children's thinking in early childhood. The term 'storying' is used by Whitehead (2010: 106) to describe personal narratives shared between young children and their caregivers in early interactions between them. She uses this term as a way of distinguishing 'personal narrative activity from the published or traditional stories current in a community'. We suggest that as children begin formal education, narratives can act as a bridge, spanning and connecting children's early knowledge and understanding of science and technology, or versions of these subjects that they will experience in school, nursery or playgroup. This early knowledge and understanding has been gained through interaction and shared personal narratives with caregivers. These narratives are 'basic and spontaneous' and are not to be confused with published forms. However, elements of published cultural narratives may be included in the story being told. For example, when dressing a young child in a red coat the caregiver's narrative may proceed as follows:

> We're getting ready to go to the big shops. We need to get lots of food for Holly's party. We need to put on your coat and go in the car and be back in time for Holly coming out of school. Holly likes you in your red coat, doesn't she? She calls you 'Little Red Riding Hood' and pretends to be the wolf.

Trevarthen (1995) suggests that children are born expecting to communicate and share meaningful experiences with caregivers. His research found that from birth children have a desire to communicate and actively seek to 'chat' with caregivers, thus beginning the 'narrative' of communication between them. In these early conversations both participants take active roles and mutually encourage each other. For example, in the conversation above, while the adult talks to the child, the child too would be contributing through eye contact, smiles, gestures and vocalisations, thus encouraging the adult to continue. Through such exchanges, young children eagerly learn the language and all other peculiar habits and beliefs of their community. These habits and beliefs include those relating to scientific and technological activities and thinking, such as the importance of planning what we will make or do. The following four short cameos of a young child at play illustrate how early storying contributes to the development of scientific and design-related thinking.

Cameo 1: Identifying and classifying animals

Yorgi (16 months) is refining his already developing scientific skills and concepts. When playing with his toy animals he is skilled at classifying them through the sounds they make. These sounds have been internalised by him though stories read to him about animals and those shared with him when playing alongside his animal toys. For example, farm animals are identified and classified according to his perception of their type. Sheep-like animals say 'bah, bah', cow-like say 'moo', pig-like make a remarkable nasal grunt. Wild animals are also categorised in this way: 'rawagh, rawagh' mimicking a lion for all big cats, 'hoo, hoo' for a monkey, and an upward arm movement with very little accompanying sound represents elephants. Vehicles used for transporting the animals, as with all machinery (including the vacuum and coffee maker) of course, are represented by the sound 'mmmm, mmmm'. When systematically arranging the habitat of his wild animals, he is developing an awareness that the giraffes and zebras cannot possibly be housed with the 'big cats' without serious consequences. The shared storying has told him so. Through visiting zoos this concept will be developed: animals will be housed according to classification, and the personal narratives shared by the adults that accompany the visits will confirm this. Through nature programmes on television (a type of cultural narrative) the characteristics of the natural habitats for each of these animals will be revealed, together with their feeding relationships.

Cameo 2: The night sky

Through observing the night sky with adults, Yorgi is able to identify the Moon and stars. On seeing them he automatically rocks backwards and forwards in a rhythmic movement accompanied by his 'singing' to encourage his caregiver to share the rhyme 'Twinkle, Twinkle Little Star' and the song 'I See the Moon'. Trevarthen (1995) describes this type of interaction between child and caregiver as a 'rhythmic story' that has all the features of a narrative, including 'an introduction, build-up, climax and resolution'.

Cameo 3: Building and making

Yorgi shares with his caregiver his new developing skill of building with commercially produced interlocking bricks. As the physical skill of building is practised, habitats are created to house toy people and soft animals. 'Bob the Builder', along with a policeman and fireman from the set of bricks, has various adventures that require structures and equipment made from the bricks. With each adventure is an accompanying 'story'. The picnic bench has to be made longer for all three figures to be seated. Yorgi, when seeing a tall tower with 'Bob' on the top will put his hands up to his mouth and exclaim 'Oh no!', knowing that from past experiences and the shared stories, 'Bob' will soon suffer the consequences of a tower design lacking in safety features!

Cameo 4: Arranging the home for the 'new baby'

Through recent changes to his home in preparation for a younger brother, Yorgi shares with his parents the many narratives about 'his new baby'. When members of the extended family visit, he is able to take them upstairs to explain and report (through vocalising and many arm gestures) the new order of his and his baby's bedrooms. In each room he directs his hands and arms with accompanying long vocalisations, as he exchanges the 'stories' of the possible positions for soon-to-arrive new furniture. At the mention of the word 'wardrobe' he immediately takes up a position in the corner of his bedroom and gestures and laughs. As he 'assists' in arranging and rearranging his clothes and soft toys into various temporary containers the narrative between him and his mother includes the benefits and disadvantages of these items being placed in easy and difficult to reach locations.

Commentary

What, then, do the above cameos tell us about the development of scientific and technological thinking through personal narratives with young children? Can we relate the way in which Yorgi's thinking was developing to some of the research and theory that was discussed in Chapter 2? In Cameos 1 and 2, Yorgi is developing the essential scientific skills of observation and classification. In some senses these skills are 'natural' and pre-programmed, but by telling stories as he does them, and incorporating elements of the cultural narratives that surround him, they become much more powerful. In Cameos 3 and 4 his understanding of the 'client' (be it 'Bob the Builder' or his baby brother) developed through storying makes his technological behaviour (joining and arranging elements) more meaningful. As Early Years practitioners we need to remember to utilise and maximise this basic and spontaneous form of narrative to develop, refine and expand children's thinking.

Opportunities that arise spontaneously need to be recognised as potential learning experiences and incorporated into daily classroom activities. For example, in one Early Years setting, children arrive unprepared for bad weather and very wet after a sudden deluge. After sharing in their stories of how and why they got so wet this situation becomes a 'natural' starting point for investigations of materials that are waterproof, designing clothes to protect body, legs and feet. Opportunities that adults have planned can also be purposeful. For example, rearranging the classroom provides opportunities for discussions with children about possible design and layout of furniture, and for sharing stories of how it was and how it could be improved – 'human factor' research with teacher and children as designers and clients.

Using cultural narratives as starting points

The cultural narratives that are of most significance to children are the nursery rhymes and songs, traditional and folk tales, myths and legends, originally told orally and now fixed in print. Added to oral and published narratives are those increasingly important narratives within digital media such as computers, television and films. Using stories as starting points for science and technology is an established feature of Early Years practice; several publications have been produced over the years to support teachers in planning for this. For example, the Collins Primary Science scheme (Howe 1990) uses traditional tales and rhymes as starting points for a range of scientific activities. In 'Threads of Thinking', Nutbrown (2011: 87) explores the notion of 'nourishing children's thinking through stories'. Using 'The Tooth Ball' (Pearce 1987) as a starting point, she describes how, 'after telling this story to her class of five-year-olds, a teacher introduced some work on wrapping and packaging'.

For designing and making activities, stories offer the opportunity to identify with a character and empathise with his or her needs. For example, in Raymond Briggs's 'Jim and the Beanstalk' (1997) the giant has poor eyesight, little hair and no teeth. This provides the opportunity for pupils to design glasses, wigs and false teeth for these fantasy needs, a project undertaken by the Reception class at Trinity Primary School in Taunton. Examples of stories in which the characters have clearly identifiable needs are given in Table 3.1, which also shows how the same stories could be used to support scientific learning.

TABLE 3.1 Story books as starting points for D&T and science

Title	Author(s) and publisher	Science links	Needs/wants (D&T)
'The Lighthouse Keeper's Lunch'	Ronda and David Armitage, Scholastic	Humans – nutrition	Something to protect and scare birds; a packed lunch
'Who Sank the Boat?'	Pamela Allen, Puffin	Forces – floating and sinking	A boat that will carry some animals without sinking
'Owl at Home'	Arnold Lobel, Mammoth	Materials	A house to keep the winter out; something to get Owl up and down the stairs quickly
'Mr Gumpy's Outing'	John Burningham, Puffin	Forces – floating and sinking	A boat to carry all the passengers without sinking
'Whatever Next!'	Jill Murphy, Picture Mac	Forces, Earth and beyond	A rocket like baby bear's to go to the Moon
'Good-night Owl!'	Pat Hutchins, Puffin	Sound	A sound-proof house for Owl
'Jim and the Beanstalk'	Raymond Briggs, Puffin	Life and living processes	New teeth, glasses and a wig for the giant
'Peace at Last'	Jill Murphy, Macmillan	Sound	Ear muffs for Father Bear
'Can't You Sleep Little Bear?'	Martin Waddell, Walker Books	Light	A light for Little Bear's cave

Learning 'embedded' in a familiar cultural context both stimulates and extends children's deeper understanding. Narrative provides a wonderfully supportive framework for young children's learning, as Berger (1997: 29) explains:

> When we are dealing with concepts, notions, or ideas, we make sense of them by contrasting them with their opposites, that is why when we read or hear the word rich, we automatically contrast it with poor, and when we read or hear the word happy we think of the word sad. If everyone has a great deal of money rich loses its meaning; rich means something only in contrast to poor.

Through such stories and rhymes young children gain an enormous amount of knowledge about how things work: permanent and reversible changes, the effect of gravity, properties of materials etc. Young children are inspired to explore scientific theories and design problems inherent in such narratives; the 'basic and spontaneous' become opportunities for embedded tasks (Donaldson 1978). In the following case study (Learning story 3.5) a traditional tale was used to instigate real scientific discovery and technological solutions.

Learning story 3.5

Material from traditional tales

Judy Cooper, Year 1 class teacher at Broad Chalke C of E First School, Wiltshire, describes her work with 'The Three Little Pigs':

> As a starting point the children went on a walk around the village to observe houses in terms of their materials and different styles. They were able to identify similarities and differences. The walk enabled the children to discuss building materials with confidence. The story of 'The Three Little Pigs' was very much enjoyed. They worked in groups to build houses that were then tested to see if they could be blown down.

TABLE 3.2 Learning outcomes for science and literacy from 'The Three Little Pigs'

Literacy	Science
Traditional stories	Observation, description and exploration of materials
To extend vocabulary; develop ideas and opinions; to collect words associated with houses	Name and describe the building materials used in 'The Three Little Pigs'
Record observations from sorting materials into sets, e.g. hard/soft, rough/smooth, weak/strong	Mind-map knowledge of houses and the materials used for building
Children to talk about their own homes, using photographs brought in as stimulus	Gather evidence of features and materials of homes in the local area from an observation trail
Share the story of 'The Three Little Pigs'. Use the story as a stimulus to raise the question of suitability of different materials for building a house	Explore and describe a collection of building materials using appropriate senses
Use reference books and evidence from observation to discover different types of homes and materials used to build them and record findings	Explore and recognise similarities and differences in building materials
Write sentences using 'I saw . . .' sentence structure to describe features of houses and materials used in building	Investigate and test the suitability of materials for building a house
Record science investigation – testing materials	Use straw, sticks and bricks to build three houses and then try to blow them down. Reinforce work on forces from last term. Use hairdryer for increasing force
Design own home using information for investigation, observation, research and discussion	

Judy brought literacy and science together to very powerful effect. As can be seen from the teaching objectives for this unit of work (Table 3.2), reading, writing, speaking and listening activities informed and inspired activity in science and vice versa. The children followed the Three Little Pigs in their search for a 'safe house'.

From this concrete example of the need for selecting the 'best' material children were supported in their more abstract investigation of materials. Had the children been asked to compare the properties of materials without the background of the pigs' dilemma, they may have found it difficult to articulate difference and similarity. The weakness of the straw used by the first little pig provides an extreme example against which the children can measure other materials. The story itself and the conversation arising from its reading can prompt new descriptions that can be used for further exploration and discovery.

In this Year 1 classroom the display boards and cupboard tops reflected the learning of the children. In order to design their own 'dream homes' and avoid the disaster that struck the homes of the first two pigs the children researched and tested materials, looked at the shape and features of houses and tried out their theories on houses made by the class. Having completed their investigation the children were then able to apply their understanding to design and make their own houses (Figure 3.1).

FIGURE 3.1 Making a house as part of a topic on 'The Three Little Pigs'

Commentary
Not only did this traditional tale provide an ideal starting point for young children's work on materials, it enabled the teacher to bring in other aspects of their scientific understanding and apply them creatively to current learning. The effects of forces on materials may be a complex concept for six-year-olds but children are very familiar with the repeated chant of the wolf as he huffs and puffs and blows houses down.

Summary

This chapter first explored sustained shared thinking and dialogic talk as approaches to teaching and learning science and technology that are based in socio-cultural perspectives. We have considered some of the challenges for teachers in developing these reciprocal ways of talking with children that require change to culturally established patterns of interaction. We have drawn on these concepts to reflect on transcripts of talk in Early Years settings and classrooms. Later in the chapter we have asserted the primacy of narrative in children's learning about themselves, the cultures they inhabit and the physical environments they explore. Learning in science and D&T involves 'telling stories', whether the spontaneous narratives that develop between parent and child or the more structured forms of narrative involved in describing a sequence of stages in making or explaining the development of a scientific idea over time. We have explored ways in which Early Years practitioners can exploit this interplay between culture, literacy, science and design through discussing children's personal narratives and by using traditional tales or rhymes as starting points. These themes will be picked up and developed in subsequent chapters.

Discussion points

- How might you develop your own participation in sustained shared thinking with children?
- What kinds of talk have you experienced during your own science and technology education? Would you describe them as 'dialogic'?
- What different books, poems and television programmes can you think of that might lead to productive learning in science and/or technology?

4

Outdoor learning in science and technology

Sarah Earle

Purpose of this chapter

After reading this chapter you should have an understanding of:

- how outdoor learning can support learning in science and technology;
- what quality provision of science and technology looks like outside;
- the role of outdoor learning in education for sustainable development.

Introduction

Much of science and technology learning lends itself to working outside; add to this the increasingly popular interest in outdoor learning in Early Years practice and its relevance becomes self-evident. To provide *enabling environments* is an overarching principle of the EYFS Statutory Framework (DfE 2012: 4). Early Years providers have embraced this wholeheartedly, with free-flow between indoors and outside spaces becoming the norm. The outdoors is just one of the areas of the learning environment where resources and activities are placed, with children spending time both inside and outside depending on their preference for self-initiated activities or those under adult direction. We need to consider what scientific and technological learning is taking place in the outdoor area and how to support or extend it. However, not all young children will have an immediately available outdoor space, and as children move through the school the proportion of time spent outside diminishes (Bianchi and Feasey 2011: 5). Thus this chapter will serve two purposes: to explore how learning can be taken outside – particularly when facilities do not include a 'free-flow' area – and to examine what quality provision for science and technology can look like outside.

Why go outdoors?

Perhaps the title of this section should be 'why stay indoors'? Why should learning take place inside a classroom? Perhaps it is our mental model of education that needs to be expanded! More detailed examples will be explored in the rest of the chapter, but it is useful to highlight some key features of outdoor learning from the outset. Learning outside can:

■ Be bigger: large construction and vehicles for sitting in can be explored outside;

■ Be messier: working with soil is not a problem when you are outdoors;

■ Be independent of the weather conditions: with the right clothing and footwear children can explore the outdoors whatever the weather;

■ Use natural resources: finding a leaf or stick that is the same or different is easier to resource than creating a box of classroom resources for the same task;

■ Be more independent: children do not feel so enclosed or closely watched;

■ Support children to understand risks: teaching them to be aware of and manage risks rather than to be afraid;

■ Help children to connect with nature: developing educational values for sustainable development.

Before moving on to the details of supporting outdoor learning, it is important to consider what is meant by the outdoors. It includes 'free-flow' outdoor areas, which are part of the learning space, often just outside the classroom, which enable children to move freely between the inside and outside. The outdoors also includes every part of the school grounds, whether that is a concrete playground or a large field. There is a lot of potential just outside the classroom door that is not only free, but also does not require a permission slip to go there. This is where the children play each day, so they and we may not 'see' the science and technology in front of them. Skilled adult intervention can prompt them to pause, for example, to notice the plants and animals that they run past each day. Outdoor learning also includes the local environment beyond the school gate: the local park or stream or shops; the traffic noise survey; the building materials trail; the nature walk etc. It can extend further still, to the school coach trip to the zoo, the farm or the beach. With such a range of places to consider, it is surprising that we spend so long inside the classroom!

EYFS and Key Stage 1 curriculum links

Outdoor provision is an essential part of the *enabling environment* in the statutory guidance for the EYFS:

Providers must provide access to an outdoor play area or, if that is not possible, ensure that outdoor activities are planned and taken on a daily basis (unless circumstances make this inappropriate, for example unsafe weather conditions).

(DfE 2012: 24)

The *Development Matters* (Early Education 2012) guidance also details use of the outdoors and local areas. For Key Stage 1, guidance is more implicit, carried in the idea that children should 'explore the world around them' (DfE 2013: 147), but specific mention of the outdoors is mainly confined to the non-statutory notes. For example, in the Year 1 Plants notes and guidance it states that:

Pupils should use the local environment throughout the year to explore and answer questions about plants growing in their habitat. Where possible, they should observe the growth of flowers and vegetables that they have planted.

(DfE 2013: 148)

Thus in Key Stage 1 children are encouraged to explore the world around them; study plants and animals within their habitat; use their local environment to observe how living things depend on each other and compare materials in other places. It is also important to remember that learning outside can happen whether or not it is directed by a national curriculum!

Early Years themes and contexts for learning

Many scientific and technological discoveries are already taking place in the continuous outdoor play provision (sand, water, etc.) of Early Years settings. It may be just a case of practitioners 'seeing' the opportunities and drawing out the skills and language involved in activities that are already taking place. However, it may also involve providing extension or focus to challenge the children to develop their skills and understanding. Table 4.1 contains some examples of typical outdoor activities and how they link to science and technology. Further details about these topics can be found in the relevant 'thematic approach' chapter and a list of resources can be found in Table 6.2.

Going for walks

Exploration of the local environment could take the form of a focused 'welly walk' in search of different shaped leaves, or a 'journey stick walk' where items from the walk are stuck or tied to the stick to help remember the places visited. These walks could be inside or outside the school fence, but because they are local this

TABLE 4.1 Science and D&T links for typical outdoor play provision

Outdoor area	Example activities	Science and technology links
Sand	Feeling wet/dry sand, pouring dry sand through sieves Using tools to dig/build tunnels/castles	Properties of wet/dry sand Use of tools Exploration of stability of tunnels/castles
Water	Pouring between containers Washing dolls Making boats, sinking boats	Properties of a liquid Floating and sinking (forces)
Vehicles	Driving the cars, turning the wheels, scooting	Pushes and pulls (forces)
Construction	Building towers Building dens	Testing materials, language of materials
Role play	Garden centre Building site Fire service 'Muddy kitchen' Archaeologist	Role of science and technology in real life

enables children to revisit these places easily, perhaps with parents. By exploring the locality with a particular focus the children are prompted to look closely at a place, perhaps noticing things such as bird nests that they have previously walked past. When asked to focus on a particular sense, such as hearing, their careful listening should lead them to notice new things about their environment. Asking children to predict what they will hear before the sensory walk can tell practitioners a lot about what they already know and also support them to listen when out in the field. While on the walk, children could try to identify the source of the sound and whether it is 'natural' – made by wind, water or a living creature other than humans – or 'industrial' (such as an engine or building sound). The volume (loudness) of the sound can be measured with a datalogger and recording the sound could act as a memory prompt back in the classroom as children try to identify the sound and remember where it was heard.

Science and technology trails

'Let's Go Science Trails' is a Primary Science Teaching Trust (formerly AstraZenca Science Teaching Trust) project in which a cluster of primary schools in Haringey developed Science Trails to make the most of outdoor areas in urban London (www.pstt.org.uk/funding-and-projects/projects/lets-go-science-trails.aspx). The trails include advice on looking for plants, birds, natural/manufactured materials, light sources, use of electricity and forces in the playground. Before going on a trail with children it is important to discuss with them what they will be asked to do; for example, when going on a 'minibeast safari' (hunting for small invertebrates) children could be asked to 'find something small that moves,' or challenged to 'see how many different minibeasts you can find,' including examples with different numbers of legs/wings/eyes etc. It is also important to brief any adults who are supporting the trail, so that they know how best to support the children's learning.

Or how about a technology trail? Children can look for 'interesting things made by people' on their trail, such as road signs that light up to tell traffic to slow down or bus stops with electronic indicators. How does the bus stop know when the next bus is coming? Children could think about how the bus and stop might be communicating with each other (using a radio? A mobile phone? A satellite in space?). Interesting things might not be limited to hi-tech examples; perhaps an unusual design for a park bench or an ornamental gate might capture children's interest. They can then be asked to consider what they think the artefact is made from or how it was put together. Building sites – though often nowadays hidden behind tall hoardings – can be sources of fascination for young children. Occasionally sites provide 'windows' in the hoardings for children to observe metal structures being lifted into place by cranes or concrete being poured. As well as learning about the uses of different materials children can be encouraged to talk about the technological process of building (e.g.: 'Who decides what the building is going to look like?' 'What do the builders need to do first?' 'How do they know which bit goes where?'). This can greatly enrich children's construction play when they return to the classroom.

Scientific process skills

Process skills are the thinking skills that children need to develop in order to engage in scientific and technological enquiry. These skills include observation, comparison, raising questions, predicting, investigating and drawing conclusions from their findings. These and others will be returned to in later chapters; however observation and comparison are the process skills most relevant to this discussion. For example, the outdoors is the perfect place to develop observation skills, with its huge natural variety and ever-changing environments. We can support children to notice, describe and explain these variations and changes. To enhance their observation skills, children can be challenged to create a nature colour pallet (using double-sided tape on a pallet shape or on a colour swatch from a paint shop), collecting small samples of natural materials to 'match' the colours on their swatch.

The ability to compare, to talk about similarities and differences between places, objects, materials and living things is a key feature of the 'Understanding the world' Early Learning Goal (DfE 2012: 9). For example, children can be prompted to identify the loudest or quietest sound on a nature trail. Such noticing and comparison can develop into question-raising as children seek to find out why flowers tend to be brightly coloured or why no grass grows under the trees. We then might prompt children to consider how they might go about finding the answers to their questions: 'What do you think? Is there a way we can test your idea?' Such hypothesis-forming and testing is an integral part of science. *Development Matters* (Early Education 2012: 2) suggests that an enabling environment should '. . . support children to take risks and explore'. Being outdoors is more free, less enclosed and observed, and thus feels more 'risky' both to children and their practitioners. However, by developing their understanding of risk, children are able to become more independent.

Story books

Story books can provide an interesting context for outdoor learning. They can be used to spark interest, to set up a problem or to raise questions. For example, there are many Julia Donaldson books that link to the outdoors. Children could look for nuts like the mouse in 'The Gruffalo' (1999), finding habitats along the way, such as the snake's logpile house. 'The Gruffalo's Child' (2004) could provide the inspiration for following tracks: 'Aha! Aho! A track in the snow! Whose is this track and where does it go?' (Donaldson 2004: 5), while 'Stick Man' (2008) could be the stimulus for exploring uses for sticks or the changing seasons.

Another book extensively used for outdoor learning is Michael Rosen's 'We're Going on a Bear Hunt' (1989). The class can replicate the bear hunt, deciding which places or materials can act as the swishy, swashy grass or squelchy mud. Alternatively they could go on their own hunt for 'minibeasts', materials or members of staff who have left an evidence trail. A different example is Jez Alborough's 'Duck in the Truck' (1999) where the truck becomes stuck in the mud. Here there is potential for recreating the scene and using different tools to push or pull the truck out of a patch of mud, linking to the science of forces and the exploration of tools in D&T.

Intervening to develop young children's understanding

One way of intervening in children's outdoor learning is to introduce challenge to the continuous provision areas of the learning environment. For example, children can be set challenges such as: 'What can squirt water the furthest? Can we build a raft to cross the shark infested waters? Can we make a waterway with tubes or guttering to transport items downstream?' Children often introduce their own challenges, such as: 'What if we try this now?' When this happens it is our role as practitioners to support these interests, by encouraging children to talk about the results of their inquiries or suggesting new things to try. The activity is child-initiated, but adult-extended. For example, when one child in a Bristol nursery showed an interest in fixing cars by using a plastic screwdriver on toy cars, the adult asked: 'Have you checked the wheels on the trike?' This led to the creation of a garage for large wheeled vehicles.

Provision of supportive or extending resources can happen at many levels, ranging from individual activities – such as providing windmills, streamers and bubbles to investigate the effects of wind (see weather boxes in Chapter 10) – to the provision of common resources for the whole school or setting. Schemes such as Scrapstore Playpod (www.playpods.co.uk), which contains a range of waste materials to stimulate creative and cooperative play, can support this whole-school approach. Somewhere in between these two ends of the spectrum is the outdoor science box or bag (Bianchi and Feasey 2011). This can be a box of generic resources or a set of rucksacks to support independent science explorations. Such a kit may contain (at different times): magnifiers, binoculars, nets, containers or sample bags (for collecting specimens), magnets, torches, clipboards, paper/labels and pencils for recording or map-making. Electronic recording equipment could be added to the bag/box to add further interest, for example, digital cameras, Easispeak microphones (available from www.tts-group.co.uk) or dataloggers (discussed below).

Many schools and settings are developing their grounds with outdoor learning in mind. Children can be involved in the redesign from the outset, whether it is siting planting boxes at the edge of a tarmac playground or redeveloping a whole field (see Learning story 4.1). Creating a 'Darwin thinking path' (Bianchi and Feasey 2011) is a novel use of the school grounds. Every day, Charles Darwin would walk along his path around Down House, giving him time to think: a reminder to children that scientists need thinking time as well as 'doing' time. A thinking path could be simply a few markers to signify the way; the siting of inspirational words/pictures/questions at points of interest; or a larger project where sensory gardens are developed en route. Visits further afield provide children with new experiences. The specialist environment of a farm or zoo cannot easily be replicated in the school grounds. As with other outdoor experiences, it is important to guide children with a clear focus for their observation, to avoid the most memorable part of the visit being the trip to the zoo shop! Inclusion of such trips should be considered when planning for the term or the year, deciding when and where they will have the most impact to justify the travel and entry costs.

Forest school

Forest schools have proliferated across the UK since the 1990s. With roots in the Scandinavian model of complete outdoor kindergartens, there is an increasing

Learning story 4.1

Millbrook School field

Sue Thorn, science subject leader at Millbrook Primary in Swindon, was given an empty field to develop following a new school build. She aimed to not only create something that was aesthetically pleasing and a fun place to be, she also hoped to create opportunities for outdoor learning and raise the profile of science in the process. By involving the children and community in the development of a 'sensory garden' it has become very much a whole-school project.

Many areas have been created: an activity trail, a willow dome, a wild meadow and fruit trees leading to a working garden. The wild meadow and 'bug hotel' provide new habitats to encourage wildlife and enable the children to examine a variety of 'minibeasts', while the activity trail has been used to consider what happens to the body during exercise. The raised beds outside nursery have been so successful that a working garden has been created to enable every class to tend its own patch, supported by a gardening club. The children prepare the soil, sow the seeds, tend and water the plants (Figure 4.1), and finally harvest, wash, chop and eat them. Being involved in every stage of producing fruit and vegetables provides the children with a valuable insight into plant lifecycles.

FIGURE 4.1 Planting the lettuces

variety of provision. So what turns an outdoor learning experience into a forest school? The following list is a summary of principles from the Forest School Association (www.forestschoolassociation.org):

- regular and long-term sessions;
- takes place in woodland or natural environment (e.g. fields or beach);
- learner-centred;
- aims for holistic development, fostering resilient, confident, independent and creative learners;

- offers learners the opportunity to take supported risks appropriate to the environment and to themselves;

- run by qualified forest school practitioners (Level 3).

The regular sessions build a relationship between the learners and the environment, supporting respect for nature, understanding of interdependence and of the changing seasons. 'The natural landscape offers the resources and props for play' (Tovey 2007: 83), with plant material being transformed in imaginative den-building. It is also more challenging than an artificial play area, with uneven ground and varied climbing heights. Knight (2011: 16) emphasises the importance of forest school learning occurring over time; it is not about one-off activities, since 'children who are given longer opportunities to participate in forest school sessions exhibit play that is progressively deeper and more meaningful'.

The hands-on, child-initiated learning promoted by forest school is based on a view of children as competent learners (Tovey 2007). They are offered the opportunity to take risks and many of the games played develop this understanding. For example: '1, 2, 3, where are you?' is more than a fun hide-and-seek game; it helps children to realise that they can find an adult even when they cannot see one (Figure 4.2). As well as developing confidence in being outside, there is also much potential for developing scientific and technological skills in such an environment. For example, three-year-old Thomas attended a forest school as part of his Nursery provision. From this developed not only a love of climbing

FIGURE 4.2 Hide and seek in the long grass

Learning story 4.2

Victoria Park Forest School

Each Thursday afternoon at Victoria Park Primary in Bristol, the Year 1 children don their welly boots and waterproofs to take a short walk up the hill to an area of waste ground where they have been given permission to run a forest school. The nearby park is a prettier destination, but would not allow the children to interact with the environment in the same way, for example, by collecting foliage or den-building. To allow both Year 1 classes to experience forest school, each class goes on alternate weeks. The first time a class are taken to the 'forest' they walk the boundary; a key part of the safety rules of forest school is to have clear line that the children do not cross – in this case a path. Other rules include: 'make sure you can see your adult' and 'no touching rubbish', which neatly covers anything from crisp packets to discarded syringes. Each adult helper is assigned four or five children to supervise on the walk and to support during the afternoon, under guidance from the teacher.

Activities range from tying sticks together to snow sculptures or finding the smallest and largest leaves (Figure 4.3). What do the children gain from such experiences? The smiles on their faces are clear, and being out in the greenery provides a stark contrast to the tarmac of the playground. The school's policy declares aims such as: 'building self-esteem, independence and collaboration; promoting awareness, respect and care for other individuals and for the natural environment'. Children are learning to take acceptable risks, work in teams, take responsibility for their own safety and care for a local habitat. Perhaps a justification

FIGURE 4.3 Which is the biggest and smallest leaf you can find?

for taking them throughout the year is to develop their 'noticing' of how a real place changes over time. For example, when one child commented, 'Oh look, there's flowers on the trees', this led to a meaningful discussion about the changing seasons. Nancy Low, forest school leader and Year 1 teacher expresses the wider benefits of the experience as follows: 'It is fantastic to see children who struggle in the classroom excel in the outside environment. I get to see a different side of the children, which helps me to know them better.'

trees, but also a persistent interest in habitats. Now aged four, Thomas still creates woodlouse houses at every opportunity and has extended this to homes for worms, snails, slugs and – on holiday – crabs, which became known as 'crabitats'!

However, it is important that a forest school session is not seen as 'the science for the week'. It is a great context for learning science, but that is not really the principle aim of the experience. True, the values of curiosity and wonder – together with the skills of observation and comparison – can be supported by forest school sessions, but tree-climbing is not really focused on learning about the science of trees! It does nevertheless develop an intuitive awareness of the strength of branches and the variety of tree sizes and types. Such experiences could lead to the development of scientific questions and hypotheses, which can be discussed at a later time, such as: 'How thick does a branch have to be to take my weight? If it bends will it break?' Of course, exploring such questions practically needs to take place through models, since it is neither safe nor ethical to test-to-destruction branches or children!

Education for sustainable development

Outdoor learning experiences, such as those described above in a forest school, gardening club or on a 'bear hunt', provide more than just new experiences and opportunities to do things in a real context. They should build an appreciation of the natural environment; a connectedness that some argue is under threat from the way today's lifestyles are concerned with indoor activities, driving rather than walking, and safety fears (Prince 2010: 275). Education *for* the environment, rather than merely *about* it or *in* it, should instil values that promote humans as part of living ecosystems, dependent upon them and with responsibilities towards them. Children should be helped to 'form an ecological awareness from an early age' (Tsekos et al. 2012: 111), by seeing that their actions have consequences; by pulling up the plant or squashing the spider they have killed it and potentially reduced biodiversity. By dropping litter they endanger the wildlife; using this as an opportunity to discuss where the litter goes can lead on to consideration of the mantra 'reduce, re-use, recycle'. Global issues are hard to grasp at a young age, but local action is not. There are further opportunities to deal with larger issues as many settings work towards 'eco-school' status (www.eco-schools.org), an award programme providing a framework to help schools become more sustainable.

Risk assessment

Risk assessment is the name given to the type of planning that needs to happen before an outdoor activity to consider the safety of the participants. A generic risk assessment will consider the risks associated with general use of the outdoor area, while specific risk assessments are needed for specific activities or outings. Dynamic or ongoing assessments are the consideration of risk during the activity, for example, if the weather changes. Each school or setting will have its own proforma for risk assessments, often adapted from the local authority guidance; there should also be an educational visits coordinator who will support the staff to carry these out.

A risk assessment considers the hazards involved in an activity or environment and the 'risk' – the likelihood that harm will occur from a given hazard. Some schools calculate a risk rating by multiplying the severity of harm by the likelihood it will occur. The aim of any risk assessment is to manage the identified hazards, to avoid them if possible, or to do what is reasonably practicable to minimise their effect. It is important for children to experience a wide range of activities, so risk assessment should help them to do this safely, not stop them. For example, a key feature of forest school is to create: ' a "safe enough" environment, not risk free . . . the area is made as safe as reasonably possible, in order to facilitate children's risk taking' (Knight 2011: 15). Children can be involved in the risk assessment process, for example, by helping to draft the reminders list for the outing. Schools, settings and local authorities will have their own guidance on child–adult ratios. It may sound strange that there is not a set ratio for outings that everyone follows, however, the Health and Safety Executive assert that the decision about how many adults to take 'should not be a simple numerical calculation' (DfE 1998). Adequate supervision will depend on the needs of the children, the experience of the adults and the outdoor environment being visited.

Access to suitable clothing and footwear is one way to support use of the outdoors. Many settings now have either central stores of wellies and waterproofs, or ask parents to ensure they are in school. Likewise, in the summer, parents will be asked to apply/provide sun cream and sunhats. Such steps ensure children can use the outdoor areas spontaneously and go on 'welly walks' whatever the weather. In fact, a change in the weather is a good reason to go outside, to see what happens to the world when it rains or snows. Considering the risks in advance means that children are prepared; for example, it makes possible the building of snowmen, since the children will already have their wellies in school!

Thinking about how to manage the children outside can support them to develop independence because they are given clear guidelines from the outset, know how far to go and how to recognise and respond to the return signal. Some settings with large outdoor areas will let the children choose when to be outside. Others with smaller areas operate a turn-taking system, for example, taking a bib or sash from a hook near the door when going outside. Since there is a limited number of sashes, the number of children outside is also limited. Children need to know the boundary, easy when there is a fenced free-flow area, but a temporary barrier or markers can do the same job. Placing cones or drawing a chalk line can provide a clear signal; the children can learn to police themselves and each other! It is also important that they know when to return; an agreed signal of a whistle or bell is typical. For older children who may be working further away in groups, stopwatches or flags could be used (Bianchi and Feasey 2011: 53).

ICT links

Digital images can provide both reminders of particular outings and opportunities for sorting, ordering and observing closely. If children are the ones taking the pictures using digital cameras or tablets, then technology can support learning from the outset. Asking the children to use the equipment makes them the ones making decisions about the important features of the environment, supporting development of their observation skills. Comparison skills can also be developed if photos are taken of the same place over time, for example, by making a 'seasons PowerPoint slideshow'. A recording of sounds on a trail provides opportunities for discussion, for example: 'Where did we hear this sound? Do you think it was made by something natural or a machine?' Out in the field a datalogger can provide numerical information about sound, light and temperature. The children can look at the display and notice how the numbers are changing, identifying the brightest, loudest or hottest places. By using snapshot logging they can record readings in particular locations, which can then be downloaded to display a bar chart. Children can then add labels to the bars along the x-axis from their notes of where each reading was taken. Continuous logging will allow the 'story' of the trail to be told, with children identifying highest and lowest points on the resulting line graph. Position-linked datalogging utilising GPS (Davies 2011) can provide such readings in a map form, enabling children to trace the changing conditions along the route of their walk.

Related designing and making activities

Building shelters or dens can be an outdoor activity rich in learning potential. To enable the learning from such activities to be extended from making to designing, it is important to discuss its purpose with children. For example, the shelter could be from the Sun or the rain, for one person or five, or for a particular person or character. We might provide specific building resources such as plastic sheets, or children could be challenged to find the best natural materials for the purpose of, for example, making the darkest den. Positioning the shelter site where there are already some structures might support inexperienced children to succeed. For example, creating some shade under the play equipment could lead to the children hunting for sheets and pegs, while asking the children to create a hidden den in a wooded area will lead to a hunt for sticks to lean against a tree and foliage for camouflage.

Providing a meaningful purpose for designing and making activities is not only motivating; it can also be more challenging, since pupils will have to 'do it for real', working to a design specification and ensuring they complete the project on time. For example, planning a meal from the plants that children have grown in the nursery garden and harvesting them in time for the party can help children develop problem-solving skills. Real purposes can also be provided in fantasy contexts; for example, 'Mr Gumpy's Outing' by John Burningham (1970) – in which the boat topples over after too many animals join the trip – could provide the stimulus to design and make a boat from natural materials that can hold a certain number of plastic animals. Returning to Jez Alborough's 'Duck in the Truck' (1999), the children could be challenged to create a bridge over the mud, or design a vehicle that will not get stuck.

Summary

Outdoor learning provides children with stimulation, space and resources that are just not possible inside the classroom. By planning the learning focus and considering how to minimise risks, children can learn safely outside, whatever the weather. Encounters with a wide range of environments provide real contexts and widen the scope for science and technology. Outside they can make a giant skeleton out of PE equipment or construct a racing water channel, go bird spotting or build a den in the woods. Let's go!

Discussion points

- Think of some everyday examples of indoor activities with a science or technology focus. Why does this learning need to take place in the classroom?
- How can children become more independent through use of outdoor learning?
- How can schools support children and teachers to become risk-aware rather than risk-averse?

5

Documenting children's learning

Rebecca Digby

Purpose of this chapter

After reading this chapter you should have:

- gained insight into the purposes and processes of documentation;
- explored approaches to documenting learning;
- made links between documentation and formative and summative assessment;
- considered how you might document children's learning in science and technology.

Introduction: what do we mean by the term 'documentation of learning'?

The phrase 'documentation of learning' is increasingly used as an umbrella term for a repertoire of formative assessment processes within Early Years education in the UK. These include: observations, diaries, journals, stories, pictures and narratives that seek to gain insight into children's achievements, attainment and progress. With such a broad phrase taken from Early Years practice in international contexts, it is perhaps inevitable that multiple interpretations of its meaning have emerged and thus differences in how learning is documented in practice. While difference and diversity in practice are crucial in order to take account of the unique contexts and cultures to which children belong, the potential for misinterpretation of the *purpose* of documenting learning is high when we take processes from one context and apply them to another. This chapter, therefore, aims to clarify the meaning of the term by questioning whether 'documentation of learning' is more than an expression used to describe a range of approaches to assessment. We will focus on the variety of meanings that are intended to be conveyed by the phrase, with links made to the relationship between documentation and children's learning of science and technology. We will also illustrate key principles of documentation in practice through a series of case studies.

At its most basic, 'documentation' is a written or pictorial record of an event that has occurred. Commonly within the UK education system, when partnered with 'learning', we have come to understand it as a teaching technique for gathering information both during and after a learning experience to be stored and used at a later date. Turner and Wilson (2010) consider this a narrow interpretation as it likens the process to the simplistic collection of data, which implies that documenting learning requires active engagement on the part of the practitioner only *after* the learning process has happened. They argue that if documents are collected, revisited and shared only at the end of a learning process, then we lose valuable opportunities to gain insight and new meanings into learning.

Practitioners within the Reggio Emilia approach to Early Years education (Rinaldi 2006) have explored documentation of learning beyond these simple perspectives. They understand it as both a tool to excite interest in the process of learning and as a pedagogical philosophy that seeks to know and value children. When we look at documentation from this position, it becomes more than a technical tool. Instead, it is an attitude to teaching and learning that requires us to listen, observe and evaluate the nature of children's experiences. Described as 'making learning visible', documentation 'embodies the essence of getting closer to children's thinking; it helps teachers understand and support their learning processes as well as their attainment of knowledge' (Turner and Krechevsky 2003: 41).

To enable learning to be 'made visible' using this approach, we need to collate a wide variety of material that is both multi-sensory and multi-dimensional in nature. This can include drawings, photographs, pictures, transcribed conversations, artefacts, annotations, videos and exhibitions of children's learning. In order to be representative of formative assessment, these materials should include the voice of the child, practitioner and parent. This will promote multiple discussions and interpretations focused on how children learn, how they come to know and the thoughts and feelings that accompanied this process. Once arrived at, shared interpretations of learning can be used to develop hypotheses and lines of enquiry with children. These are then explored through the use of provocations and 'open-ended' materials such as sand, water, clay, blocks, cardboard, pots, tubing etc. Rinaldi (2006) sometimes calls these 'intelligent materials' as they have many possibilities for interpretation and use by children, thus providing the potential for future investigations and learning to be further documented and analysed. Through active engagement in these processes, we recognise children as capable, competent researchers of the world around them, working with others to co-construct meaning (Turner and Wilson 2010).

The documentation of learning within Early Years education in the UK has also been influenced by practices within the Pre-school curriculum Te Whàriki (New Zealand Ministry of Education 1996). It is from this approach that the now common use of 'learning stories' has emerged. These narrative assessments, in which adults and children tell and retell stories of learning and developing competencies, take place in Early Years settings that are recognised as communities of learners (Carr and Lee 2012). As with practice in Reggio Emilia, all participants in children's learning take an active role in the development of learning stories. Emphasis is placed on practitioners developing awareness of the habits and values that children acquire in the process of learning. With a focus on the socio-cultural nature of learning, learning stories attempt to capture the learning to be found in culture, history, relationships and the environment. Most importantly, they are underpinned by the principle that they act to construct learner identities. Therefore, through active contribution to learning stories, we support children to develop agency and a sense of identity of themselves as learners (Carr and Lee 2012). Dialogue plays a crucial role in this process, so we need to regularly revisit learning stories with children to provide a provocation for them to initiate conversation, engage in sustained shared thinking (see Chapter 3) and develop a sense of valued participation. The act of revisiting the learning story, moreover, provides new and deeper insights into the learning profile of the child through meta-cognitive reflection. Through engagement in their own learning stories children can become experts in understanding their learning processes, a process akin to that by which they 'are active in creating their own understandings' through assessment for learning (Black et al. 2002: 15). Learning stories can also help us to identify children's learning dispositions and key competencies so that we can gain a deeper and more holistic understanding of them as learners.

If we understand the documentation of learning as much more than a simple label for assessment techniques and draw on its intended practices, it offers us opportunities to gain insight into the attitudes and processes through which children engage in learning experiences. These insights hold great potential to help us to explain how children understand, interpret and make connections to the world (Turner and Wilson 2010); paramount to the effective facilitation of learning and to ensuring that we make provision for children to progress in their learning. Additionally, by supporting children in gaining understanding of their own processes, dispositions and attitudes towards learning, we encourage ownership over learning and respect for genuine interests and enquiries.

Key features evident in the documentation of learning

Documenting children's learning:

- promotes mental and cultural habits that recognise the child as a capable and confident co-constructor of learning;
- requires active engagement from children, practitioners and parents both during and after a learning event has occurred;
- seeks multiple perspectives including the voice of the child, practitioner and parent;
- values multi-modal sources of data including visual, written and audio in order to give holistic insights into learning;
- facilitates insight into children's learning processes, feelings and thoughts as well as providing a representation of learning events;
- supports an enquiry-led and investigative approach to learning;
- encourages meta-cognitive thinking through reflection and (re)interpretation.

These features can be interpreted as guiding principles to support practitioners in developing a deep understanding of children as learners. Essentially though, they remind us of the respect that should be given to children as the protagonists in this process.

The relationship between documentation of learning and early science and technology

The features that define the documentation of learning have much in common with the processes children undertake as they engage in early scientific and technological enquiry. Primarily, this is because both value a process-driven approach and involve thinking and reflection in order to get to the heart of children's knowing and understanding. Children's early learning in the domain of science begins with exploration that is experiential in nature and often situated in a play context (de Boo 2000). As with technology activities such as designing and making, we should underpin learning opportunities with a 'hands-on and minds-on' approach to effectively support children's developing understanding of concepts (Millar 2010). The documentation of learning, which requires active engagement from children, practitioners and parents both during and after the learning process has occurred, would seem therefore to provide complementary practice through which children's learning can be formatively assessed. More-over, Harlen and Qualter (2004) argue that we enhance practical experiences in science through the discussion and sharing of ideas with others, as children need opportunities to think about what they are doing and why they are doing it.

Documentation processes, such as the development of learning stories, which value dialogue in order to 'make learning visible', and the promotion of meta-cognitive reflection through the co-construction of meaning, can be used as powerful facilitators in this process. Furthermore, the emphasis on learning dispositions as promoted in learning stories holds great potential as a focal point for us to explore and support the development of the positive and enquiring attitudes essential to developing children's understandings of the tentative nature of science.

Elicitation activities such as observation, questioning, floor books, mind-mapping and concept cartoons, discussed below, are firmly established as approaches to formative assessment for learning in science and technology. Used as part of the process of documenting learning, they can act to provide us with insights into children's existing knowledge and understanding from a wide range of perspectives. Crucially, elicitation has a meta-cognitive dimension (Ollerenshaw and Ritchie 1997) in that it encourages children to gain understanding of their own learning processes as ideas are explored and changes in thinking are identified, promoting children as active agents of their own learning.

Observation and questioning

The elicitation of children's current knowledge and understanding through observation is recognised as a fundamental assessment tool within Early Years practice. To ensure that observations provide insight into learning and, where appropriate, effectively engage young children in reflective activity, it is important that we document:

- the context for learning;
- the nature of the activity (e.g. independent, collaborative or scaffolded);
- the process of learning (i.e. the events within a learning sequence);
- dialogue and interactions/non-interactions;
- attitudes and dispositions to learning;
- competencies and achievements;
- next steps for learning.

To gain an holistic view of a child's developing skills, concepts and attitudes in science and technology, observation is best carried out over a range of activities in a variety of social contexts; for example, when the child is with an adult, or a group of peers, or working independently. In addition, a balance between adult-initiated and child-initiated activities will support the collection of a broad range of perspectives. It is important to recognise that while many observations will take place from a distance (non-participant), some will occur as we interact with children (participant). Where the observations are participatory, it is important that we immerse ourselves in the child's lines of enquiry in order to gain a sense of her developing capabilities and competencies. Focusing observations on what children *can do*, rather than noting what they are *not achieving* (a deficit model) leads to a deeper awareness of these capabilities, and asking open questions can support the process of gaining insight into children's ideas and understandings. In the quest to co-construct meaning with children, our questions should be inquisitive and genuinely enquiring in nature. The following question stems are a useful starting point:

- How can we be sure that . . . ?
- Is it always true that . . . ?
- What does that tell us about . . . ?
- How do you . . . ?
- What is the same and what is different about . . . ?
- How would you explain . . . ?
- What is the best way of . . . ?
- What might happen if . . . ?
- What if . . . ?

Open questioning can also support the co-construction of meaning, particularly when we invite children to contribute to their own learning stories, both during and after learning experiences. Acting as both a tool for the practitioner and the child, this process promotes a sense of ownership for children as they engage in the learning process.

Floor books

A floor book is essentially a hand-made book of plain pages in a large format in which practitioners and children work collaboratively to write or draw ideas, observations, predictions, questions and explanations. When working with young children, it is best to compile the book on the floor so that all those participating can access and contribute to its creation. Whether completed over one session or revisited during a number of sessions, floor books have a number of advantages as an activity for documenting learning:

1   *They are motivational*: learning is enhanced if we build on the existing ideas that children hold (Ollerenshaw and Ritchie 1997). In order for children to share their ideas they need to feel part of a secure learning environment where their ideas are valued and accepted. The act of visibly recording what a child says, even if they cannot read it, provides a strong message to children that what they say is important. It shows children that they can become actively involved in decision-making processes.

2   *They develop language skills and the concept of taking turns*: as children become used to learning in this way they can begin to think how their ideas might be recorded in sentences, or as questions. Taking turns and listening to what others say are key skills for successful collaborative learning; observation of children's interactions in this context can provide the practitioner with insight into learning dispositions.

3   *They provide opportunities for the practitioner to model and share with children the writing process*: while creating a floor book, children will observe and may become curious about how their words are being transformed into writing. They will see the practitioner using the conventions of writing.

4   *They can slow conversation, allowing time for thought*: recording children's ideas as they say them can be problematic and requires some practice on the part of the practitioner, however it also requires the children to understand the need for pauses. This provides ample opportunity for children to think, develop and refine their ideas, or retell them, so aligned with the principles of the documentation of learning.

5   *They record for assessment and evaluation*: contributions can be initialled, or each child's ideas can be recorded in a different colour. The floor book then provides a document to be reflected upon during subsequent sessions or with individual children, thus building a foundation for meta-cognitive activity.

Mind-mapping

Mind-mapping refers to a range of techniques for making visual representations of ideas and is closely associated with the development of thinking skills. In Primary science, the most common form of mind map is the concept map (Novak and Gowin 1984), a formative assessment technique more appropriate for slightly older children than the floor book – for those towards the end of Key Stage 1. During the process of constructing a concept map, we need to encourage children to think about how they see the connections between ideas and thus clarify their own thinking. The resulting map usually consists of words associated with a particular area of learning, arranged across a page, with annotated arrows drawn to connect those words that children see as linked, e.g.:

Sun ——— gives us ⟶ Light

We can use this process and the resulting maps to gain insight into children's thinking and to identify where ideas may need to be challenged or developed. Concept maps can also be useful as a way of helping children to be more aware of their learning, particularly if they actively revisit their maps throughout their learning experiences by explaining and retelling their developing and changing ideas to other children, practitioners and parents.

Concept cartoons

A further way of gaining access to learners' scientific ideas, supporting the meaningful documentation of learning, is to use an approach developed by Naylor and Keogh (1997, 2000) known as 'concept cartoons'. Each cartoon depicts an everyday science-based situation for children to think about, with three or four comments representing common 'alternative frameworks' written in speech bubbles by cartoon children. For example, in one cartoon three children are watching another child play with a toy car. Their three statements are:

1   'If I wind this car up twice as much it will go twice as far.'
2   'I think it will go twice as fast.'
3   'It won't make much difference.'

There are a number of ways in which we might use this cartoon: children could be invited as a class or a group to decide which character they agreed with (and why); they could indicate their preferred statement on a mini-whiteboard and discuss with a partner; or try the activity out. A strength of the technique is that children feel less anxious about exposing their own ideas as 'wrong' – the idea belongs in the cartoon to the character. It can also support children who find it difficult to express their own concepts in words; they can explore an idea closest to their own thinking and work with it, evaluate and perhaps reject it. The ideas in the cartoons can be developed and made more meaningful to young children by acting them out with props or with puppets taking on the characters' roles. Practitioners often use a similar approach to gain access to children's thinking through role play. By making 'wrong', 'silly' or debatable statements clear and obvious, young children can be prompted into revealing their own under-standing. Statements such as 'Please get me my coat – I'm really hot in here', or 'I think that the batteries have run out of this push-along toy!' can prompt discussions that will generate rich material for the documentation of both children's ideas and their learning through consequent lines of enquiry.

What does documentation of learning look like in science and technology contexts?

The following learning stories illustrate the documentation of children's learning across a range of science-rich and technological contexts. Largely drawing on observation and questioning as elicitation activities, they provide a snapshot of different approaches to documentation and insight into how we might understand some of its principles in practice.

Learning story 5.1

Documenting sustained enquiries: insight into children's learning processes

Practitioners at Blagdon Pre-school in north Somerset felt very strongly that a focus on planning for an enabling learning environment rather than for specific areas of learning would support children in developing their investigative and enquiry skills. As a result the environment was set up with distinct areas for children to use a range of open-ended resources to develop their own lines of enquiry. A clear set of values underpinned the practice within the setting, and opportunities were provided for children to:

- enquire with a genuine purpose in mind;
- hypothesise and look for evidence;
- deviate from a plan;
- go down blind alleys and store knowledge for another time;
- take time;
- use relevant resources, including other people for their enquiries;
- attend to details;
- think alone;
- bounce ideas off others.

Four-year-old Jacob's sustained interest in one line of enquiry was documented and revisited over a period of 18 months. An initial interest in how water flowed from a water butt in the playground and several visits to a nearby site where pipes were being replaced underground, led to Jacob independently investigating how water flows through different vessels and channels. The practitioners documented Jacob's play and experimentation through photographs and discussions, and interactions with peers were recorded as a narrative. The enquiry culminated with an exploration of phenomena related to the concept of forces through collaborative water play. This led to connections being made with an interest in volcanos and how they erupt. The following are excerpts from the lengthy and ongoing narrative of Jacob's learning journey:

1   Jacob discovers how to get the water to come out of the water butt (Figure 5.1).
2   Jacob had watched the others with the lengths of guttering and how they were able to move the water into the water tray. This had clearly intrigued him. Some pipes and guttering were introduced into the resources available outside. He began to connect a length of pipe to the water butt. When he turned it on he watched the water flowing along the pipe and come out the other end.
3   Jacob began to adapt his design by adding more pipes. He soon discovered that the water did not always go where he thought it would. This puzzled him and he would stop to look where the water was going and try to find out why. He discovered that by changing the height of the pipes he could change where the water went.
4   Jacob connected several pipes together. 'What's going to happen?' he asked. He discovered that by lifting and lowering the pipes he could change the flow of the water. While Jacob was unable to articulate what he was trying to do, he was clearly following a logical plan based on each discovery.
5   Jacob repeated this activity again and again as he consolidated his new knowledge about water flow. The water no longer needed a pipe to flow. 'Look the water is coming down!' he exclaimed (Figure 5.2).

FIGURE 5.1 Jacob discovers how to get the water to come out of the water butt

FIGURE 5.2 'Look, the water is coming down!'

Commentary

This learning story provides an example of an extended narrative that documents the processes and lines of enquiry in which a child engages at each stage of an ongoing investigation. Clearly, the documentation helps to make 'learning visible' and provides evidence of how scientific concepts begin to be assimilated, and the development of skills and disposition for science and technology, such as; curiosity, raising questions, the development of hypotheses and emergent ideas about designing, construction and the nature of forces. Additionally, used as a framework for reflective discussion, the learning story supports practitioners in developing an acute awareness of learning processes and insight into how connections have been made between prior learning, the immediate environment and wider context, as well as how these experiences have helped to shape future lines of enquiry and exploration. This information has proved vital for practitioners in making decisions about which resources, learning environments and adult interventions will act to promote progression in learning while maintaining a genuine respect for the child's interests and his ownership of the investigation.

Learning story 5.2

Active engagement of all participants during and after the learning process

Practitioners at The Red Room Pre-school situated in the grounds of Chewton Mendip C of E VA Primary School hold learning journals at the centre of their practice. Used to share learning between the home and setting, they aim to present a holistic picture of children's interests, strengths and significant events in their lives. As a 'live' document, they are updated regularly by keyworkers and parents and carers. Children also contribute to their journals by adding examples of learning and talking to keyworkers about their photographs and past experiences. Thus, many perspectives are drawn upon to build an image of the child as a learner. In the example below, the dialogue between two children is transcribed providing insight into their progressive understanding about the properties of materials. The pair work collaboratively to transport ice from one location to another demonstrating an interest in the material's potential for construction. This line of enquiry is later developed at home and the resulting igloo captured in photographs by parents.

Context

It was very cold and water in the water tray had frozen overnight. To play outside the children had to wear coats, hats and gloves. Joshua and Cameron came outside and looked into the water tray. They both moved over to the sand pit. Cameron began to dig in the sand and Joshua picked up a spade.

Joshua: It's for the ice. (*Joshua began to scrape some ice on the playground and on the platform bike with the spade.*)

Cameron went into the garage area and came back with a hammer. He hit the ice with the hammer until the ice broke. Cameron then took the hammer into the sandpit.

Cameron: It makes the sand a bit cold. (*He looked up at a staff member.*)

FIGURE 5.3 'There's only a little bit of snow'

Cameron: There's no ice in the sand because I'm making it a bit gooder. There's only a little bit of snow. (*As he dug in the sand; see Figure 5.3.*)
Joshua: It's too cold. (*He went back inside.*)

Cameron returned to the water tray and filled an upturned step with ice. He put it onto the back of a platform bike and pedalled it over to the sandpit.

Cameron: I've got some more ice.

Cameron ran along the sandpit cover and jumped two feet together into the sand.

Cameron: I've got a run up.

Joshua began to tip the ice onto the green area.

Joshua: I'm unloading, Cameron give me a hand. (*Joshua fetched the large spade and began to shovel up the ice.*)

Cameron gave Joshua a bucket and Jonas began to fill the buckets with ice. Cameron found a spade and began to help to fill the bucket.

Cameron: Take it to the ice house.

Joshua pushed the ice onto his spade with his hand. They filled the bucket and placed it onto the back of the platform bike (Figure 5.4). Joshua pedalled the bike back to the water tray and emptied the ice back onto the tray.

FIGURE 5.4 They filled the bucket and placed it onto the back of the platform bike

Achievements
- Comments and asks questions about the weather (natural world).
- Develops understanding of weather changes; cold and ice.

Next steps
Look at ice melting in the Sun by adding salt. Make an ice picture using natural objects in water and let it freeze overnight.

Commentary
Through analysis of the narrative learning story and the accompanying images documenting an extended enquiry at home, the practitioners identified the 'characteristics of effective learning' demonstrated by each child (Table 5.1). Grouped under the headings 'Playing and Exploring', 'Creating and Thinking Critically' and 'Active Learning', they provide a comprehensive set of early scientific and technological skills and dispositions, applicable across other areas of learning. The formative tracking of skills in this way supports practitioners in building a picture of children's strengths and those areas for focus in next steps for learning. Significantly, however, it is through seeking multiple perspectives on children's learning that a broader picture of children's competencies, capabilities and achievements can been accessed, and insights made into a child's approaches to investigation.

TABLE 5.1 Documentation of Joshua's and Cameron's learning story

Playing and exploring: engagement	Creating and thinking critically: thinking
Finding out and exploring • Showing curiosity about objects, events and people • Using senses to explore the world around them • Engaging in open-ended activity • Showing particular interests	**Having their own ideas** • Thinking of ideas • Finding ways to solve problems • Finding new ways to do things
Playing with what they know • Pretending objects are from their experience • Representing their experiences in play • Taking on a role in their play • Acting out experiences with other people	**Making links** • Making links and finding patterns in their experience • Making predictions • Testing their ideas • Developing ideas of grouping, sequences, cause and effect
Being willing to have a go • Initiating activities • Seeking challenge • Showing a 'can do' attitude • Taking a risk, engaging in new experiences and learning by trial and error	**Choosing ways to do things** • Planning, making decisions about how to approach a task, solve a problem, reach a goal • Checking how well their activities are going • Changing strategy as needed • Reviewing how well the approach worked

Active learning: motivation

Being involved and concentrating
• Maintaining focus on their activity for a period of time
• Showing high levels of energy, fascination
• Not easily distracted
• Paying attention to details

Keeping on trying
• Persisting with activity when challenges occur
• Showing a belief that more effort or trying a different approach will pay off
• Bouncing back after difficulties

Enjoying achieving what they set out to do
• Showing satisfaction in meeting their own goals
• Being proud of how they accomplished something
• Enjoying meeting challenges for their own sake, rather than external rewards or praise

Learning story 5.3

Documentation as a vehicle for meta-cognitive thinking and reflection

Having recently extended to two sites, St Michael's Pre-school and toddler group in Winterbourne, Bristol were keen to ensure a continuing sense of belonging and cohesion among different ages and learning groups. As a result, the learning environment on each site was organised to mirror the other. Distinct areas of learning with easily accessible resources and displays were all considered to enhance children's interactions and collaborative exploration. In particular, the practitioners were keen to support children in developing their ideas and interests through enquiry. In response to curiosity about volcanos after sharing the interactive question and answer book 'You Choose' by Nick Sharatt and Pippa Goodhart, an adult-initiated investigation was planned for identical twins in order to model a volcanic eruption and lava flow (Figure 5.5). Following the activity, the twins were keen to record their experience through drawings and mark-making. These were stimulated by the photographs that documented the process of preparing and carrying out the investigation. An interactive display with narrative to illustrate the learning experience drew attention from other children in the centre and led to a small group creating a collaborative volcano story. The following extracts illustrate the initial investigation and the lines of enquiry pursued:

Luke: The volcano could burst over the top.
Jack: The volcano could explode! It could be really hot.
Matthew: And smoke could be coming out of it.
Jack: And flames coming out.
James: And fire.
Practitioner: What else?
Ethan: A dog fell into the volcano.
Jack: They found an easy jet in the volcano and he flew away.

FIGURE 5.5 Modelling a volcanic eruption and lava flow

Luke: And lava . . . and it was sticky boiling lava.
Jack: It all bubbles up like it did to us!

Commentary
Although the documentation of learning sought to identify children's learning processes and understanding of skills and concepts in this example, the emphasis was on documentation as a tool for developing lines of enquiry through the reflective review of learning experiences. Engagement with photos narrating the learning process, rather than just with the outcomes of the activity presented children with a reference point for reflection. This was led by the practitioner who used questioning to elicit understanding about the physical processes involved in the 'lava' erupting. Spontaneously, this understanding was represented through drawings and further discussion between the twins. The documentation of their learning through a display, made easily accessible to children, captured others' interests and imaginations and led to engagement in collaborative lines of enquiry. In this case, children's emergent understanding about physical processes was further demonstrated, through story.

Learning story 5.4

Documentation as a vehicle for meta-cognitive thinking and reflection II
As identified in the principles of the documentation of learning, meta-cognitive engagement and reflection can also promote agency and ownership over the learning process. In the following example, children's learning in scientific enquiry was first documented through photos, annotated conversations and one-to-one interactions. Layers of tracing paper were then overlaid onto previously documented learning and used to capture children's reflections on their experiences over a three-week period. The practitioner, a final placement PGCE student in Bellefield Primary and Nursery School, Trowbridge, sought to emulate the principles of the setting, which included play-based exploration and responsive planning, and found the documentation of learning invaluable in this process. The extract from the learning story (Figure 5.6) illustrates children's observations on an exploration of the outdoor environment following their interest in making maps and journeys. Their subsequent reflections were overlaid on the document using tracing paper.

Commentary
For the practitioner, the process of engaging in documentation supported the understanding of both children's nascent scientific processes and attitudes to learning. Captured in the images and accompanying commentary are children demonstrating their curiosity and inquisitiveness in making sense of the world around them. Their questions and predictions of how things grow and where they come from were used to inform the planning of further lines of enquiry. By actively encouraging children to reflect on their learning experience, the practitioner gained a deeper insight into existing knowledge and alternative frameworks further supporting this process. Following this, children led the documentation process by taking their own photographs and creating drawings of different locations, which were used to create a visual trail representative of children's understanding of the characteristics of different environments.

The children used magnifying glasses to look closely at the treasure they found. Many of the children were interested in the different colours they found on the bark of the tree.

Development matters
Developing knowledge, skills, understanding, and attitudes.

22-36 months: Notices detailed features of objects in their environment.
30-50 months: Can talk about some of the things they observe such as found objects. Shows care and concern for living things and the environment.
40-60 months: ELG - They talk about the features of their own immediate environment and how environments might vary from one another.

Isabella was excited when she found some treasure and was keen to share it with the other children

The children talked about the different features of the leaves they found.

'This leaf is pointy' - Finley
Another child chose a dead leaf as their treasure because 'it makes

FIGURE 5.6 Extract from a learning story: outdoor explorations

Making summative judgements on children's learning

As illustrated above, learning stories and the documentation of learning are akin to the formative processes within 'Assessment *for* Learning' (Black et al. 2002). While supporting the development of a holistic picture of the learner and providing rich material to inform children's future lines of enquiry, documentation can also aid practitioners in making summative judgements about children's progress towards the Early Years Foundation Stage (EYFS) Early Learning Goals (DfE 2012) and, later, in making decisions about whether children have met statements of expected attainment by the end of Key Stage 1 (DfE 2013). Judgements on children's attainment can be reached through analysis of the wide variety of documented learning, which provides a comprehensive evidence base of progression and achievement. Documented learning can also help us carry out moderation of assessment judgements across a Foundation Stage setting, Key Stage, whole school, or even, where relevant, clusters of schools. Although at the time of writing changes are expected to the current system of assessing children's attainment in Key Stage 1 through levels, it is worth noting that – whatever the system – engagement in the process of documentation of learning supports the practitioner in making secure judgements of a child's competencies, progress and attainment.

ICT links

Although there is some debate about the advantages of using ICT with young children, it is becoming increasingly embedded within teaching and assessment practice. Indeed, the use of digital technologies such as cameras, video and word processing software has become part of the daily documentation of learning by both practitioners and children within many settings. It is particularly useful for managing the collation of a wide variety of forms of children's learning such as drawings, artefacts, performances and works in progress. Crucially, it also enables the process of learning, engagement in sustained shared thinking and non-verbal interactions within environments to be captured for reflection and analysis. Additionally, 'apps' and software packages are available to support practitioners with formative and summative assessment of learning. However, it must be stated that while these can offer benefits in terms of the manageability of assessment, they cannot substitute for the discourse, reflection and critical analysis of learning that informs our understanding of children as learners.

Reporting to parents and carers

Most schools arrange structured meetings between parents/carers and practitioners during the year to discuss children's progress; a formal report is usually produced annually, identifying a child's attainment and achievements over the course of a year. However, as Early Years practitioners we are also likely to have frequent, informal conversations with parents and carers about their children. These can often provide rich evidence of children's learning in different contexts that can then be documented alongside learning, which is captured within the setting, thus exemplifying a holistic perspective on learning. Conversations with parents and carers should be seen as two-way processes of information-sharing; as in Learning story 5.2, opportunities can be created for the sharing of the knowledge being acquired by the child via photos and written annotations. At its best, this process of formative reporting involves a child guiding their parent or carer through their own documented learning and stories. In an activity such as this, a child and parent or carer can identify developing competencies and capabilities together and add their own reflections and comments, thus creating another perspective to the documentation. Engaging in this process can support parents and carers in understanding the importance given to the *processes* used in learning experiences as well as the outcomes, particularly relevant to understanding the nature of learning in science and technology contexts.

Summary

This chapter began with an exploration of the meaning of documentation of learning by defining the term and discussing the principles that underpin the practice drawn from the Reggio Emilia approach and the Te Whàriki Pre-school curriculum in New Zealand. We have emphasised the relationship between early science and technology learning and its documentation, while outlining a range of elicitation activities for formative assessment such as observation, mind-mapping, floor books and concept cartoons. All of these strategies can be used as interactive activities for documenting children's learning in technology and science-rich contexts. We have presented examples of the documentation of learning through learning stories, illustrating how principles have been translated into practice. The inclusion of parents' and carers' perspectives in the documenting process and avenues for reporting to parents have also been discussed along with consideration of how we can use the documentation of learning to inform summative assessment judgements.

Discussion points

- What do you see as the key benefits of engagement in the documentation of children's learning?
- Do you see any potential issues for practitioners? Parents and carers? Children?
- How might you document children's learning in science and technology-rich contexts?

Planning for science and technology in the Early Years setting

Rebecca Digby and Sarah Earle

Purpose of this chapter

After reading this chapter you should have:

- an understanding of how planning can support learning in science and technology in the Early Years Foundation Stage (EYFS) and in Key Stage 1;
- access to analysed examples of long-, medium- and short-term planning;
- considered how you might plan to support learning in science and technology-rich contexts.

Introduction: planning in Early Years practice

Although there is not one formula that leads to 'good' planning in the early years – since plans necessarily need to take account of individuals and their unique contexts – there are core principles that can support the process. First, planning should start with the child. If we make the most of the close partnership between planning and formative assessment it is possible to understand a child's sense of agency – their way of being, seeing and responding to the world (Edwards 2001) – so ensuring that the effective facilitation of learning can take place. While Chapter 5 on documenting children's learning provides guidance on approaches to formative assessment within science and technology contexts, it is helpful in our planning to see it as grounded in social constructivist learning theory (Black and Wiliam 2009). This theory recognises that:

- learners come with a range of prior learning;

- the process of linking 'old' and 'new' knowledge is continuous and active (or constructivist);

- the construction of knowledge involves experience and interaction with knowledgeable others;

- learning is facilitated by language and communication (inner speech) – talk drives learning.

Observation and interaction – by both practitioners and children in a reciprocal relationship – play key roles in the planning process. They enable the practitioner to gain a genuine understanding of the prior learning a child brings to a range of different learning experiences, and to recognise how a child constructs and co-constructs knowledge in different socio-cultural contexts. It is therefore essential that we understand observation and interaction as processes that support purposeful formative assessment, in turn informing planning, so that appropriate provision for learning can be made.

By maintaining a broad overview and resisting the temptation to 'over-plan', we are more likely to be successful in providing a breadth and balance of relevant learning experiences for children. An overview approach allows space for the consideration of how to make meaningful connections between areas of learning and how best to make provision for progression in learning. Crucially, however, sustaining a broad overview also promotes flexibility and openness to possibilities; to responding to children's motivations, interests and emergent lines of enquiry. Underpinning the planning process is a recognition that, at its best, the construction of a learning experience is a collaborative enterprise between practitioners, parents and carers and the child. By understanding children as active participants in the learning process, we support the concept that they are competent and capable learners, so promoting their autonomy, imagination, decision-making and problem-solving capacities (Rose and Rogers 2012b).

Approaches to planning for learning in Early Years practice have traditionally been structured around long-, medium- and short-term aims. More recently though – to take greater account of children's emerging interests and developing lines of enquiry – these have been replaced with systems that are more flexible and responsive to the child (Brodie 2013). When planning in this way, objectives and aims are more loosely defined to allow for daily and weekly adaptation of activities and so personalisation of children's learning experiences. However, regardless of the approach taken, it is still useful to consider the principles of long-, medium- and short-term planning, and what they might look like in practice, as illustrated in Table 6.1.

TABLE 6.1 Principles into practice: long-, medium- and short-term planning in Early Years practice

Long-term planning	In practice
• Establishes a clear ethos and aims for areas of learning • Considers appropriate provision for the physical environment, both indoors and outdoors • Ensures progression, breadth of experience, and coverage of the statutory curriculum	• Provide a wide range of open-ended and stimulating resources • Provide adult support for planned and spontaneous activities • Respond to children's interests, interacting with them and engaging in talk focused on their experiences with materials, objects, people and events • Encourage children to observe, enquire, question and experiment • Collaborate as a team ensuring that practitioners and children contribute to the ethos and aims of the learning environment

Medium-term planning	In practice
• Plans sequences of learning for a period of weeks with a clear start point/event and defined ending • Focuses on organising coherent topics around clusters of learning objectives • Shows contexts for learning and learning activities • Provides an overview of how learning outcomes will be achieved • Shared with all stakeholders	• Use prior knowledge and formative assessment of children to plan engaging activities, taking account of differing needs and interests • Identify learning objectives, which are differentiated when appropriate • Identify and organise appropriate trips, visitors, resources and other provocations for learning • Involve all practitioners in the setting in the planning process • Invite children to contribute to planning for learning • Inform parents about the topic and invite them to become involved

Short-term planning	In practice
• Weekly, daily or activity based • Shows the working notes for the structure and content of a planned learning experience • Contains details of key questions, success criteria and outcomes, teaching strategies and resources, differentiation and personalised provision	• Ensure planning is responsive and informed by daily formative assessment; activities are adapted according to children's motivations and interests • Change resources and provocations for learning daily or weekly • Use as a working document, provide copies of plans for all practitioners to annotate with their observations, interactions and assessments • Identify where and with whom practitioners are working, the questions and vocabulary they might use and how learning may be personalised to individuals and groups of children

Planning for science and technology learning

As with other areas of an Early Years curriculum, planning within a science- or technology-rich context must be flexible and responsive as it is essential for children to be given the freedom to explore their own ideas and to make choices. This is in order that they experience the science and technology as inherently practical, led by questions and the expression of ideas and theories. This freedom helps to promote children's engagement in enquiry and creative endeavour, which lays the foundations for successful learning in science and technology.

It is important to consider the separate development of attitudes, skills and knowledge in science and technology as well as children's holistic learning. An environment that fosters enquiry and develops children's confidence as creators will support a disposition for science and technology. Harrington's (1990) 'creative ecosystem' theory suggests that this is achieved through providing a non-threatening atmosphere for learning, encouraging play, ownership over experiences and ensuring respect for thinking time. Additionally, by encouraging children's curiosity and exploration of the world around them, we support them in fostering intrinsic motivation for learning as well as an understanding of the core principles of science and technology. This requires open-mindedness on the part of the practitioner, an ability to 'see' the science and technology potential in topics and activities.

To provide a relevant starting point and a meaningful context for children, planning for science and technology may be set within thematic 'topic' areas such as 'ourselves', 'dinosaurs', or perhaps issues related to the environment and sustainability. Alternatively it may begin with a research question responsive to children's curiosity and engagement with open-ended resources such as water or sand play. Planning will also need to consider appropriate experiences and the provision of sufficient support in a balance of adult and child-initiated activities with the aim of promoting a 'hands-on and minds-on' approach to learning (Millar 2010). Additionally, since early science begins with exploration often situated in a play context (de Boo 2000), it is paramount that we give careful consideration to the learning environment.

In England, making reference to the EYFS Early Learning Goals (DfE 2012) or National Curriculum Programmes of Study (DfE 2013) can support planning for progression. For example, a practitioner can consider an earlier descriptor when deciding upon how to pitch an activity, or look at later descriptors when trying to provide challenge for learners. When planning leads to an end goal, such as designing biscuits for a party, it is important to consider the steps needed to achieve the aim and plan progressively so that the children have practised the skills required. Within a thematic topic, progression can be planned for in the form of questions designed to support and extend children's thinking. For example, the dinosaur topic described below in Learning story 6.1 lists a number of probing questions that the practitioner can ask, some of which would be more appropriate for the beginning or end of the week. Planning for progression in the learning environment will also take into account the complexity of the materials provided, with those that provide more challenge possibly saved until later in the session, or requiring an adult to support their introduction. Essentially, by making progression explicit in planning, with reference to descriptors or goals, it becomes easier for us to track children's progress. Learning story 6.2 provides examples of medium- and short-term planning in Year 1.

Learning story 6.1

Foundation Stage long- and medium-term planning in a science-rich context

Nicki McBeth, a practitioner in reception in Batheaston Primary School, Bath, aims to promote the school ethos in her planning. Priding itself on being a school of creativity, Batheaston values the outdoors as a rich environment for learning, and on 'Mike's meadow' adjacent to the school grounds, a community-built straw-bale classroom is often used by Nicki as a stimulus for enquiry and investigation. Recognising children as individuals and involving parents and carers in all aspects of learning are also highly regarded principles within the school, which can be evidenced in the learning experiences planned for children by Nicki.

The following examples (Figure 6.1, Table 6.2) illustrate a sequence of long- and medium-term planning for a topic developed in response to children's interest in dinosaurs. The case study demonstrates how many of the principles discussed throughout the chapter can be translated into practice. In particular:

■ maintaining a broad overview in order to identify meaningful links between areas of learning;
■ identifying opportunities for children to develop their understanding of scientific concepts, skills and dispositions;
■ promoting enquiry and creative endeavour within a science-rich context;
■ providing learning experiences that utilise a range of resources, contexts and environments;
■ recognising children as active in the planning process;
■ sharing planning with parents.

Personal, social and emotional

Exploring other cultures and beliefs – learn about Chinese New Year (Year of the Dragon).

Explore feelings around being happy, sad, excited and proud. The children will learn how to recognise these emotions in themselves and read other people's body language to identify these emotions.

Communication, language and literacy

Phonics – phase 3 – continue to learn new phonemes and tricky words. Begin to apply in reading and writing.

Look at non-fiction books about dinosaurs and use for research. Learn about the contents and index page. Use to find information.

Problem solving, reasoning and numeracy

Problem solving and comparative language – use facts about dinosaurs as a stimulus. Counting beyond 20 and ordering numerals. Begin language of addition. Combine two groups of objects. Partition given number of objects. Name solid shapes. Solve puzzles. Begin the language of subtraction.

Dinosaurs/Ice Age winter

Inspire days
Visit to 'The Bristol Museum'

Parent info/support

Check welly boots and daps for size!

Parent workshop –

'Supporting Early Writing'
February 2nd @ 5pm–6pm

Understanding the world

The children will think about past and present events in their own lives and contrast this with how we know about the lives of dinosaurs. They will become paleontologists exploring dinosaur bones, fossils and carrying out their own digs. They will also construct their own volcanic eruption and ice experiments to explore theories behind dinosaur extinction.

Creative development

Imagine you are a dinosaur hunter!

Read the story 'Katie Goes to London' to follow her adventures. Create our own dinosaur environments. Travel back in time – to a world of dinosaurs. Find a dinosaur skull and fossils to use for observational drawing.

Physical development

Games – begin to practice simple games skills such as sending and receiving a variety of balls i.e. throwing and catching and rolling.

Gym – sequencing movements on the mats, practising gym skills including jumping, climbing, rolling and travelling. Use the apparatus safely – including the gym wall bars.

FIGURE 6.1 Nicki McBeth's long-term planning

Outdoor environment

Bird hide – the children will watch out for the birds and wildlife living in our local environment.

Welly walk – look for signs of winter.

Meadow area – visit the meadow to look for birds, wildlife and signs of winter or early spring! Dinosaur fact mission.

Key learning skills

Communication skills – show you what we think and feel in lots of ways e.g. drawing, music, dance and pretending.

Enquiry skills – ask questions about why things happen and what or how things work. Talk about what we have found out.

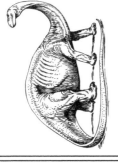

Grand finale

Dress up day – come into school as a dinosaur or palaeontologist!

Eco

Look at how we can be responsible citizens in our local environment, such as looking after wildlife during the winter months. Make bird feeders for our outside environment.

Roleplay area

Museum and shop – (downstairs) a shop with dinosaur-related items to sell, money, mark making, role play. (upstairs) – Palaeontologist lab

Equalities

Gender – look at the life and times of Mary Anning and her role as a palaeontologist in early Victorian Britain.

Children's questions

How do we have books about dinosaurs if they lived millions of years ago?

Are there dinosaurs on other planets?

What did they eat? How do we know what they ate?

How big or small are dinosaur bones?

Children's suggestions

We want to...

Create a time machine outside using our wicker tepee.

Look for dinosaur bones and find clues about dinosaurs.

Find bones and put them together to make a skeleton.

Look for a T-Rex's teeth.

FIGURE 6.1 *continued*

TABLE 6.2 Nicki McBeth's medium-term planning

Understanding the world	2012	Spring 1	Theme: Dinosaurs/Ice Age		
WK	Development matters— What we want the children to learn	Related scale points	Activity	Assessment opportunities I can . . .	Opportunities to explore and apply
Week 1 9/1/12	**Dinosaurs** **Find out about past and present events in their own lives, and in those of their families and other people they know.** (Sp6) Use time-related words in conversation. **Investigate objects and materials by using all of their senses as appropriate.** (Sp4) **Ask questions about why things happen and how things work.** (Sp5)	Complete a simple program on a computer. Begin to differentiate between past and present.	• How do the children know about their own past? Discuss photos/ memories/other people's memories . . . • Explore and discover how scientist/palaeontologists know about dinosaurs. • How do the children know about themselves? How is it different? • Show children an area in the playground where it is believed there might be dinosaur bones. • Carry out an archaeological dig with the class so that they find a range of bones and put together a dinosaur. • Introduce Mary Anning and provide children with a little bit of background info on her life. • Show children Jackie T's real fossil that she found – explore the fossil using all our senses, discuss what sort of dinosaur it might be from? • What clues have we got?	*How do we know about dinosaurs?* *Why are there no photographs of dinosaurs?* *Who finds dinosaur bones?* *How do we know it is a dinosaur bone?* *Where do paleontologists find dinosaur bones?* *Why do we sort dinosaurs into groups?* *How can we sort them?*	• Teacher: Audio-visuals – walking with dinosaurs. • Fossil hunting – tough spot – clipboards, mini microscopes. • TA-led: Make potato carved footprints. How does each dinosaur differ? What might a water-based dinosaur's footprint look like? • Use real chicken bones for children to explore so that they can invent their own dinosaur once they have found the bones in the tough spot. • Find own ways to sort dinosaurs. • Design and make own dinosaurs using playdough. • Make own skeleton picture using mini cocktail sticks of a dinosaur. • Researching dinosaurs using books and note-making using mini clipboards. • Children to play – 'being a paleontologist' and dig for bones and then build dinosaur using: www.tvokids. com/games/dinodig

TABLE 6.2 continued

Understanding the world	2012	Spring 1	Theme: Dinosaurs/Ice Age		
WK	**Development matters—What we want the children to learn**	**Related scale points**	**Activity**	**Assessment opportunities I can . . .**	**Opportunities to explore and apply**
Week 2 16/1/12	**Find out about and identify the uses of everyday technology and use information and communication technology and programmable toys to support their learning.** (Sp7) **Ask questions about why things happen and how things work.** (Sp5)	Use time-related words in conversation Complete a simple program on a computer. Begin to differentiate between past and present. **Build and construct with a wide range of objects, selecting appropriate resources and adapting their work where necessary.** (Sp8)	Ask children how they would sort dinosaurs, e.g. wings, tails, if they can fly, if they are plant or meat eaters. Introduce the idea of sorting them into carnivores and herbivores using: www.childrensmuseum.org/themuseum/dinosphere/games/earlyreader/earlyReader_3.htm Plenary: Introduce dinosaur egg! Explore and discover the dinosaur timeline, how different reptiles are believed to be linked. Look at how long the dinosaurs lived. Plenary: Watch dinosaur plays BIRD WATCH – DINOSAURS LINKED WITH BIRDS	*How big were some of the dinosaurs?* *Which was the biggest?* *Which was the smallest?* *How do we know? Do we know for sure?* *How many Class 1 members does it take to equal the height of a T-rex?*	• Teacher-led: Audio-visuals – walking with dinosaurs. • TA-led: Paint and design own dinosaur using : www.4kids.tv/games/play/dinosaur-painting • Chalk drawings in the playground of dinosaurs. • Tough spot: Dinosaur habitats. • Children to play sorting dinosaurs game into herbivores and carnivores: www.childrensmuseum.org/themuseum/dinosphere/games/earlyreader/earlyReader_3.htm

Learning story 6.2

Key Stage 1 medium- and short-term planning in a science-rich context

Judith Davis at Ashley Down Infants School values Lighting Up Learning's enquiry-based cross-curricular structure for planning. A whole term will hinge on a research question, such as, 'How does our garden grow?', which lays the foundation for medium-term planning (Figure 6.2). The learning cycle begins with a number of 'wows' to catch the children's interest. In this case it is a day spent outside rotating around a number of activities: planting, making bird feeders, reading 'The Tiny Seed' by Eric Carle, minibeast hunting, making natural collages and clay sculptures.

In the following weeks the children move to the 'immersion' and 'have a go' phases where there are a number of learning activities to support their developing understanding of plants (Figure 6.3). For example, modelling the parts of a plant out of pipe cleaners and tissue paper and investigating what happens to plants when their environment is changed. The final 'challenge' phase requires the children to apply what they have learnt, for example, by creating an instruction booklet about how to look after plants.

This case study shows an enquiry-based approach to science and technology in practice. There is a particular focus on:

- cross-curricular learning;
- a progressive structure for skills development;
- opportunities for children to develop their understanding of scientific concepts;
- opportunities for children to draw on prior knowledge and apply 'new' knowledge to different contexts;
- encouraging learning experiences in a range of contexts.

The enabling learning environment

The physical environment needs to be organised in a way that enhances opportunities for learning, supporting children to be enquirers, researchers and creators. Resources should be easily accessible, to enable children to select and store them independently. There are many ways in which resources can be stored, each with their advantages or disadvantages. Most commonly, practitioners favour either simple class-based systems or a central coordination of resources, which, although ensuring a larger collection of resources can be accessed and brought into the classroom temporarily, can mean that spontaneous opportunities for learning cannot be built on when they present themselves. With class-based systems, many settings have clearly designated areas for different types of activity, for example construction, puzzles, collage etc. (Figure 6.4). Drawers or boxes should be labelled and may be colour-coded so that children know where to look. Consideration of progression could support decisions about which equipment to make available (e.g. construction kits with increasing levels of challenge).

✿WOW!

Day of outside learning

Birth of a butterfly
Grow own fruit and veg garden

Year: 1 Term 5 weeks 27-31

Details of activities we plan to do to answer our research project question.

🐜Huuuuummmm! Immersion

- Children to share thoughts about the stages of growth for plants
- Children make observations and predictions about butterfly larvae in classroom
- Explore outside environment
- Sow, plant, grow and harvest own fruit and veg garden
- Investigations to explore what happens to seeds if environment is changed.

Research project: How does our garden grow?

🐞Challenge!

- Write non-fiction instruction/explanation book about plants
- Read the story of Flower Garden (Eve Bunting). Children to create a text about becoming a city gardener.
- Look together at the story of The Tiny Seed – Eric Carle
- Mini science observations each week

🐢Have a go!

- Children to research plants or living things such as mini beasts on the Internet and non-fiction books to write an instruction or explanation text
- Children to look at the flower images of Georgia O'Keefe and William Morris and produce print pattern using natural objects
- Create a 3d model showing part of a plant
- Use research and information gathered to produce a news bulletin to be filmed. Children to research plants on the Internet and find suitable images for their non-fiction texts

FIGURE 6.2 Ashley Down Infants School medium-term planning

This term we are developing the following skills

ELLI skills:	SMSC skills	Talk skill:
I can decide upon a question to investigate I can explore something new for a sustained period I can make a guess because I use what I know I can make a model to explain something more clearly I can use self-talk to help order my plans (first I will...) and say what could happen next	**SEAL, Rights respecting and values for life** Empathy: I know that all people have feelings, but they might show them in different ways. I can be supportive of others and try to help them when they want it. Social skills I can work well with a group, cooperating with others to achieve a joint outcome. I can make a wise choice about my work and behaviour. Article 14 Children have the right to choose their own religion and beliefs. Parents should help them decide what is right and wrong and what is best for them. Forgiveness	I can make and share predictions I can respond to what others say

Research project weekly planning Our research project question is: How does our garden grow?

WOW part of the learning cycle Term: 5 Date: WB 23.4.12

Lesson number and NC link	Learning objectives	Skills	Success criteria Process or product	Introduction	Main teaching and learning time (including differentiation information)	Plenary opportunities /key questions	AFL notes (including assessment of speaking and listening)
Science WOW Lesson 1 NC Day of outside learning	Introduce research project Enquiry Sc1. 1 - collecting evidence. Sc1. 2a- first hand experience. Sc1. 2f- explore using senses. Sc2. 5a, b and c - different plants in local environment.	ELLI/SMSC: Social skills I can work well with a group, cooperating with others to achieve a joint outcome. I can make a wise choice about my work and behaviour. TALK: I can respond to what others say	Familiarise with outside area Explore enquiry skills in preparation for research learning	Introduce research question. Watch episode of Mr Bloom's nursery from C beebies. Discuss how we are going to prepare our own garden for growing. What will we need to do/look out for? Mindmap ideas and use question prompt words to generate any questions i.e what happens if... How long will what if we change... Does...	Explain that we are going to have a day of learning outside. (Set up tables children rotate around activities during day.) Introduce activities: Photography- capturing what they see. PLANTING PLANTERS WITH SEEDS AND PLANTS FOR OUR GARDEN Making bird feeders Mini beast hunt/spotter Making and eating a fruit and veg salad Planter decorating/sign making (laminate) Make a natural collage out of things they find Make a clay sculpture using things they find Read 'The Tiny Seed' by Eric Carle INCLUDE TIME FOR LEARNING QUESTIONS THROUGHOUT	Reflection time during day Use of key question box	

FIGURE 6.3 Ashley Down Infants School short-term planning

This term we are developing the following skills

ELLI skills:
- I can decide upon a question to investigate
- I can explore something new for a sustained period
- I can make a guess because I use what I know
- I can make a model to explain something more clearly
- I can use self-talk to help order my plans (first I will...) and say what could happen next

SMSC skills

SEAL, rights respecting and values for life

Empathy: I know that all people have feelings, but they might show them in different ways. I can be supportive of others and try to help them when they want it.

Social skills: I can work well with a group, cooperating with others to achieve a joint outcome. I can make a wise choice about my work and behaviour.

Article 14 Children have the right to choose their own religion and beliefs. Parents should help them decide what is right and wrong and what is best for them.

Forgiveness

Talk skill:
- I can make and share predictions
- I can respond to what others say

Research project weekly planning
WOW part of the learning cycle

Our research project question is: How does our garden grow?

Term: 5   Date: WB 23.4.12

Lesson number and NC link	Learning objectives	Skills	Success criteria — Process or product	Introduction	Main teaching and learning time (including differentiation information)	Plenary opportunities /key questions	AFL notes (including assessment of speaking and listening)
Science Lesson 2 — NC parts of a plant model making	To recognise and name parts of a flowering plant.	ELLI/SMSC: I can make a model to explain something more clearly. TALK: to focus upon the main points and to remember specific points that interest them	Core: I can record and describe parts of plants. Extension: I can record and describe plants labelling roots, leaves, stem and flower. Support: I can recognise that a plant has different parts.	Share espresso parts of a plant interactive activity. Take a range of plants and use visualiser to look at and name all the parts. Include correct vocal stem, root bud leaf flower stigma. Pay attention to the flower and what is found there. Discuss what each part of the plant is for. In TP children each have a plant to dissect and name parts	INCLUDE TIME FOR LEARNING QUESTIONS THROUGHOUT. Children to show what they have learnt about the parts of a plant by making a model from pipe cleaners, tissue paper, string etc showing the detail of the different parts. With talk partner discuss the different parts, what have they forgotten to add, what does each part do? Photograph each child and plant model. Support: I can make a model of a plant showing stem leaves and buds. Core: I can make a model of a plant showing stem leaves buds flower stigma etc. Extension: I can also explain what each part is for	In teams use their bodies (ie lying on the floor) to recreate the parts of a plant.	

FIGURE 6.3 continued

FIGURE 6.4 The learning environment organised into distinct areas with easily accessible and labelled resources for construction, sand and water play at St Michael's Pre-school, Winterbourne

TABLE 6.3 Planning an enabling environment: materials for exploration, designing and making

Sand	Water	Malleable materials
Dry/wet sand	Recycled materials	Playdough with:
Recycled materials	Boats and people	Rolling pins and cutters
Dry sand and wheels	Water wheels	Textured rollers
Dinosaurs	Funnels and pipes	Syringes
Vehicles	Funnels, jugs and bottles	Moulds
Bottles and jugs	Coloured water	Plastic numbers/letters
Stacking beakers	Bubbles, pipes and blowers	Scales
Spoons and scoops	Toy animals	Tea set
Buckets and spades	Popoids, stickle bricks etc.	Plates and cutlery
Sieves	Tea set	Small sticks
Duplo	Water clocks	Straws
Small wooden bricks	Foam numbers and letters	Plastic scissors and knives
Sticks and leaves	Containers with holes	Different types of dough, for example,
Animals	Pipes and gutters etc.	salt dough, stretchy dough
Sand moulds	Washing dolls	
Sieves and treasure	Floating and sinking objects	
Tiny things	Shells	
	Squirty bottles and water pistols	
Alternative materials:		
Compost	Clear tray over colourful paper	Clay
Lentils	with shiny objects	Plasticine
Rice	Saucepans and wooden spoons	Cornflour and water
Leaves	with coloured water	
	Washing clothes	
	Ice	

Varying the equipment available stimulates children's interest and encourages exploration and enquiry. The use of 'open-ended' or 'intelligent' materials (Rinaldi 2006; see also Chapter 5) can provide rich opportunity for investigation. Table 6.3 provides some ideas for the range of materials that can be provided. In a recent literature review of creative environments for learning in schools, Davies et al. (2012) identified research suggesting that classrooms that were used flexibly were supportive of children's creativity. In particular, by moving or removing furniture from within the classroom environment to allow children to develop their own exploratory space, we can foster risk-taking and facilitate the development of independent lines of enquiry. Additionally, Vecchi (2010) has demonstrated, through a series of case studies in schools in Reggio Emilia, the importance of sensory qualities such as light, colour, sound and micro-climate in learning environments, and how these influence children's and young people's perceptions of how creative they are able to be within them. She recommends the use of small spaces ('mini ateliers'), acoustically but not visually separate from the rest of the class to enable pupils to work quietly in groups.

A further important feature of the visual environment we need to consider when looking to stimulate children's creativity in enquiry is displays of work in progress (Addison et al. 2010). Bath Opportunity Pre-School (BOP), a setting in Bath that caters for a wide variety of complex needs, works in this way to provide children with a visual presentation of their learning processes and a prompt for further investigation. Learning in science and technology within the setting is promoted through play and sensory exploration, which supports children in developing a positive sense of themselves and the world around them. To realise this in practice, children are encouraged to follow their interests through 'sensory integration': a neurological process that supports the organisation of sensation between the body and the environment. Figure 6.5 is a display panel illustrating the processes children engaged in during an ice balloon activity that took place in different environments to promote a rich sensory experience.

Use of the outdoor environment is discussed in more detail in Chapter 4. Here it is sufficient to note that many settings tend not to plan opportunities for learning indoors and outdoors separately, rather considering the enabling environment as a whole. However, those without a free-flow outdoor area will need to plan how the outdoors can be included in their provision, considering the use of large, messy or natural materials. Recognising children as competent learners, The Red Room Pre-school in Chewton Mendip, Somerset, uses a wide variety of large, natural and open-ended resources to extend learning. The outdoor environment is planned to be responsive to children's current interests and they are encouraged to free-flow their play from inside to outside. Figure 6.6 illustrates how areas of learning have been created to provide children with opportunity to develop their own lines of enquiry. The role-play area is on raised decking and with a walkway back down to the lower play area. A garden area along the path and in the extended play area is used to dig for minibeasts and

FIGURE 6.5 Ice balloon activity display at Bath Opportunity Pre-school, Bath

FIGURE 6.6 Outdoor learning environment at The Red Room Pre-school, Chewton Mendip

plant seeds and bulbs. There are sensory plants in the border and a very small covered 'pond' for tadpoles. The water tray and resources including guttering and hose are next to the water tap. In the extended play area children have access to a big sand pit. Plastic vegetable racks are used to store the sand resources.

Planning for adult-initiated and child-initiated activities: the role of the adult

The role of the adult in the Early Years classroom is a recurring theme in this book, particularly within Chapter 3 and its consideration of sustained shared thinking. Planning for such a role is not easy, since the temptation is to lead the learning and plan what the child will do. However, it may be more fruitful to plan for what we or other adults could do or say in order to successfully facilitate children's enquiries and investigations.

For example, consider the two cameos below and identify the small adult interventions.

Cameo 1

Susie enjoyed riding bikes, drew and painted using circular marks, used wheels with dry sand and was fascinated with turning taps on and off. She had worked briefly with the water with little interest. When nursery staff provided old bicycle wheels, she became very excited and was determined to make the water turn the wheel. She tried to balance the wheel on the edge of the water tray and then carefully put gutters across to support the wheel. The teaching assistant (TA) working with her observed without intervening. This was unstable and although the wheel frequently slipped and fell, she persevered for several attempts. The TA said, 'It keeps wobbling, doesn't it? I wonder if there is something that would make it more steady?' The child looked around and eventually found that the milk crates formed a stable base to support the wheel, exclaiming 'That's it! That's not wobbly now! I done it, look!' She called the TA to see the wheel turning. The TA responded, 'That's fantastic! What is making your wheel turn?' The child replied excitedly, 'The water. The water goed on the top and it goed round and the wheel goed round and round like that.'

Cameo 2

As part of a topic on gardens, the role-play area in the nursery was turned into a garden centre, the children planted seeds, played with compost in the sand tray and enjoyed filling up flowerpots with compost. Real plants and artificial flowers were on sale in the garden centre. Lily went to the art area, using collage materials available, scissors and glue; she collected a large piece of paper; cut a long strip, which she used to make the stem of a flower. She collected a small piece of paper; put some glue over it, folded it over the top of the stem and decorated it with collage materials to make a flower. She then made several more flowers, which she put in the garden centre to be bought by other children. The next day, without saying anything, we put some long art straws in the art area so Lily and her friends made some more flowers.

Commentary

The 'planning' of what to do or say next in these cameos came from an understanding of the children; observation leading to intervention and additions to daily plans. To ensure effective adult intervention, the ethos of supporting independence and child-initiated play needs to be shared with all staff in the setting. One way of doing this is to make it explicit on activity plans, with 'encourage independence' being a key teaching point. Other planned teaching points could include decisions as to which vocabulary will be introduced and modelled, together with possible questions and extension tasks. The aim of such planning is to be enabling rather than restrictive.

Involving parents and carers

Parents and carers have a key role in supporting children's learning, but they too may need support with making meaningful connections between learning at school and the home environment. Ethos and planning can be shared with parents in a number of ways: on home visits; in newsletters or information booklets; at the beginning and end of a session; on notice boards and on the school website. Sharing planning with parents is supportive in a number of ways: helping them to understand the purpose of activities in the setting; supporting their discussions with their children and inviting them to become involved, as the following example demonstrates. A parent read a notice about plans for a topic about toys and offered to bring in his collection of old toys. He talked to the whole class, showing them each toy and encouraging the children to ask questions and share their own experiences. The children then played with the toys and became very interested in the moving toys, particularly the robots. In the following days the children explored moving toys, they designed and made robots with recycled materials and Duplo, and incorporated robot role play into their games.

Summary

This chapter has introduced the process of planning as the development of a clear set of principles and aims. We have emphasised the need for planning that begins with and is responsive to the child while maintaining a broad overview. We have focused discussion on the construction of planning as a process involving practitioners, children and parents and carers, together with the establishment of an engaging learning environment, which draws on open-ended resources inside and outside of the classroom. Within the context of science and technology, we have focused on planning for enquiry, creativity and the development of concepts, skills and dispositions. Flexibility and a mindfulness of children's interests and enthusiasms – identified through careful observation and interaction on the part of both practitioners and children – have also been given attention. Finally, we have explored planning as a coherent and appropriate range of experiences for children, which are progressively refined and adapted through long-, medium- and short-term plans, and in practice, as illustrated through case studies.

Discussion points

- What do you consider to be the key principles of planning for learning?
- Examine the case studies. How do the plans promote the facilitation of young children's learning?
- How might you plan to support learning in science and technology-rich contexts?

Guidance on teaching thematic science and technology topics

Sowing the seeds – a thematic approach to plant life in Early Years education

Alan Howe and Christopher Collier

Purpose of this chapter

After reading this chapter you should have:

- knowledge of the ways in which plant biology can be taught through age-appropriate practical activities;

- familiarity with the concepts and misconceptions relevant to this field of study;

- an understanding of how plant biology can be contextualised to make it a relevant and engaging topic for young children;

- an appreciation of how an understanding of plant life can help children appreciate the importance of plants to our ecology and our planet.

Introduction

Plants are amazing things. They are delicious and deadly, gorgeous and ghastly, and are some of the biggest, smallest, tallest, heaviest, most useful living things on the planet. We eat them, burn them, shade under them and have found a million different uses for them; from building our houses to decorating our homes, from spicing our food to relieving our aches and pains. The 'big ideas' about the plant kingdom add up to this – we can't live without them. We need to understand and investigate plants, and ensure as many different species continue to grow simply because they are so vital to our existence. As educators we argue that it is essential that children begin to understand this branch of science so it's our job to sow the seeds of understanding that will blossom into a real appreciation of plant life. (Plants get everywhere – try rewriting that sentence without the plant clichés!)

This chapter will start by outlining relevant concepts in relation to plants (structures, diversity, conditions for growth, lifecycles and classification) at both practitioner and appropriate child levels. It will consider the scientific process skills needed to investigate the plants as living organisms. The chapter will go on to suggest learning activities within broad Early Years themes such as 'gardening', 'food' and 'the seasons', illustrated with case studies, children's story books, curriculum and ICT links.

Conceptual development at 3–7 years

During their early years, children will become aware of plants as a group of objects that have characteristics in common – they have leaves, flowers, they are green (usually) and they grow. Children will not immediately understand them as living things – they are more likely to categorise them as 'not living' if asked. Through experience they will begin to recognise some common flowering plants as having leaves, flowers, stems and roots, then plants can be classified into different groups by their similarities. A little later they will begin to understand plants need water and light to grow, and they can die. Children will become aware that seeds, which come from plants, grow into new plants. Later on they will realise that plants have many things in common with animals but only plants can make their own food. They will become aware that plants come in an incredible range of shapes, sizes and colours, and that organisms as diverse as oak trees and moss are both plants. Hopefully, they will understand that plants are very useful and attractive and are worth growing and looking after.

During their time in Key Stage 1 children are required to gain further knowledge and develop some challenging concepts. They should be taught to identify and name a variety of common plants, including garden plants, wild plants and trees, and those classified as deciduous and evergreen. They should be able to identify and describe the basic structure of a variety of common flowering plants, including roots, stem/trunk, leaves and flowers. They should explore and compare the differences between things that are living, things that are dead, and things that have never been alive; recognise that most living things live in habitats to which they are suited; describe how different habitats provide for the basic needs of different kinds of animals and plants; and understand how they depend on each other. By the end of Key Stage 1 they need to be able to identify and name a variety of plants and animals in their habitats, including micro-habitats; describe how animals obtain their food from plants and other animals; use the idea of a simple food chain; and identify and name different sources of food. Finally, they should observe and describe how seeds and bulbs grow into mature plants, and find out and describe how plants need water, light and a suitable temperature to grow and stay healthy (DfE 2013: 148–53).

The above seems a rather daunting list of requirements to be achieved over the four years on which this book focuses. Table 7.1 summarises the key concepts relevant to this area of science and the kinds of subject knowledge required by practitioners as they develop children's appreciation and understanding of plants as living things. Read on to find out how such demands can be met through some fun and fascinating approaches.

Early Years themes and contexts for learning

We have seen in Chapter 4 how learning outdoors is a fundamentally important aspect of education for 3–7-year-olds. In addition to the benefits of providing space for large-scale, messy, independent activities, the local environment can provide essential resources for learning in this area of science. Teachers have found certain themes to be rich in possibilities, as described below.

Gardening

Gardening is very much part of our culture; we love to visit historic gardens, arboreta, botanic gardens, parks and garden centres. Gardeners have a wealth of expertise and knowledge about plant species, habitats, seasonal patterns and ecology. By introducing children to gardening we can tap into this dimension of our culture and provide a very rich and engaging context for learning. Gardens are also spaces where generations can meet – older gardeners can be valuable sources of gardening knowledge and enthusiasm. For a comprehensive discussion of the benefits of school gardening, from broadening children's understanding of ecological complexity to shaping their environmental values, see Blair (2009). It can also be argued that gardening is a political act, where children can become aware of environmental issues and take action towards a more sustainable future (Ralston 2011).

There are a number of organisations that promote school gardens and gardening. The Royal Horticultural Society (www.rhs.org.uk/schoolgardening) runs a campaign for school gardening and their website includes resources and details of continuous professional development (CPD) activities. Garden Organic, the national charity for organic growing, also has web-based resources and offers school visits to its Warwickshire headquarters (www.gardenorganic.org.uk).

Charities such as the Earth Restoration Service (www.earthrestorationservice. org) and the Conservation Foundation (www.conservationfoundation.co.uk) also

TABLE 7.1 Conceptual understanding: plants

Key concepts in the Early Years curriculum	Subject knowledge for practitioners in the Early Years curriculum
Flowering plants have leaves, flowers, stems and roots	A flowering plant has two main parts – above ground is the shoot system comprising stem, leaves and flowers. Below ground is the root system. Each part of the plant comes in a diverse array of colours, sizes and shapes. Studying them is a good way to introduce the concept of biodiversity.
There are many different kinds of plants and animals (biodiversity)	The main function of the **leaf** is making food by photosynthesis. Many plants have flat, thin leaves making them efficient at trapping light energy and exchanging gases, and they often have pronounced midribs and veins for transporting water to the leaf and food away. There are many different forms (needle-like, prickly, hairy, spotty, striped etc.) and colours.
	The **stem** supports the leaves. It transports water from the root system to the leaves and food away from them. Like leaves, stems come in a variety of forms and colours: hollow or solid; round or square; upright, branching or horizontal to the ground; smooth or rough (e.g. the bark of woody plants).
	The **flower's** main function is sexual reproduction. Flowers, too, come in a wide variety of sizes, colours and forms, from simple flowers such as lilies or buttercups, to composite flowers such as daisies that have a mat of fertile yellow flowers in their centre.
	Plant **roots** have two main functions – to introduce water and dissolved minerals into the plant and to anchor it. Some plants store food as starch in thick, swollen roots, e.g. carrot. Others develop delicate, branching root systems to take up water from a larger volume of soil.
	A number of different parts of the plant are eaten as a vegetable: lettuce, cabbage (leaf); parsnip, swede (root); broccoli (flower); and celery (stem). Vegetable is a culinary rather than scientific term, whereas fruit has a specific meaning to a scientist – it's a ripened ovary containing seeds. Therefore a cook calls a tomato or a pepper a vegetable, a biologist calls each one a fruit.
Plants need light and water to grow	For a plant to be healthy and grow it has to be able to make its own food by photosynthesis and for this to happen it needs water from soil, carbon dioxide from air and a source of light energy (usually sunlight). From these simple raw materials the plant makes food, which is transported from where it is produced (principally the plant's leaves) around the plant so that new stems, roots and flowers can be made.
	The green pigment chlorophyll found in abundance in plant leaves is vital for photosynthesis. It absorbs light energy and transfers it in a form of energy that can be used to assemble sugars. In simple terms carbon and oxygen from carbon dioxide and hydrogen from water are combined to make a sugar molecule of carbon, hydrogen and oxygen (carbo-hydr-ate; -ate refers to oxygen). The waste product of photosynthesis is oxygen. In summary: carbon dioxide (CO_2) + water (H_2O) + light energy $\rightarrow$ sugars (CH_2O) + oxygen (O_2)
Seeds grow into flowering plants	Flowers and fruits play a role in the lifecycle of flowering plants In the early years, children will learn that flowering plants form fruits containing seeds, that these seeds are dispersed in different ways, and that they will grow into new individuals given the right conditions.

TABLE 7.1 continued

Key concepts in the Early Years curriculum	Subject knowledge for practitioners in the Early Years curriculum
	Plants can reproduce asexually (for example, by sending out horizontal stems – runners – which take root) or sexually. The flower is the structure in which sexual reproduction takes place. Pollination is the process of pollen from one plant being moved to the stigma of another. Pollen may be moved from one plant to another by the wind (e.g. grasses) or by insects – bees are very important flower pollinators. Once on the stigma the next stage of reproduction occurs – fertilisation. The pollen grain grows a tube from the stigma to the ovum. It is here that the male sex-cell contained in the pollen grain unites with the female ovule. Finally the fertilised ovule becomes a fruit containing the seed.
	Once the seed is produced it is dispersed, thus avoiding overcrowding of the adult plant. Seed dispersal might be by wind (e.g. sycamore helicopters), water (e.g. coconut palms that float), animals (hooked to their fur or eaten and pooed out), or by explosion (a sudden explosion scattering the seeds as the fruit dries out, e.g. gorse bushes).
	Finally the seed will germinate given the right temperature, moisture and oxygen. Light is not needed – the seed has a store of energy to draw on until it has leaves and is capable of making its own food.
Distinguish between living, non-living and dead	In Table 8.1 we point out that, in comparison with animals, plants are not so obviously carrying out the seven processes that are common to all living things. Despite this, plants do indeed carry them all out. Taking each in turn:
	Move – fast movement in plants is rare (the venus fly trap being an exception), but over time plants will move their shoot system in response to a stimulus, e.g. daisy petals open and close over the course of a day
	Respire – plants break down the food made by them and energy is released
	Sense – plants sense light, gravity and water
	Grow – most plants increase their size for the whole of their life (unlike animals)
	Reproduce – plants make new individuals sexually (flowers and seeds) or asexually (e.g. runners)
	Excrete – plants produce oxygen as a waste product of photosynthesis (a process that is made visible by the bubbles of oxygen produced by underwater plants such as pond weed)
	Nutrition – plants make their own food through photosynthesis
	The mnemonic MRS GREN is a helpful aide memoire for these processes.
There are many different kinds of plants (biodiversity)	The division of living things into plants and animals is explained in Table 8.1. It is usually obvious to young children that flowering plants with a stem, leaves and roots are plants. However there are other groups that are members of the plant kingdom that may be less obviously so because they do not show all of these features:
Plants can be classified into	**Mosses** – have no stems, flowers or real leaves; in contrast to flowering plants mosses are unable to transport food and water through their bodies so form tufty

TABLE 7.1 continued

Key concepts in the Early Years curriculum	Subject knowledge for practitioners in the Early Years curriculum
different groups by their similarities	cushions that are low to the ground and are found in damp places. Their lifecycles have two distinct generations, one of which produces a filament and capsule containing spores that are dispersed by the wind.
	Ferns – they have stems, leaves and roots enabling them to transport food and water, but no flowers or seeds. Like mosses, they have two generations. The large leafy generation is most familiar to us. It produces spores that are visible on the underside of leaves.
	Conifers – seed-bearing plants; seeds are protected by cones but not enclosed by them (yew and juniper are exceptions that enclose their seeds in berries).
	Flowering plants – bear seeds that are enclosed in a fruit; includes some trees, e.g. oak, and shrubs, e.g. holly.
	Algae – e.g. seaweed, pond slime, blanket weed; mainly live in water, are green and photosynthesise so are usually treated as plants by primary teachers but actually have their own kingdom separate from plants.

Early Years activities that develop children's understanding of plants support their development towards the big idea in science that *organisms are organised on a cellular basis, organisms are dependent on or in competition with other organisms, diversity of organisms is the result of evolution.*

Sources to develop background subject knowledge further:

Collier, C., Davies, D., Howe, A. and McMahon, K. (2011) *The Primary Science and Technology Encyclopedia.* London: David Fulton.

Harlen, W. (ed.) (2010) *Principles and Big Ideas of Science Education.* Hatfield: ASE.

Howe, A., Davies, D., McMahon, K., Towler, L., Collier, C. and Scott, T. (2009) *Science 5–11: A Guide for Teachers*, 2nd edn. London: David Fulton (Chapters 10 and 11).

Peacock, G., Sharp, J., Johnsey, R. and Wright, D. (2012) *Primary Science: Knowledge and Understanding (Achieving QTS Series)*, 6th edn. Exeter: Learning Matters (Chapter 2).

Wenham, M. and Ovens, P. (2010) *Understanding Primary Science*, 3rd edn. London: Sage (Chapters 2, 4 and 5).

offer support of various kinds. Gardening can be undertaken on many scales, from the planting of a classroom window box to a whole-school initiative. Rye et al. (2012) describe a whole-school garden programme, which, it is claimed, enhanced science education for a range of diverse learners, including those with special educational needs. They recommend that for a large-scale programme to be successful, an infrastructure is necessary that includes administrative and senior staff support, the creation of a shared vision with all those interested, the identification of funding opportunities (local partners could include retail businesses, university departments or community groups), the development of community support and careful long-term plans for the use of indoors and outside. With such planning and investment schools can make a considerable difference to their environment, and create a rich learning resource for years to come.

Food and cooking

In 2013 the British Nutrition Foundation (BNF) published the results of a survey that found that among over 27,500 children across the UK, nearly a third of Primary school-age children think that cheese comes from plants and one in ten Secondary school children believe that tomatoes grow under the ground. There are concerns among educators that children do not have sufficient experiences of food production or knowledge of unprocessed foods. There is potential here for the Early Years educator to address this deficit.

Durmas (2013) reports on a project that gave a group of six-year- olds a range of opportunities to explore food in a variety of ways. These included field trips, interviews of experts, observations of food production, fruit and vegetable growing, model-making (of farms and factories) and the cooking (of jams, pickles, yoghurt and breads). One outcome of this extensive project was that the researcher found children become significantly more adept at recognising and categorising food plants. While schools may not have the capacity to embark upon such a major initiative, some elements of Durmas's project can be replicated. Activities such as trip to a 'pick your own farm' then cooking the produce back at school, or a trip to the local supermarket and a discussion of where the food on the shelves has come from can begin to connect for children their knowledge and experiences of food.

There are many resources to help the school integrate food and cooking activities in the curriculum. At times, discussions about the ingredients and their origins can emerge from such activities and enhance children's understanding of the diversity and usefulness of plant life. Websites such as www.cookschoolfresh. co.uk and www.focusonfood.org offer lots of advice.

Looking after our world

This might not be a common theme for Early Year learning but may be one that becomes increasingly relevant and important to young children in the future. There are well documented concerns among educators that children don't spend enough time outside, and can even find the outside rather frightening (see Prince 2010 for a discussion). Many teachers will certainly be interested in the ways in which children can develop an appreciation of the 'natural world', which can lead later on to a love of the outdoors and a desire to look after it. Both the previously discussed topics of food and gardening can lead to further thinking about relevant questions. Where does our food come from? How can we look after our land? Should we put chemicals on our crops? What shall we kill and what shall we keep?

The key concepts needed for an understanding of environmental issues that can be developed in the Early Years curriculum include:

Biodiversity

Ecologists and environmentalists tend to see biodiversity as a good thing (and it usually looks pretty, too). We can ensure children encounter a wide range of living things, plants included, so that they begin to appreciate the range of life on Earth – from the tiniest moss underfoot to the tallest tree shading the playground. One technique for drawing attention to this is carrying out a 'bio-blitz'. The Bristol Natural History Consortium (2013) describes this as a great outdoor, family event where expert naturalists and members of the public work together to do a fast and intensive survey of all forms of life in a natural space.

Interdependence

This chapter should really be read in conjunction with Chapter 8 where we look at animal life. Animals are totally dependent on plants to fix the Sun's energy. Learning about food chains (what eats what eats what . . .) – noticing the ways in which insects pollinate plants, the way plants feed insects, looking for small creatures under leaves or in the bark of a tree – all these observations point to the interdependence of living things.

Cycling of materials

What better way to illustrate the way in which we recycle materials than starting a compost heap! Children can set up enquiries into biodegradability. Let them bury a selection of objects – say the leftovers from a packed lunch; an apple core, a plastic bag, a paper bag, a crisp packet. Return in a week or so and observe. What has changed? Where have the items gone? This kind of activity can lead to thinking about rubbish, pollution and how we might care better for our immediate environment.

There is further guidance on how this topic can be developed in Chapters 5 and 8.

Scientific process skills

One advantage of working with plants is that they are easy to get close to. They are often the subject for observational work in the classroom – you may well have seen children drawing a daffodil or a vase of flowers for an art or science activity. To get the most out of such a 'science rich' opportunity, activities can be structured around the development of observational skills. A start point could be to allow the children to handle a collection of plant material: a bunch of flowers, some daisies picked off the field or a bag of vegetables from an allotment. Children's attention can be drawn towards the smell and feel of flowers, the strength or delicacy of stems, the spikiness or softness of leaves. Observations could be focused on any of the following: colour, shape, pattern, size, texture, aroma, form, function. After children have really explored the material and talked about their findings they will be better equipped to make a record of them (see the tips in the ICT section below on making observations).

The second way to structure observations is over time. This is essential where plants are concerned. Children can plant seeds in all sorts of ways – as 'hair' in an egg shell, in cotton wool in a plastic bag taped to the window, in a seed tray, in the garden, on wet tissue. Regular observations can then be made and discussed. This approach gives children a chance to record data in some way, and look for patterns. Ask children to observe when the first signs of germination are evident, when the root and shoot start to emerge and grow, how the seed coat splits and falls away, how the 'seed leaves' begin to form and turn green. Observations of the local flora are also straightforward to make and record over time. This is actually a branch of 'real 'science called 'phenology' (not to be confused with the pseudoscience of feeling bumps on heads – phrenology) and has provided evidence that our seasons are changing. There are an increasing number of 'citizen science' projects where the public are asked to submit records of seasonal events (e.g. the first leaves on an ash tree, the first blackberries of autumn) that contribute to our understanding of climate change. Have a look at www.naturescalendar.org.uk for some surveys children can get involved in and ideas for what to look out for.

From observations, other skills can be developed. Question-raising should emerge from the activities outlined above. Where does the flower's smell come from? How long before all the seeds germinate? Can plants live in the dark? What will we see inside a blackberry? Simple investigations can be set up to test predictions: 'All the cress seeds will germinate on the same day'; 'My plant will grow taller than yours because I gave it more water'; 'The plant will grow one centimetre overnight'; 'Slugs don't like red lettuce'.

Plants can be sorted and classified in many ways – biologists still argue about the finer points of the classification of the plant kingdom. Again, starting with a collection of plant material or some good quality photographs, children can be asked to suggest how plants are similar to and different from each other. There are a number of common misconceptions about plant life to watch out for in discussions. The correct scientific ideas are:

- Trees *are* plants.
- 'Flowers' are just one part of a plant.
- Some plants have no flowers (e.g. moss and ferns).
- Grasses have flowers (they are wind pollinated).
- Any plant could be a weed – effectively a weed is an 'unwanted plant'.
- Some plants don't need soil to survive (e.g. mistletoe).
- Evergreen trees do drop leaves, just not all at the same time.

- 'Vegetable' isn't a correct scientific classification – so some vegetables are fruit (e.g. marrow), some are stems (celery), some are roots (carrot), some are leaves (e.g. spinach) and some are even swollen underground stems (potato)!

- Mushrooms aren't plants (they are fungi).

- Seaweed isn't technically a plant (it is algae) – biologists even argue about whether the term 'plant' is useful!

EYFS and Key Stage 1 curriculum links

Young children who are exposed to new experiences both indoors and outside, encouraged to observe and explore their world and given opportunity to talk and think about their learning will experience no major discontinuity between early learning about the natural world and investigative practical activity at Key Stage 1.

However, in the proposals for the new Key Stage 1 curriculum (DfE 2013: 140) there has been a considerable increase in the expectations for children's *knowledge* about plants, compared with the previous curriculum. In Year 1, pupils should be taught to:

- identify and name a variety of common plants, including garden plants, wild plants and trees, and those classified as deciduous and evergreen;

- identify and describe the basic structure of a variety of common flowering plants, including roots, stem/trunk, leaves and flowers.

While many of the activities discussed in this chapter will be familiar to both Early Years and Key Stage 1 teachers, it is the concept of 'identification' that separates the demands of the two curricula. It is likely that when children become absorbed in looking at, growing and cooking plants in the ways described above, they will be curious about them and begin to develop a repertoire of plant names. As discussed further in Chapter 8, conceptual development and language development are closely linked. As a general rule we would advise that the exercise of identifying and naming organisms should emerge from children's interests and observations of local flora. There is no definitive or recommended list to be learned but here are some suggestions:

- Garden plants: roses, daffodil, tulip, pansy, daisy (all flowering plants).

- Wild plants: nettle, buttercup, lords-and-ladies, bluebell, hart's tongue fern, wild garlic.

- Trees: oak, silver birch, alder, willow (all deciduous); yew (evergreen); pine (evergreen and coniferous – which means having cones).

There are some good identification guides available, although most demand some interpretation and reading skills, so children usually need help to use such resources. See www.forestry.gov.uk for a simple online tree identification key. Science and Plants for School (www.saps.org.uk) produces useful guidance on how to begin to make identification keys with children, so they better understand how to use them. Schools themselves could also produce their own simple identification sheets, adapting those available online to reflect the local flora. Don't be afraid to make up names for unidentified specimens (after all, that is what people have being doing for centuries). Children can have fun inventing provisional names for newly discovered plants.

Story books

As well as the traditional tales: 'The Enormous Turnip', 'Jack and the Beanstalk' (children might also enjoy the Raymond Briggs version, 'Jim and the Beanstalk'), there are many stories that can provide contexts for children's learning about plants; some suggestions are shown in Table 7.2 below.

TABLE 7.2 Story books as starting points for looking at plants

Book title (author)	Ideas
'Oliver's Vegetables' (Vivien French)	This is a story about a boy who doesn't like eating vegetables until he tastes some that he digs up in his grandparent's garden. It could be a starting point for a gardening project.
'The Tiny Seed' (Eric Carle)	This book might provoke questions about how plants grow from seeds and how they can travel far from the adult plant that grew them. This could lead into collecting and observing different kinds of seeds (conkers, coconuts, sycamore 'helicoptors', 'velro-like'; burrs) and how they disperse. E.g. *Do tiny seeds grow into tiny plants?* (Children could make a comparison between the fruit of tiny *Lobelia* seeds and bigger radish seeds.
'One Child One Seed: A South African Counting Book' (Kathryn Cave in association with Oxfam)	Perhaps not a 'story', but certainly a narrative, this is a book about a South African girl as she grows a pumpkin and the different parts are used for different purposes. It could lead to looking inside pumpkins, estimating how many seeds there are in a pumpkin, and of course growing pumpkins.
'Ten Seeds' (Ruth Brown)	Growing plants can be frustrating and disappointing when they don't grow as you might expect. In this story, only one of 10 sunflower seeds survives. As well as helping children deal with any gardening disappointments, this book introduces ideas about the animals who eat plants and is a very gentle introduction to ideas about natural selection.

Learning story 7.1

Runner bean pods

In Heidi's Reception class, the children looked closely at runner bean pods (which are actually fruit, containing bean seeds). What follows is a lovely example of children becoming curious about an object that adults tend to take for granted. The children are keen to record their observations using digital cameras and make an imaginative link to a story they have heard.

Teacher: Where did you find that bean?
Child: In there.
C: Where's the bean?
C: I want to go and have a look at the bean.
T: Where did that come from Tilly?
C: There.
C: Bet it was inside there.
T: Do you think? Do you want to have a look inside and see if you're right?
C: It's nice.
C: A bean.
T: Can you open it?
C: Yes. Going to open it.
C: Take a picture?
C: I've got a bean there what I want to take out.
C: I've found a pink bean.
T: Oh!
C: A pink one.
T: Let me have a look?
C: Inside the pink . . .
C: Can I snap it?
C: It's a pink bean.
T: Yes, of course you can.
C: It's a magic bean . . .
C: And another one.
T: We've been reading 'Jack and the Beanstalk', haven't we, in our classes.
C: I see another one.
C: Take a picture of that. Can we take a picture of it?

ICT links

There is a wide range of online resources available for teachers. One of the best places to start is Science and Plants for Schools (www.saps.org.uk). The organisation works closely with the biology community, consults with teachers to make sure their work is what they need, and talks to scientists to ensure information is topical and up-to-date. On their website you will find a link to their flickr image library (www.flickr.com). Of course children can create their own library of digital images using simple cameras, digital microscopes and visualisers. Close-up images of daisy flowers, dandelion seeds, prickly leaves and tangled roots, projected onto a screen, could all be starting points for talk and learning. Figure 7.1 shows how a digital microscope can be set up in the classroom in a way that allows children easy access to it as an aid for observation

Learning story 7.2

Leaves
In Bishop Henderson School's Reception class, the children have collected some leaves from the school grounds and the teacher is encouraging close observation.

Teacher: Do you want to have a look with a magnifying glass? Have a little look. And you can look with your eyes, you can touch them.
Child: They feel weird.
Child: They're hard.
Teacher: They are quite hard.
Child: Hard.

FIGURE 7.1 A digital microscope in use – is it a seed or coal?

Child: And bouncy because when you press your thumb on them they go boing, boing, boing, boing . . .

Teacher: They weren't like that earlier in the summer were they? What's changed? How . . .

Child: They've gone different colours.

Teacher: They are different colours.

Child: And it's wet.

Child: Really green.

Teacher: They were bright green, weren't they, before?

Child: My ones at home are purple.

Teacher: You've got some different ones at home have you?

Child: Now they've gone that colour.

Teacher: Why do you think that?

Child: Because it's not summer any more. And they've got colder.

In another class in the school, the children had been dipping the school pond and were examining something puzzling under the digital microscope. They were tiny (3mm), egg shaped, smooth black objects that had been scooped from the pond water. A fascinating discussion ensued, as the children tried to make sense of them. One child declared them 'coal' (the school was in an old mining area and they had recently been to the local museum). Other children were not so sure and continued to observe them under a higher magnification, with the image projected onto the whiteboard (see Figure 7.1) Another child suggested they 'looked a bit like seeds'. From conversation it was decided that these hypotheses could be tested. A small group went back to the pond to collect more material on which to conduct the tests – coal should burn, while seeds should germinate if they were planted.

and a prompt for questioning. Even at 10x magnification and good lighting, surface features of seeds, petals and leaves can be seen from a whole new perspective. Most digital cameras are now good enough to allow for images to be 'blown up'. When making images it is important to remember some 'rules' to make them clear and useful:

- more light usually means better photos – take items outside or near a window whenever possible;
- teach children about 'focus' and how to avoid blurry photos;
- use the 'macro' setting if the camera has one (usually indicated by a flower or tulip icon on the camera);
- tiny objects can be kept still and flat by mounting on some card with double-sided sticky tape.

Once images have been created, review them on a big screen if possible. Try beginning with a close-up or closely cropped image. It can be quite a puzzle to identify something commonplace, such as a daffodil petal, from a magnified section. Flower petals are very good at reflecting light, so under magnification they can look like they are sprinkled with glitter powder!

Also available online are time-lapse videos of seeds germinating, shoots growing, flowers bursting and fruit forming. These life processes are made much more visible by collapsing days into seconds and can be awe inspiring. (begin with www.bbc.co.uk/nature/life/Flowering_plant and www.naturefootage. com/stock_video/plant_timelapse_video.htm). Time lapse is tricky to do in the classroom, but taking photos from exactly the same spot over a number of days of weeks, perhaps of a tree or garden, will remind children how their environment is changing slowly and imperceptibly.

Related designing and making activities

We have described how some of the most fun ways to learn about plants are through food-related activities. Food preparation has remained a part of D&T in the National Curriculum for England (DfE 2013: 183) and includes the requirement to understand 'where food comes from'. When undertaking cooking activities, try to present ingredients to children in their 'raw' form where possible, with stalks, leaves and dirt still attached. Try to take time to tell children that highly processed ingredients like sugar, flour and cocoa come from plants. Simple activities such peeling, cutting and preparing fruits and vegetables can also teach children about the shapes, textures and smells of common foodstuffs – scientific learning can go hand-in-hand with the development of skills for designing and making.

Clark et al. (2003) note that young children's priorities in Early Years pro-vision include the importance of friends, food, drink and cooking and outside play. The report goes on to say, however, that too often, children under five are not consulted about the provision they are offered. Developing a garden or an outdoor wildlife area can be an excellent context for such consultations. Such projects can become one big D&T venture for a class or the whole school. If you search the web for case studies of such projects you will find some inspirational stories that show how, on a minimal budget with maximum enthusiasm, schools can make a difference to their local area by planting trees, flowers and vegetables and redesigning outdoor spaces (see, for example, Lancashire's Good, Best and Innovative Practice Awards at www.lancsngfl.ac.uk). Importantly, many of the best projects involve the children through the consultation and decision making process. Who uses this space? What do they like to do there? How can we make it nicer? What plants would people and animals like to see? Hard landscaping decisions can also involve scientific thinking. How do we suppress weeds? Which wood is best for making a climbing frame? What are the pros and cons of artificial grass versus real grass?

Summary

We have shown how learning about plants is a vital part of young children's education, one that can lead to a lifelong love of the things many adults enjoy – cooking, gardening or just spending time outside enjoying the scenery. It can also lay foundations for an appreciation of the natural world and even a desire to look after the environment. We have also shown how the topic can be made relevant for children through the familiar contexts of gardening and cooking, which lend themselves to a wide range of practical activities and enquiries.

We have shown how the curriculum requirements for Key Stage 1 can be connected to children's early experiences of plant life, and how knowledge and understanding can be developed appropriately. We have discussed the role technologies can play in bringing seemingly 'inanimate' objects to life so that children begin to appreciate that plants and animals share many of the same processes.

Discussion points

- Why might children think that plants are not alive?
- When outside in a wood or garden, how can children be encouraged to focus on both the tiny details and the 'big picture 'of the place or space?
- At what age would children be able to understand that plants don't need food? How would you explain the idea to a seven-year-old?

A thematic approach to humans and animals in Early Years education

Kendra McMahon and Christopher Collier

Purpose of this chapter

After reading this chapter you should have:

- an understanding of the key ideas about animals including humans that children in the Early Years context should develop and why these ideas are important;

- ideas about thematic contexts for children's learning about animals;

- an insight into how practitioners can support children's learning about animals through enquiries in science and D&T.

Introduction

Children are interested in animals and curious about their own bodies. Many children will have first-hand experience of animals as pets or through hobbies, or through playing outdoors. They are very likely to have learned a great deal about a wide range of animals and their habitats through media such as books and television. They will share common experiences of how their bodies work and grow as well as having physical and sensory differences as unique individuals. Social concerns about healthy lifestyles draw on ideas about what humans need to stay alive and well. There are two values underlying this topic: that we should learn to live in a way that respects and protects living things and that we need to understand and look after our environment.

For teachers, this means that children will have a rich bank of ideas to draw on in discussions and knowledge to share with others. The challenge for work in this area of science is not so much about explaining the concepts or finding meaningful contexts; the challenge is about finding ways of learning more about living animals and humans that are hands-on, ethical and accessible. Observing animals in their natural habitats takes time and patience. Some children may be frightened about handling real animals and they don't always keep still to be sketched or photographed! Unlike learning about a torch, you can't take a human apart to see what is inside, but we can explore our senses, and compare and measure what our bodies can do. Learning from secondary sources is also important, but should be part of a broader enquiry.

This chapter will start by outlining relevant concepts in relation to living processes, classification, human and animal biology, habitats and sustainability at both practitioner (adult) and appropriate child levels. It will consider the scientific process skills needed to classify animals, undertake fieldwork and appropriate attitudes to be developed towards living things. The chapter will go on to suggest learning activities within broad Early Years themes such as 'ourselves', 'underground' and 'water', illustrated with case studies, children's story books, curriculum and ICT links. Related D&T activities such as designing a home for an animal will also be included.

Conceptual understanding of humans and other animals

This chapter encompasses a very broad range of concepts. Some can be considered together as learning about the characteristics of a range of specific animals: what are they like, what do they do and what are they called? One scientific approach to this diversity is to look for commonalities: what are the similarities and differences between animals; how can we classify them? Considering the characteristics of living things in general with a particular focus on animals helps us to identify themes such as feeding and growth and to look for the ways in which different animals meet the challenges of staying alive and reproducing. Taking a broader view of the relationship between animals and their environment leads us to think about habitats and the relationships between different groups of animals, such as in food chains. Another useful biological strategy is to look for links between the 'structure and function' of a particular body part to help explain how it works – again this connects to understanding the characteristics of living things in general, such as excretion and respiration, and the particular environment it is in. This helps us to ask relevant questions. Why is a worm like it is? How does it feed and breathe? Does it have babies? Do worms need to sleep like humans do?

Table 8.1 below summarises the key concepts children should learn and provides a synopsis of the subject knowledge a practitioner would need to support this.

TABLE 8.1 Conceptual understanding: animals

Key concepts in the Early Years curriculum	Subject knowledge for practitioners in the Early Years curriculum
Distinguish between living, dead and non-living	In comparison with plants, children find it relatively easy to see animals as alive because they more obviously carry out the seven processes that characterise life. Most obviously they move (often very actively, in search of food or away from danger). They also obtain food (by feeding on plants or other animals), respire (usually the way a complex animal exchanges gases as part of the process of respiration is observable), sense, excrete and reproduce. Animals do also grow, which in an adult is the process of replacing worn out cells with new ones rather than actually increasing an animal's size, but, as is the case with plants, this is really only measurable rather than visible as it happens gradually over time (see Table 7.1 for further details).
There is a major division of living things into plants and animals	In the early years children will learn that there are two large groups that can be used to classify living things: plants and animals. These are in fact only two of the five kingdoms that many biologists use to classify all living things; the others are fungi, monera (e.g. bacteria) and protoctista (e.g. algae and seaweed).
Feeding relationships are shown as food (energy) transfers	Although children will learn later that plants and animals differ at a cellular level (plant cells are made of a rigid material called cellulose), at a young age it is differences in the way they feed that help children distinguish between the two kingdoms. Plants are able to make their own food; animals either eat plants (herbivores), animals (carnivores) or both (omnivores). Animals can also move to change location, whereas plant movement might involve opening and closing flowers or growth in a particular direction.

The feeding relationship between plants and animals can be represented as a food chain or food web that shows the direction of energy transfer from plant to animal. An arrow shows the movement of chemical energy from plant (producer) to animal (primary consumer), and from animal to animal (secondary consumer), e.g. grass → rabbit → fox. Simple food chains such as this can be part of a larger food-web which depicts a set of feeding relationships. |
| Animals can be classified into different groups by their similarities

Living things are found in certain environments because they have features that enable them to survive (adaptation) | Animals are divided into two main groups: vertebrates, which have a backbone, and invertebrates, which don't. Vertebrates include:

Fish – live in water, have gills for gas exchange ('breathing'), have scales, lay eggs.

Amphibians – newts, frogs and toads; adults live on land in damp places and breathe with lungs or though their moist skin; at an earlier stage in their lifecycle tadpoles live in water and have gills; eggs are laid in water.

Reptiles – lizards, snakes, tortoises; dry, scaly skin, lay eggs in soft shells; dinosaurs are extinct reptiles.

Birds – lay eggs, have feathers and wings.

Mammals – humans, bats, whales, dolphins; feed their young milk that is secreted from the mammary gland; most give birth to live young. |

TABLE 8.1 continued

Key concepts in the Early Years curriculum	Subject knowledge for practitioners in the Early Years curriculum
	Animals and plants are adapted to survive and thrive in specific conditions. Adaptation to a particular environment is the result of small differences that occur between individuals. In competition with other individuals of the same species, the one which is best adapted to its environment is more likely to survive and pass on its features to its offspring. An example of animal adaptation is the difference in dentition between carnivores and herbivores. Meat eaters have prominent incisors and canine teeth for killing and tearing apart prey; plant eaters have lots of grinding molars for chewing plants which are hard to digest.
Different parts of animals have different functions	Younger children will become familiar with the names of external body parts. Later they will learn that the bodies of complex animals are organised into systems made up of specialised tissues and organs. In humans there are seven main systems:
	Digestive system: mouth, teeth, tongue, oesophagus, stomach, intestine, liver, anus. The function of the digestive system is to break food down into smaller and smaller pieces until it is possible for food to pass into the body. Young children will be most aware of the start of this process in the mouth where food is broken down mechanically by teeth and chemically by saliva. They will also be aware of undigested food being expelled from the anus as poo (faeces).
	Excretory system: kidneys, bladder, liver, urethra, skin. Its function is to remove the waste products of metabolism from the body, so poo is not included. However with primary-age children this distinction is not usually made so is included in the study of excretion along with urine (wee).
	Circulation system: blood, heart, blood vessels (veins and arteries). Blood is the main means of transport for materials (oxygen and carbon dioxide, food, waste products) around the body. It is pumped around the body in vessels by the heart which produces a surge of blood in the arteries each time it beats. Children can feel this as their pulse. Arteries take blood away from the heart, veins takes blood back to it.
	Respiratory system: lungs, nose, mouth, trachea (wind pipe). Breathing is only part of the respiration process, but it is the part that children will be aware of. Oxygen is absorbed into the blood stream in the lungs as a result of breathing. The oxygen is involved in the chemical process known as respiration that releases chemical energy from food for movement and other life processes. It can be represented by the equation:
	glucose + oxygen $\rightarrow$ carbon dioxide + water + energy
	Carbon dioxide is a waste product of this process, and is expelled by the lungs.
	Nervous system: nerves, sense organs (eye, ear, tongue, nose, skin), brain. This is the system that enables different parts of the body to communicate with each other. Information from sense organs is received by the brain. It controls the body's response to this information, maybe sending nerve impulses to muscles to control their movement. We are able to consciously control some responses (e.g. running) but some actions are involuntary (e.g. pumping of the heart, or reflex actions).

TABLE 8.1 continued

Key concepts in the Early Years curriculum	Subject knowledge for practitioners in the Early Years curriculum
	Skeletal system: bones, muscles, tendons. Our skeleton protects vital organs (e.g. the rib cage protects the heart and lungs) and enables us to move (muscles pull on bones which move about joints). Muscles are only able to contract, not lengthen, so operate in pairs pulling in opposite directions (e.g. biceps and triceps in the upper arm).
	Reproductive system: testes and penis (males), ovaries, uterus and vagina (females). Younger children will learn the biological name for external reproductive organs and be aware that humans along with other animals reproduce – that is form new individuals. Later they will learn about the process of reproduction in humans – that it is sexual, that it involves the female egg being fertilised by the male sperm and that bringing the two together is achieved by sexual intercourse.
Staying healthy involves eating a balanced diet, exercise and sleep	A balanced diet includes: **Carbohydrates** (bread, rice, pasta, potatoes, sugar) for energy. **Proteins** (beans, meat, fish, milk) for growth and repair. **Fats** (oils, butter), small amounts are required for correct functioning of nerves. **Vitamins and minerals** for specific functions, e.g. vitamin C for preventing scurvy, a skin disease. **Water**, required for all chemical processes that take place in the body. **Exercise** improves the strength of muscles, including the heart muscle and muscles associated with breathing. It can contribute to reducing obesity.
Medicines are drugs we take to help our body work	The focus in Early Years is on drugs that are helpful to the body (medicines). Later children will learn that some drugs can be harmful, and that some of these are illegal. Different drugs act at different sites in the body. For example, asthma medicines reduce inflammation in the airways of the respiratory system enabling sufferers to breathe more easily.

Early Years activities that develop children's understanding of animals support their development towards the big ideas in science that *organisms are made up of cells, organisms require a supply of energy and other materials and that organisms are in competition for them, genetic information is passed from one generation to the next.*

Sources to develop background subject knowledge further:

Collier, C., Davies, D., Howe, A. and McMahon, K. (2011) *The Primary Science and Technology Encyclopedia*. London: David Fulton.

Harlen, W. (ed) (2010) *Principles and Big Ideas of Science Education*. Hatfield: ASE.

Howe, A., Davies, D., McMahon, K., Towler, L., Collier, C. and Scott, T. (2009) *Science 5–11: A Guide for Teachers*, 2nd edn. London: David Fulton (Chapter 9 and 11).

Peacock, G., Sharp, J., Johnsey, R. and Wright, D. (2012) *Primary Science: Knowledge and Understanding (Achieving QTS Series)*, 6th edn. Exeter: Learning Matters (Chapter 3).

Wenham, M. and Ovens, P. (2010) *Understanding Primary Science*, 3rd edn. London: Sage (Chapters 2, 3 and 5).

Early Years themes and contexts for learning

There are many opportunities for outdoor learning about animals; different habitats can be visited and explored. Many teachers begin the year with a theme that focuses on 'ourselves' as part of getting to know children and helping them feel that they themselves are at the centre of their learning. Themes of growth and change are often linked with transitions between stages of education to help support children with the emotional and cognitive challenges this can present. A place or theme that is revisited at different times during the year would offer new possibilities depending on the season.

Learning science can, and perhaps should, be about taking action and participating in making changes for the better. Projects could focus on ways to protect or improve the environment in the local community or to help children look after their own health. School grounds can be developed to offer a range of habitats and micro-habitats by making smaller scales changes such as a 'minibeast hotel', or a larger project such as a pond. Children might think about how they could use a local play area differently to help them stay fit and healthy. The broad Early Years themes explored below – ourselves, minibeasts, water and Spring – have been chosen to cover a range of concepts and approaches to learning.

Ourselves

Young children enjoy exploring their senses – what they can see, smell, taste, hear and touch – and this offers rich opportunities to develop descriptive language as they find out what their bodies can do. Taking part in cutting up fruit and vegetables for snacks can also be a regular part of the daily routine in food preparation; the range of fruit and vegetables offered could be varied and extended. What do children like and dislike about the flavours and textures of the food? There are clear links here with the food strand of design and technology as well as the science of senses. The exploration can begin in an informal way, such as playing with a range of musical instruments with practitioner interventions to suggest how children could make comparisons. Which sound is louder? Which sound is softer? How could you change the sound? What else might make a similar sound? Providing mirrors can help children to look at their eyes, ears, noses and tongues more closely, notice different parts and wonder what they are for.

Games and songs such as 'Heads, Shoulders, Knees and Toes', and 'Put Your Finger on Your Nose' can help children name the different external body parts. Still focusing on visible, external features, children could compare handprints and food prints with each other, or perhaps measure their height and find out how that compares with some other animals. How many 'Tobys' long is a crocodile? To develop comparison and measurement children could try picking things up with their feet or hands. Which hand is best? How can you prove it? Why might fingers be better than toes at picking up Lego bricks?

Invite children to draw around themselves (each other) and label the body parts they can see. Ask them to talk about what is inside their bodies too. Research (Osborne et al. 1992) has shown that young children are aware of their bones, stomach, heart and brain, probably because these are referred to in everyday language and also because they have some sensation of what they do. However, they may be less clear about what these organs look like and where in the body they are. When asked to draw their ideas about where food goes when we eat it, very few young children have a clear idea about how intestines are tubes from mouth to anus. There are two common ideas: sometimes food goes all over the body, just as it is, so a whole fish finger could end up in their forearm, sometimes food just sits in a bag (the stomach). Without an understanding that food is broken down into smaller bits and used as building blocks, a rather like Lego, it is hard for children to move beyond these ideas and some will not be ready for these more abstract ideas until later.

Considering our bodies and what they do also means thinking about how we look after them. A visit from a doctor, nurse or dentist would provide stimulation for a role play in an area of the room set up as a clinic. Although children may be able to talk about the importance of exercise for good health, they often do so in adult terms – exercise means being on an exercise bike, or lifting weights. Asking them to notice what happens in their bodies when they are skipping or playing chase might help extend their ideas. Concerns about the rise in childhood obesity in the UK mean that it is important to help children choose to eat an appropriate, balanced diet, but practitioners need to be sensitive; food choices go beyond scientific knowledge, and young children do not control the food that is provided in their homes and may have limited choice about the food offered. Culture and identity play a role in the diets people have as do the wealth and income of families.

Minibeasts

Children find animals interesting. Early Years practitioners would not be surprised by the outcome of an investigation that showed toddlers were more engaged by living animals than attractive toy equivalents; they spent significantly more time playing with them (Lobue et al. 2013). This was even true when the animal included a snake and a spider.

The most available wild animals children can study are 'minibeasts'. This is the name often given to *invertebrates* (animals without backbones) and avoids the less positive sounding term 'creepy crawlies'. The group 'minibeasts' or invertebrates, includes commonly found animals: insects (adults have six legs), worms, slugs, snails, woodlice (14 legs) and spiders (eight legs).

Children can collect and observe, then photograph and draw a wider range of minibeasts in the garden, school grounds or nearby space such as a park. The Woodland Trust has downloadable guides with colour photos to help identify a range of common minibeasts (www.woodlandtrust.org.uk). They also have 'trump cards' to help children become more familiar with a range of different animals as they play the game. The Field Studies Council produce cheap, splash-proof identification guides (www.field-studies-council.org). An alternative is to take a camera out to the location the children will be studying and create your own identification guide to match the area. Through drama or dance children could draw on their observations to move like different minibeasts – a grass-hopper, an ant or a woodlouse curling into a ball.

The children might think about animals they are not seeing, as well as those they are. For example, there is a concern about the decline in bee populations. The charity Bee Scene works with schools and nurseries to connect work on animals with plants by helping children to identify the wild flowers that provide nectar for bees (www.wildaboutplants.org.uk/beescene). An active project might survey minibeasts in a specific area before and after an intervention such as planting flowers that will attract pollinators such as butterflies or bees. This could involve the local community, with children talking to experts to plan what to plant and asking parents and others what they think of the outcome. A popular project is building a bug hotel. This involves filling a space, which could be as small as a shoe box or a large as a stack of wooden pallets, with sticks, hollow bamboo, bricks with holes in, pieces of bark and anything else the children think that minibeasts might like to live in.

Water

The theme could be as broad as water, or refer to a more specific place: 'the seaside' or 'our pond'. Looking at animals living in water, or nearby, offers a contrasting habitat to compare with minibeasts on land. This may mean planning a visit. Perhaps this would be a good opportunity to ask children what they need in a place to keep them alive and well – food, drink, shelter or warm clothes, and somewhere to go to the loo! The discussion could be developed later to consider what the water animals need to stay alive and where they might find what they need.

An alternative to a wild location might be a zoo or aquarium visit. Garden centres can be a surprisingly good and free source of cold water and tropical fish to look at. Children could imagine themselves living underwater; many will be familiar with the well-researched television programme 'Octonauts' (BBC CBeebies) in which cartoon charters encounter a range of sea creatures and learn about them. Encourage children to contrast animals in different habitats: how do they move, feed and breathe?

Most children think of animals as being large, furry, four-legged land mammals (Bell 1981). How do children see animals such as fish, crabs, sea anemones or corals? The research suggests they tend to see them as separate groups rather than subsets of animals. It is worth mentioning at this point that children often do not see humans as animals and this is reinforced by everyday uses of the word such as: 'No animals allowed except guide dogs'.

Is a shell found on the beach a living thing? (In case you weren't sure: it isn't.) Research into children's ideas about what makes something 'living' goes back to work by Piaget in the 1920s. Characteristics such as movement, growth, not being 'man-made' or having a face may be used by children as criteria to decide whether something is alive or not (Piaget 1929; Osborne et al. 1992). Instead of rote learning of the list of characteristics of living things (see Tables 7.1 and 8.1) it may be more productive to explore with children what different body parts different animals have and how they contribute to keeping them alive to gradually build a rich body of knowledge about the variety of life in a range of habitats.

Spring!

A good start point for this theme might be to ask: what season is it: Winter or Spring? How do we know? What is changing? Go beyond the usual clichés of chicks and daffodils to what the children can actually observe in the local area. Alternative titles for similar themes might be 'Changes' or 'Growing up'.

To explore lifecycles at first-hand it is possible to keep chickens, though many settings and schools opt to incubate eggs until they hatch and then return the chicks when they are older. This can be made particularly exciting if, like Fen Marshall (formerly head teacher at Hawkesbury Upton Primary School), you take the trouble to source a range of eggs of different sizes and colours. Small amounts of frogspawn can be kept and when the tadpoles emerge they can be fed on blanched lettuce until they have grown into froglets, when they will need to be released, preferably to the place the frogspawn came from. Visiting a farm to look at and bottle-feed new born lambs or kids is very popular. Other opportunities for learning about the lives of animals might be learning about how some animals wake from hibernation or looking out for migratory birds (such as swallows, swifts and house martins) when they return from warmer climates where they have spent the Winter. Links can be made with Spring festivals such as Easter with themes of growth and renewal. It is possible to buy cocoons and pupae to hatch out a moth or a butterfly and see the astonishing process of metamorphosis at first-hand.

Research into children's ideas about what happens inside a chicken egg before it hatches reveals a variety of ideas (Russell and Watt 1990). An unusual but intriguing idea a few children have is that there is an 'assembly of compete body parts'– legs, head, body and beak – waiting to be put together. A more common idea is of a complete animal in limbo and waiting to hatch, and the most common was of miniature, but complete animal, gradually increasing in size. It is rare for children under the age of seven to present the idea that the material inside the egg transforms into a structurally refined animal. Perhaps this shouldn't be surprising as to really understand this we need an advanced concept

FIGURE 8.1 Bottle-feeding a lamb

about matter as tiny particles that can be formed into different materials. Consistent with this, children will predict that an egg gets heavier as the animal inside 'grows' rather than understanding that the material is reorganised but not added to. They could be challenged to think about where the new material would come from – how would it get in?

Inviting a parent to bring a baby into the room would stimulate children to think about how they have changed since they were babies. Another way of making a link with home is asking them to bring in photographs of themselves as babies or toddlers. Among other changes such as from crawling to walking, babbling to talking, they might talk about changes to what they can eat as they grow teeth. Children's first baby teeth are lost at about the age of six, usually the lower incisors. Different cultures have different stories about what you should do with your baby teeth when they come out and children could share and find out about these. Instead of a tooth fairy many cultures have a 'tooth mouse' and in some Asian countries the custom is to throw the tooth and shout a request for it to be replaced by the tooth of a mouse – a tradition probably based on the fact that, unlike humans, rodents have teeth that continue to grow throughout their lives.

Process skills

Learning about animals will draw on a wide range of process skills: questioning, recording, measuring and drawing conclusions and presenting findings. In this chapter the focus is on the scientific process skills needed to identify and classify animals, undertake fieldwork and develop appropriate attitudes towards living things.

How to catch an animal: techniques and ethical issues

Often the best way to study animals is by observing them as they go about their normal behaviour in their natural habitat, but sometimes it is good to carefully catch them for a closer look. Children can be taught some ways to do this using IT (see Chapter 7 for more on using magnification techniques and close up photos). Children need to be shown how to collect animals carefully and have respect for them and then afterwards return them to where they were found.

Some minibeasts can simply be caught by gently using your hands, or scooping them into a collecting pot. Very small minibeasts, such as ants or flies that could be damaged by fingers, can be picked up using a paintbrush, or a 'pooter' – a small collecting pot with a clever system so the child sucks on one tube and the minibeast is sucked into the pot through a second tube. One way of collecting a range of minibeasts is to place a sheet or upturned light coloured umbrella under a bush and then tap or gently shake the bush so that flies and beetles tumble down where they can be collected. Adults should be a positive role model for the careful handling of minibeasts. The author of this chapter has been practising handling large spiders (as large as Incy Wincy) and not responding like Little Miss Muffet. Animals living in ponds can be caught by sweeping a net through the water; practitioners could suggest skimming the top or taking a deeper sweep, or even scraping some of the muddy bottom to see what different things can be found. Empty ice cream tubs make good containers for children to see what they have found with the white plastic providing enough contrast to see more clearly.

Unless the school keeps animals, perhaps chickens, larger animals will probably be viewed at a distance or on a farm or zoo trip. The ethical issues of keeping animals out of the wild can be debated. Do children think it is okay to keep pets such as hamsters or rabbits? What about a snake, a bird or a lion cub? Invite children to offer their opinion and justify it: 'I think ... because ...'. This is also an opportunity to talk about what animals need to keep them alive and well. In the theme of this chapter, as in this area of science, curiosity needs to be balanced with care and respect for living creatures.

FIGURE 8.2 Hamster in a cage

Identifying and classifying animals

Having caught an animal, children may want to name it. The National Curriculum for Key Stage 1 to be implemented in 2014 (DfE 2013) emphasises that children should know the names of a variety of plants and animal and be able to classify them correctly, that is, according to the current scientific view. If interpreted narrowly, this could become rote learning and limit children's own observations and the connections they make as they make sense of the variety of life around them. But there are reasons for naming and classifying. As they acquire language, young children are very good at learning the names of objects and then applying this label to similar objects. It is a common belief that the child first develops the concept – say of 'butterfly' – then names it, but linguistic research suggests that encoding a concept with a word is part of what the development of a concept is. Concept development is promoted by language acquisition (as explored in Chapter 2). Naming an animal as a frog, toad, newt or amphibian is a way of assigning it to a group that has certain common features. Young children tend to focus on obvious observable features of objects to distinguish them and there is a role for adults in helping to draw attention to 'salient' or significant features. In Learning story 8.1 Year 1 teacher Julia Holder helps children refine their criterion for something being alive 'it moves' to something that moves by itself.

As critical practitioners we should also pay attention to what is not named. Children may be able to name different kinds of dogs, or perhaps dinosaurs, but

Learning story 8.1

Is it alive?

In this short transcript teacher Julia Holder at St Phillips Primary School works with a group of children who have been sorting objects/photos according to whether they are alive or not.

Teacher: Could you tell us, how did you sort yours? How did you sort it?
Child 1: Umm . . . all of these are alive and all of those are not.
Teacher: And all of those . . . including that one there?
Child 1: Yes.
Teacher: Okay. What do you think?
Child 2: They move.
Child 3: So that means it is alive.
Child 2: It being moved. It only has a helped being moved because it's got that tree.
Teacher: You're quite right. But would it move by itself? No. We said, if you listen, we said . . . umm . . . Thomas and Ashley said that we know that these things . . . umm . . . are alive because they move and then we looked at this watch here and we said but hang on, that one moves along, but what did you just say Allie?
Allie: They need batteries to move.
Teacher: They need help to move don't they. Okay. Umm . . . and then, what else did you say Thomas, how do we know that these things are alive? How do we know that they're alive?

can they name, and therefore distinguish between, different types of butterflies, or perhaps spiders? The naming of parts of our bodies can contribute to health and well-being. The non-statutory guidance for Year 1 recommends that: 'Pupils should have plenty of opportunities to learn the names of the main body parts (including head, neck, arms, elbows, legs, knees, face, ears, eyes, hair, mouth, teeth)' (DfE 2013: 149). Does this mean the reproductive organs should not be named? How do we relate this to safeguarding children, which is strengthened if children can use words that everyone understands? Schools and settings will develop their own policies on this issue.

One of the issues in learning about classification is young children's lack of understanding of how groups can be subsets of bigger groups, so the idea that an ant is an insect and an animal is difficult for many to grasp (Bell and Barker 1982). A study (Leach et al. 1992) found that even seven-year-old children, when asked to classify a selection of items (e.g. photos of animals) can do so by finding common features between items in the collection, but the groups may have different status and not be hierarchical. For example, in this topic children might group a selection of pictures of animals into these groups: colourful birds, brown birds, things that live in a pond, animals I like and creepy crawlies. Understanding of classification can be gradually built during children's education through discussion of different examples in different contexts.

Early Years Foundation Stage and Key Stage 1 curriculum links

In the Early Years Foundation Stage (EYFS) (DfE 2012: 8) there is an emphasis on health and self-care in the prime area of physical development that relates to science. Children are expected to 'know the importance for good health of physical exercise, and a healthy diet, and talk about ways to keep healthy and safe'.

As part of 'Understanding the world' children should know about similarities and differences between themselves and others, and different places and living things. The document emphasises the role of talk: 'They talk about the features of their own immediate environment and how environments might vary from one another. They make observations of animals and plants and explain why some things occur, and talk about changes' (DfE 2012: 9).

As in all themes, opportunities for playing and exploring in this context are important. There are perhaps particular opportunities for 'creating and thinking critically' as children make their own links between different animals and their habitats to form a broader picture of how living things are similar and different and how they relate to each other.

At Key Stage 1 the English National Curriculum (DfE 2013) requires that children identify and name a variety of common animals across the whole range of groups: birds, fish, amphibians, reptiles, mammals and invertebrates. They should be able to compare them, thinking about the different structures of different animals, although it is not until Key Stage 2 that the formal distinctions between the different groups of animals are required. They should learn about common animals that are carnivores, herbivores and omnivores. This is expected to take place in Year 1, along with naming the parts of the human body and associating them with the different senses.

In Year 2 children are expected to explore and compare the differences between things that are living, dead, and things that have never been alive. Building on their previous studies of particular animals, the focus extends to learning about a range of different the habitats in which different animals live and how the habitats provide for the basic needs of different kinds of animals. The curriculum distinguishes between the major 'habitats', which could be a pond, grassland, ocean, or rainforest and or 'micro-habitats'. The non-statutory guidance describes a micro-habitat as 'a very small habitat, for example for woodlice under stones, logs or leaf litter' (DfE 2013: 151). When studying habitats, the concepts of inter-dependence of living things (e.g. how a butterfly depends on flowering plants) and simple food chains can be introduced.

Children should be taught that animals, including humans, have offspring that grow into adults. The non-statutory guidance makes it clear that in the science curriculum there is no expectation that children should be learning about sexual reproduction in Key Stage 1:

The focus at this stage should be on questions that help pupils to recognise growth; they should not be expected to understand how reproduction occurs. The following examples might be used: egg, chick, chicken; egg, caterpillar, pupa, butterfly; spawn, tadpole, frog; lamb, sheep. Growing into adults can include reference to baby, toddler, child, teenager, adult.

(DfE 2013: 153)

Children are expected to find out about what animals, including humans, need in order to survive; the basic physical requirements for water, food and air. This link with health education is further strengthened by the expectation that children learn about the importance of diet, exercise, and hygiene.

Story books

In Table 8.2 there are some suggestions for story books and how they could be used as start points for children's learning about animals and human health.

It is worth noting that non-fiction texts can also play an important role in children's learning about animals. Ganea et al. (2011) demonstrated that young children were able to apply information about camouflage that they had read in information picture books to a new context that was presented and, importantly, also to real animals they encountered.

ICT links

By looking at photographs of different animals children can compare their different features. Video offers the possibility of recording animals in action: moving and feeding and often provide more information about the habitat than a still photograph. Children can do their own Internet research using images alone to answer intriguing questions that adults may not be able to answer. Do crabs lay eggs or just have baby crabs? How does a spider make its web? The organisation 'Arkive' (www.arkive.org) has collected a wide range of photographs and video clips of animals with further text providing more information available about each animal so it can be used at many levels. But children can also take their own photographs and make their own movies. This could capture unexpected animal events; Figure 8.3 shows a photograph of a grasshopper shedding skin that was taken by a six-year-old. Alternatively children could be given a camera to record a systematic survey: Where can we find spiders' webs? What do the habitats have in common? What is different about them?

Still photographs of animals taken by children could become characters in animation packages such as Puppet Pals HD, an easy to use 'app' in which children can move, grow, shrink and flip images to bring them to life against a

TABLE 8.2 Story books as starting points for children's learning about animals and human health

Book and author	How it could be used
'Sharing a Shell' (Julia Donaldson)	This book about the symbiotic relationship between a hermit crab, anemone and bristle worm could be a start point for creating a 'rock pool' for small world play in nursery settings.
'Owl Babies' (Martin Wadell)	With a powerful emotional context as three baby owls wait anxiously for the return of their mother, this story provides information about owls: where they live and how they hunt for food at night, but also some misinformation: 'all owls think a lot'. Practitioners could discuss with children which parts are true, which are not and how they could check.
'Run Little Mouse Run' (Shirley Isherwood)	This picture book with plenty of tension (and a happy ending) would be a good way of introducing ideas about predators and prey and which habitats might be safest for the prey.
'The Very Hungry Caterpillar' (Eric Carle)	This popular book is often used to introduce the topic of lifecycles. But help the children to take check the information against other sources. Beyond the more obvious questions: Do caterpillars really eat pickles and wear boots, they might find out: Which pair of butterflies wings is the larger – the top or the bottom? Or, what is the difference between a cocoon and a pupa?
'Dr Dog' (Babette Cole)	As Dr Dog warns: 'Never scratch your bum and suck your thumb'. This funny book would be a great introduction to a discussion about what we can do to keep healthy.
'One World' (Michael Foreman)	This story of two children exploring a rock pool could be used before or after a visit to a real rock pool. The children think about how they can protect habitats of the world as they have looked after their rock pool and this could provoke thinking together about how wild animals should be treated and natural environments protected.
'One Tiny Turtle' (Nicola Davies)	This book, which is part narrative, part information text, introduces the lifecycle of the endangered loggerhead turtle. It explores what we don't know as well as what we do know, offering possibilities for imagining what is happening to the turtles in the time they are out at sea and not seen by humans.
'Whale' (Nicola Davies)	In this book Nicola Davies explores how everything about a blue whale comes back to just how very big it is!

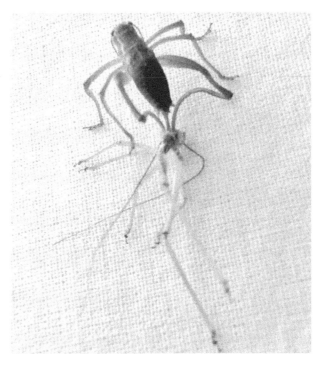

FIGURE 8.3 Grasshopper shedding its skin

Learning story 8.2

Animals inside and outside the classroom

Many of the children in the Reception class of trainee teacher John Paul Sharman had very little direct experience of animals. With the support of his teacher-mentor, John Paul planned a range of activities to introduce children to a range of animals. He was careful to check school policies, LEA guidance and legal issues before beginning. He sent a letter to all parents asking for information regarding children's known allergies. He was also careful to find out whether animal bedding or feed (for example, that containing nuts) might cause allergic reaction. At the same time he asked parents if they could help in any way with the topic of 'animals'.

The topic began gently with James bringing in his rabbit from home. James was able to talk to the class about how he cared for the pet, its need for exercise, handling (to keep it good natured) and feeding. In this way the class began to think about the needs of living things. When another pet made a visit to school, four-and-a-half-year-old Kim astounded the class and the teacher by demonstrating her expertise in the care of poodles, since her mother was a dog breeder. She explained to her peers how she 'groomed' the poodles by shampooing, 'clipping around the muzzle' and brushing their coats.

For two weeks the class hosted a colony of African land snails. The children were taught how to care for these amazing molluscs – they need regular spraying with water mist and enjoy a diet of fresh cucumber. Because the snails are very large, the children could clearly see the way they 'rasped' their way through the cucumber and how they moved on ripples of their 'foot' as they travelled up the glass side of their tank. The children made links to other experiences with snails and slugs, realising why their parents needed to keep them away from their precious garden plants.

The death of animals was a significant part of the project. One child was hoping to bring his pet dog in to share with the class, but it fell ill and died during the term. Children discussed such losses openly; they shared experiences about burying dead pets and where they had 'gone', although John Paul noticed children often talked about dead pets in the present tense and seemed to think a replacement pet was the original pet in a new guise. He felt that the discussions helped children begin to understand death and bereavement.

The next visitor to school was a horse although John Paul kept clear due to an allergy. Discussions about the care for this animal provided a good opportunity for the children to think about similarities and differences; both the horse and the snails enjoyed apples, while the differences were easier to identify. An education officer, Vicki Thomas, from the Royal Society for the Prevention of Cruelty to Animals (RSPCA), was the next visitor to the class. She did not bring any animals with her, as the RSPCA have a policy of advising teachers not to keep animals in school. During the workshop she encouraged them to think about the needs that all pets have: food, clean water, exercise, a safe and comfortable place to live and sleep, grooming to keep them healthy and 'love' (i.e. freedom from injury, fear and stress, and the opportunity to behave naturally) for all their lives. The teacher used this framework of six needs in future weeks when the children encountered other more unusual creatures. Having a visitor in class also gave the children opportunity to practise listening, raising questions and responding to a different adult in a change of routine – all aspects of 'stepping stones' to Early Learning Goals in this area.

Social development also featured in a trip to Bristol Zoo; again children were having to adapt to a new situation in a different environment. At the zoo the education officer was rather taken aback by the level of knowledge the children already had about the care of animals. For example, the children were shown a cage with a rat inside but otherwise empty. They were able quickly to identify what the zoo should provide in order to care for it properly. The children were then introduced to a python and some hissing cockroaches. They heard about the need for animals to have appropriate and varied diets and careful handling (e.g. always to stroke a python with the back of the hand to avoid transferring sweat and salts to its skin) before seeing the rest of the zoo.

John Paul concluded the topic with an 'empathy session'. Children took it in turns to be an animal. The others then asked the child how they would feel if they were hit, or mistreated, or not fed. This helped the children think back to all they had learned about caring for animals and apply it to this situation.

Commentary

This delightful case study shows how, with a considerable amount of planning and thought, children's scientific experiences of living things can be enriched enormously during the Foundation Stage. The work described above addressed many aspects of personal, social and emotional development, including those related to dispositions and attitudes, behaviour, self-control and self-care. It also shows that the local community and children themselves can contribute towards this learning. John Paul acknowledges that the topic would not have been half as successful without the parents' support.

Learning story 8.3

Mole holes

Making models of animals and animal homes requires children to draw on and develop their knowledge of animal structure, their usual habitat and even their diet.

As part of their topic 'Under the ground', children at Westleigh Infants School made model animals and habitats for them. In Figure 8.3 you can see a mole made out of air-drying clay with the key features of the animal – it is blind, but has a long nose for smelling, it has big feet, claws for digging and a short tail. An empty box has been painted to represent the underground tunnel and a model stag beetle and other small insects that the mole will eat are there too. The information used came from books that were available in the classroom and from verbal support by the teacher as the children worked.

The child who made this model took her research on moles into the field – or rather her granny's garden, where she took a long stick and poked it systematically into each of the many mole hills, moving the stick around to find the direction the tunnel went off in and then pushing it in as far as it would go. Each time she looked carefully at the stick to see how far it went in (about 50cm on most occasions), once noticing that she was moving the grass a short distance away as that tunnel was very shallow. Finally she concluded: 'That means they don't go as far down as the lava'.

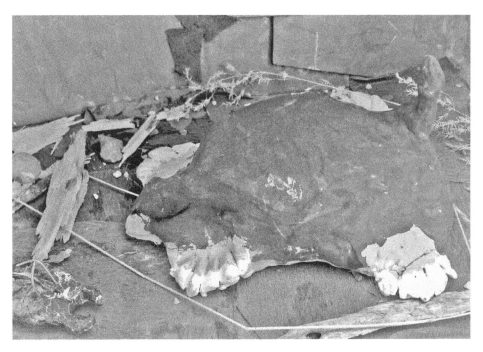

FIGURE 8.3 Home for a mole

background while adding sound. Possibilities might include turning a food chain or lifecycle into a story, or perhaps showing an animal checking out different habitats until it find the one that suits it best.

The Internet could be used as a source of information about the human body, but practitioners need to make sure children are not accessing age inappropriate or unsafe websites. We also all need to be wary of using websites with misleading or unsubstantiated information, particularly about health as many, many people and organisations claim health benefits for products or foods for which there is no good evidence. More reliable sites are those that offer government-backed health advice, or the websites of publically accountable organisations such as the BBC.

Summary

Children are fascinated by the other life forms with which humans share this planet. Knowledge of our own bodies is essential for us to make health choices during our lives. In this chapter we explored concepts of what it means to be alive, about different animals, their behaviour and lifecycles and how they are interconnected through food chains and their habitats.

We provided an overview of the curriculum requirements in England and made suggestions for meaningful contexts through which these ideas could be brought to life: ourselves, minibeasts, water and Spring. Research offers insights into some ideas about humans and other animals that children may bring to their learning and we presented case studies of real learning in action that provided further insights into what practitioners can do to support children's learning.

Discussion points

- The ancient Greek philosopher Thales defined living things as anything that can 'move by itself' and later another Greek philosopher Aristotle suggested the definition should be 'can nourish itself'. Are these good definitions of living things?

- What television programmes are children currently watching that involve animals in some way (documentary, cartoons, etc.)? What ideas are they learning from these?

- Is knowing the science of how our bodies work enough to make us have healthy lifestyles? What other factors might be involved?

- How has studying the structure of animals influenced designers and technologists to solve problems and make new products?

9

A thematic approach to everyday materials in Early Years practice

Christopher Collier

Purpose of this chapter

After reading this chapter you should have:

■ an understanding of a range of practical activities that will support children's learning of everyday materials and an appreciation of the role of the practitioner in this development;

■ a knowledge of the key concepts in materials and how children's understanding of these concepts can be developed;

■ an understanding of how play can support children's development of scientific skills;

■ ideas for design-and-make activities in the context of everyday materials.

Introduction

Does this chapter really matter? Well, yes, because, although we rarely give it a moment's thought, we inhabit a world which would, quite literally, be nothing without matter! Our very being is attributable to the existence of substance. At all times of the day we are interacting with the material world and our understanding of it influences our actions. For instance, we know that our comfort at the dinner table can be improved by placing a foam-filled cushion on the seat of a wooden chair. We question what a piece of food packaging is made of before deciding how we should dispose of it. When choosing perfume or aftershave, we know that the initial smell of the scent will change over time.

By waiting a little while before purchasing we will discover more about the perfume's lingering notes. It is unlikely that we have considered the properties of the cushion, food packaging or fragrance in terms of their hardness, bio-degradability or volatility, but it is our knowledge of them, albeit at an intuitive level, that affects our actions.

Similarly, for young children the topic of everyday materials has a usefulness and relevance to everyday situations. Very young children explore and make observations of their surroundings, only later describing these in terms of the matter with which they have interacted. So, possibly through painful experience, they will become aware of the difference between toppling over and hitting a wooden floor compared to falling on a mattress. They will happily investigate the tactile properties of their food by squishing it between their fingers. They may discover that some food sloshes about and some holds its shape. As they become older, their actions and choices will be influenced by their knowledge of materials. What clothing is the most appropriate for playing in the mud? What material should we choose for the curtains in the doll's house?

In nurseries and schools many opportunities exist for children to learn about materials through play. Perhaps they will explore the properties of liquids in the water tray and solids in the sand tray. Combine the two and sand-sculpting becomes a possibility. 'Welly walks' through the seasons and different weather conditions provide a wealth of experiences linked to the topic of everyday materials. Experiences such as these (and the many more that will be discussed in this chapter) allied to well-thought-through interventions will lead to children developing an appreciation of the fascinating material world they inhabit.

Conceptual development at 3–7 years

Progression in key concepts about everyday materials is described in Table 9.1.

Early Years themes and contexts for learning

There are many possibilities for exploratory play that will support children's development and understanding of everyday materials. By providing a range of interesting resources and settings linked by a theme that is relevant to young children, learning will be promoted that is focused on children's enquiries. In the three examples of collections below, thought was given to the objects selected so that children experience a range of properties (footwear), states of matter (bath time) and material origins (seaside). The contexts chosen are familiar to children.

- Footwear collection: include shoes with variations in grip, waterproofness and flexibility. A collection might include a training shoe, football boot, welly, canvas shoe, flipper and sandal.

TABLE 9.1 Conceptual understanding: everyday materials

Key concepts in the Early Years curriculum	Subject knowledge for practitioners in the Early Years curriculum
All matter ('stuff') called material is because it has a mass and takes up space	In everyday language 'material' is synonymous with fabric, but scientists use the term more generally to refer to all matter, or 'stuff'. It is relatively easy to appreciate that solids and liquids have a mass and occupy space. Maybe less apparent is that gases such as air also do too.
Materials can be classified by their origin	Ultimately all materials originate from the Earth (with the exception of very small quantities of material that have been brought back from the Moon or are asteroids!) but some have undergone little or no processing and are termed 'natural' materials whereas others have been modified and are classed as 'man-made' or 'manufactured'.
	Natural materials include those from the biological world (wood, vegetable or animal fibres) and those from the physical world (rocks and soils). They require little processing to be of use apart from possibly shaping, cleaning and sorting. Building stone is essentially the same material as the rock from which it was shaped. Sheep wool needs washing, teasing and spinning before it can be used as yarn, but in essence, the material remains the same.
	Manufactured materials are made from natural materials that have been changed so that their structure and composition are modified. For instance, metals are refined from ores found in rocks – metal alloys are produced by combining metals. Plastics are made from the products of the oil industry.
Materials can be classified by their properties	A property of a material is defined by how it responds to an external influence. This in turn leads to properties being grouped according to the nature of that influence:
	Mechanical properties are related to how a material responds to a force and include: • Hardness – the ease with which a material can be marked or indented. • Elasticity – elastic materials deform when force is applied to them but then return to their original form when the force is removed. The opposite of this is called plasticity. • Strength – a description of the amount of force needed to break a material. Other mechanical properties include flexibility/rigidity, brittleness/toughness, compressibility and malleability.
	Thermal properties (response to heat) include thermal conductivity, defined as how well a material conducts heat.
	Electrical properties (response to electricity) include electrical conductivity, which is the resistance of a material to the flow of electricity.
	Chemical properties (response of a material when in contact with another material) include: • Reactivity – a measure of a material's resistance to change in a reaction. • Corrosion – a specific type of reaction whereby iron or steel react with oxygen and water to form rust.
	Optical properties (response to light) include: • Transparency – all, or practically all, light passes through a transparent material with little or no interference so that the material does not cast a shadow and objects viewed through it are seen as sharp images. • Translucency – only some light passes through a translucent material so that it forms grey or coloured shadows. The material may scatter light so that images viewed through it appear fuzzy e.g. tracing paper.

TABLE 9.1 continued

Key concepts in the Early Years curriculum	Subject knowledge for practitioners in the Early Years curriculum
	• Reflectivity – a material with a matt appearance reflects light in a scattered way from its uneven surface. However, polished, smooth surfaces reflect light in a uniform way so that objects are visible in it as mirror images. **Magnetic properties** (response to magnetic fields) include: • Permanently magnetic materials (e.g. bar magnets), which attract and repel other permanent magnets. • Temporarily magnetic materials (e.g. a steel paper clip), which are attracted to magnets but not repelled. • Non-magnetic materials, which are neither attracted nor repelled.
Properties of materials determine how we use them	The uses children put materials to during design and technology projects will be determined by the properties of the material: **Paper/card** – easily cut and shaped; rigidity increases with thickness; absorbent, but weaker when wet; strength increases when folded; corrugated card is rigid along corrugations and flexible across them; papier mache forms a hard shell when dry; art straws lose rigidity when bent or flattened. **Plastic** – easily cut; rigidity increases with thickness; often waterproof; can be opaque, translucent or transparent; corruflute is a material made from plastic that is particularly rigid. **Wood** – resistant to cutting (although sheet balsa can be cut with scissors), high rigidity; absorbent after long immersion, otherwise waterproof. **Textiles** – quite easy to cut; very flexible; large range of textures; sometimes waterproof; good thermal insulators. **Mouldable materials** (e.g. clay, playdough) – easily shaped; malleable; may become rigid if allowed to dry.
Materials can be grouped as solids, liquids or gases	All materials are made up of tiny particles that bond to each other in various ways. The arrangement of particles and the way they are bonded together determine the property of a material and its state, be it solid, liquid or gas. Particles in solid materials are tightly packed together and bonded strongly to neighbouring particles so that solids have a fixed shape and volume, and are not easily compressed. Particles of a liquid are also closely packed together but the bonds between particles are weaker enabling particles to move about relative to one and other. Consequently a liquid, like a solid, has a fixed volume and is not easily compressed. Unlike a solid, a liquid does not have a fixed shape so it flows to fill the bottom of the container it is in. The particles of a gas are widely spaced out and not bonded to neighbouring particles. Therefore a gas can be compressed, has no fixed shape and a variable volume, expanding to fill the container it is in.

Early Years activities that develop children's understanding of everyday materials support their development towards the big idea in science that *all material is made of very small particles*.

Sources to develop background subject knowledge further:

Collier, C., Davies, D., Howe, A. and McMahon, K. (2011) *The Primary Science and Technology Encyclopedia*. London: David Fulton.

Harlen, W. (ed.) (2010) *Principles and Big Ideas of Science Education*. Hatfield: ASE

Howe, A., Davies, D., McMahon, K., Towler, L., Collier, C. and Scott, T. (2009) *Science 5–11: A Guide for Teachers*, 2nd edn. London: David Fulton (Chapter 2).

Peacock, G., Sharp, J., Johnsey, R. and Wright, D. (2012) *Primary Science: Knowledge and Understanding (Achieving QTS Series)*, 6th edn. Exeter: Learning Matters (Chapters 6 and 7).

Wenham, M. and Ovens, P. (2010) *Understanding Primary Science*, 3rd edn. London: Sage (Chapters 6 and 7).

- Bath-time collection: include liquids such as shampoo, shower gels, bubble bath, warm water; solids such as soap, towel, loofah; and the gases formed from perfumes and aftershaves.

- Seaside collection: include a range of natural materials (e.g. sand, seashells, water, rocks, dried seaweed) and man-made objects (e.g. parasol, sun cream, inflatable beach toys, Lycra swimwear).

Learning by exploring thematic collections is one way to contextualise learning about materials. Another way is to identify a theme and explore its potential. In fact, it's difficult to imagine themes that involve children gaining practical, concrete experiences as they learn that do not have some link to the topic of everyday materials. The three themes identified below (keeping safe, shadow puppets and being an artist) were chosen to illustrate this point. They also highlight the relationship between children's scientific discoveries and design-and-make activities. By making this connection children's learning of materials is given a purpose.

Keeping safe

Perhaps the most obvious way that learning can be made purposeful is through children testing the properties of materials and applying their newly acquired knowledge to the construction of an artefact. This theme affords a number of opportunities for children to learn in such a way. For example, a range of materials (cotton wool, paper, fabric, etc.) can be tested for their ability to insulate sound before selecting the most suitable material for making a pair of ear muffs. The reflective qualities of materials can be tested – maybe in a dark room constructed in the role-play area – before choosing which one will make the best reflector to keep us visible in the dark. Safety in the Sun can also be investigated by testing a range of sunglasses, or even by children making a pair of their own after testing the transparency of a range of materials. A word of warning though: sunglasses made from coloured acetate and the like won't actually protect children's eyes from the Sun, and we should never look directly at the Sun, even through shop-bought sunglasses. Another activity linked to the theme of safety is for the absorbent properties of different materials to be tested prior to designing a mop for soaking up classroom spillages.

Shadow puppets

Form links between science, technology and drama by providing children with the opportunity to make shadow puppets, using them to act out a story or nursery rhyme. For this to be a particularly effective learning experience, children need to have a good range of opaque, translucent and transparent materials to select from, including tracing paper and coloured acetates. A simple shadow screen can be created from an old bed sheet that can be backlit by an overhead projector.

Being an artist

Children can have a great deal of fun exploring the properties of artists' media (paint, glue, clay, paper, card, crayon, pastel etc.), beginning with experiments in mark-making. Children can explore the media in which powder paints are mixed (e.g. water, glue, cooking oil) and how these media change the properties of the paint produced and how this in turn alters the finish of their art work. Painting on a variety of different surfaces (e.g. paper, blotting paper, greaseproof paper, tin foil) will also produce different results. Working with clay, children may discover that the wet clay is elastic and relatively soft, but once air-dried it is harder and breaks. Clay fired in a kiln becomes brittle. They can also consider the properties of the clothes and aprons that they wear and equipment they use: which fabric will get stained? Which is easy to clean or wash out? How do we clean the brushes?

Scientific process skills

Collections such as those listed above can promote experiential learning in a play-based context. Young children will be exploring science in a context where they initiate their learning and their enquiries are dictated by what they find curious at the time. They are not necessarily taking a systematic approach to science enquiry while exploring, although it is likely that they will be raising questions in response to the objects they are presented with, as well as making observations and conducting tests, even if this is simply attempting to bend an object to see if it is flexible or holding it up to the light to test its opaqueness.

Initially the practitioner's role is to create the potential for learning by carefully planning the resources they will provide for such 'free' exploration. Later a degree of focus and structure can be introduced through 'guided' exploration, when the adult intervenes and makes suggestions, or 'structured' exploration, when scientific skills and concepts are deliberately scaffolded. One way practitioners have traditionally sought to intervene is through playing games with collections. The games described in Box 9.1 (page 154) provide many opportunities for children to develop science enquiry skills including:

1   Observation and question raising, leading to fair testing: games such as 'Guess the criterion' and 'Guess which object' provide opportunities for children to raise questions. The nature of the question will determine how it should be answered: by fair test, using secondary sources of information, through observation, or it might be a question that is unanswerable by

scientific methods. For example, in response to choosing a tin can from a range of packaging materials these questions were generated:

- What colour is it? (Answered by observation.)
- Is it the hardest object in the collection? (Answered by comparison and fair testing.)
- Is it a man-made material? (Answered by secondary sources of information such as web-based resources.)
- Is it the most beautiful object? (Not answered by scientific methods!)

2   Presentation of results: The game 'Sorting into groups' develops children's ability to sort into two groups (on the basis of one property), a relatively straightforward activity compared to 'Grids and Carroll diagrams', which gives children experience of sorting and presenting results on the basis of two properties or characteristics.

As well as enquiry-skill development, the sorting games can also develop an understanding of procedural schemata (see Chapter 2). These are general ways of thinking that can be applied to solve challenges and problems in a variety of contexts (Adey and Shayer 2002, Adey et al. 2003). The games are particularly good at developing the skills of classification (putting things into groups based on common characteristics) and seriation (putting things in order). The game 'Making a key' will directly support the skill of classification. Reasoning patterns developed in the context of materials could be applied to other scientific contexts such as constructing keys to sort plants and animals. The 'Domino game' develops the skill of seriation through paired comparison of objects, a way of reasoning that can be applied to other sequencing activities. These might be in a scientific context (e.g. the changes in the appearance of the Moon in a lunar cycle), or other areas of learning (e.g. sequencing events in a story). Allowing time for a child to reflect on the approach he/she took to solve a particular problem, a stage known as metacognition, should not be underestimated, as this is recognised as the primary tool for cognitive development in many thinking skill interventions (McGuiness 1999).

Early Years Foundation Studies and Key Stage 1 curriculum links

In the Foundation Stage (EYFS), developing children's 'Understanding of the world' (one of the four specific areas of learning in the EYFS) involves them being guided to make sense of the physical world (DfE 2012). Towards the end of the EYFS children will be assessed to discover if they know about similarities and differences in relation to objects and materials. Guidance that accompanies the statutory elements of the curriculum suggests that children aged 30 to 50 months old may talk about the things they have observed such as natural and found objects (Early Education 2012). The characteristics of liquids and solids could be learned at this age through children working in a practical context such as cookery. At age 40 to 60 months the guidance suggests that children could be provided with a range of materials and objects to play with that work in different ways for a variety of purposes. They will be learning that the different qualities that materials exhibit influence their use. The guidance suggests that carefully framed open-ended questions will support children's development, as will introducing vocabulary to them to enable them to talk about their observations.

In Year 1 of the National Curriculum in England (DfE 2013) children should be taught to compare and group together a variety of everyday materials on the basis of their physical properties. Non-statutory guidance that accompanies the curriculum indicates that children will become familiar with properties such as hard/soft; stretchy/stiff; shiny/dull; rough/smooth; bendy/not bendy; waterproof/not waterproof; absorbent/not absorbent. In Year 1 children will distinguish between the name of the object and the material from which it is made, and identify a range of everyday materials including wood, plastic, glass, metal, water and rock. Guidance suggests that children will work scientifically by performing simple tests on materials to determine if their properties make them suitable for a particular purpose.

In Year 2, children will build on their ability to identify everyday materials by comparing the uses to which each is put. Guidance suggests that they will investigate this in a variety of settings such as at home, the journey to school or on visits.

Story books

Here are a few suggestions for story books that can support teaching of everyday materials, beginning with a couple of traditional tales. 'The Three Little Pigs', or an alternative take on this tale, 'The Three Little Wolves and the Big Bad Pig' (1993) by Eugene Trivias, are both about choosing the right building material. 'The Emperor's New Clothes', will not only encourage children to respect the evidence that is presented to them (it is obvious to everyone who sees the emperor in his new clothes that he is wearing nothing but they choose to ignore this) but is also linked to the topic of materials by their absence! A more contemporary book about selecting clothing wisely is the Charlie and Lola book 'Snow is My Favourite and My Best' by Lauren Child (2006). At one stage in the story, Lola wonders why she can't wear her party dress in the snow.

'Lucy's Picture' by Nicola Moon (2010) is about a girl who selects objects for a picture based on their texture because she is making it for her blind granddad. It's a book that can be used to encourage children to use their sense of touch to sort materials. Authors of silhouette books such as Jan Pienkowski ('The Fairy Tales', 2005) or Clay Rice ('Mama, Let's Make a Moon', 2011) select materials for their illustrations based on their opaque, transparent and translucent properties.

Children could construct their own silhouette pictures in response to this type of book. For very young children the publisher Usborne has produced a number of 'touchy-feely' books (e.g. 'That's Not My Dolly' and 'That's Not My Dinosaur'; Watt 2004a, 2004b) designed to help develop sensory skills. On every page there is a patch of material to touch, with the writing that accompanies it describing its texture and property.

Intervening to develop young children's understanding

The science team at Bath Spa University have devised a number of sorting games that are designed to be used in a variety of ways to develop scientific skills and concepts (see Box 9.1). Play of the sort provoked by these games falls into the category of rule-based play (Hutt 1979), the rules being imposed initially through teacher intervention, although later children can organise the games by themselves.

At the planning stage the teacher needs to consider carefully a number of aspects of scientific development, including a recognition of the scientific vocabulary that might be developed, the key scientific skills that will be nurtured. More generally he/she will need to think how learning will be organised. Working in small groups allows children more time to handle and sort their collections than is available in a whole-class teaching situation. Thought also needs to be given to the choice of objects selected. It will reduce confusion if objects made from only one material such as a rubber band are chosen rather than an object composed of multiple materials. Clean household packaging can provide an excellent range of different materials – plastic cartons, tin cans, different coloured glass bottles, bubble wrap, polystyrene packing chips, cardboard packets, cellophane wrappers etc.

The adult role will initially be to establish the rules of the game. Then, perhaps through their participation, she/he can introduce new words, or possibly definitions of a variety of everyday materials, or the names of common materials. The focus could be the uses to which materials are put. Alternatively the games can be used to elicit children's understanding of materials.

Learning stories

There is a recognition that practical work by itself does not necessarily develop learners' understanding of scientific concepts and that therefore not only a hands-on but also a minds-on approach to learning in science is needed (Millar 2010). The connection between practical work (hands-on) and conceptual development through the learner being challenged by questioning and given opportunities to engage in discussion (minds-on) is illustrated by these two learning stories from the Early Years classroom.

Box 9.1

Sorting and classifying games
(Developed from Howe et al. 2009)

Sorting into groups
Give out a group of objects and ask children to sort them. Keep the number of objects small, no more than 10. There is no need to tell them what to sort for; they will have their own interesting (and, often unexpected) ideas. This gives you an insight into their thinking, not whether they can sort according to your criteria! However, you may need to demonstrate. Stick to two groups initially, e.g. . . . is red; . . . is not red. Young children usually choose colour, shape and size as a starting point. You may need to introduce the vocabulary of properties of materials such as stronger than . . . , weaker than . . .

Coloured PE hoops can be used for the sorting and overlapped for items that fit both groups, thus introducing Venn diagrams.

Guess the criterion
With the children in a circle, look at the collection of objects. Talk about what is there and the characteristics of one or two objects, particularly any unfamiliar ones. Begin to sort into two groups and ask the children to guess the criterion you are using. Then ask one child to sort them while other children try to guess the criterion she/he has used. This can be repeated many times with different criteria.

It's a good idea to start with a small collection and divide it into two groups, gradually increasing the size of the collection and number of groups over a period of time. Children can work in small groups each with a collection to sort.

With very young children, ask them to 'whisper' their criterion to you – this ensures they don't change it when the right answer is given!

Guess which object
This is similar to the game 'Guess Who?' by Hasbro, but uses objects rather than pictures. Choose one object from the collection but do not reveal which it is. Children ask questions based on different criteria to try to discover which object it is, e.g. Is it made from wood? If the answer is 'no', remove all wooden objects and further questions centre on those that are left. Only allow 'yes' or 'no' answers. Choose a child to select the object while others try to find out which one has been selected.

Give us a clue
Select an object from a collection but do not reveal choice. Provide clues one at a time until children are able to identify the object. Base clues around the intended learning outcome, e.g. if the focus is housing materials the clue might be 'The object can be used on a roof'.

Mystery object

Put one object from the collection into a closed box or bag without giving the children a chance to see what it is. Pass the box around the children and give them the opportunity to feel, shake and listen before asking one question about its hidden contents. Continue until object is identified. A small group each with a box ensures children's interest is maintained.

Spot the criterion

This works best with Key Stage 1 children. Split the class into groups and give each group a small collection and a coloured pencil. Ask each group to sort their collection in three different ways and to record these ways on a sheet of paper. They then sort using a fourth criterion, leaving the objects so arranged but without recording the criterion. Each group moves to the next collection and tries to guess the final criterion used by the previous group. They then record their own three ideas for sorting in a different colour on the sheet and leave the objects sorted in a fourth way.

This can be continued as long as is thought appropriate. It allows you to find out a great deal about how the children are thinking, and each group's responses can be easily identified. This activity could be used at the start and end of a topic to help the teacher to assess changes in the children's thinking.

Adding to a collection

Select an object and choose a criterion but do not reveal it. Children take it in turns to add one more object ,which is accepted or rejected depending on whether it fits the chosen criterion. Children have to identify criterion being used. This is a game that offers plenty of opportunity for the teacher to introduce the names of new properties of materials.

Domino game

Can be used to identify similarities or differences (differences are easier to begin with). Each child holds an object from a collection. One child is asked to place their object on the floor; the others are then asked if their object is different in any way from the object on the floor. One child is asked to place their object alongside the first and the criterion is recorded. Children are then asked for an object that is different to the second object on the floor. The process continues until all objects are on the floor. The game can be made more difficult by insisting that criteria can only be used once, e.g. shape, size, texture, material, etc. This game can be made competitive.

Finding similarities

Children work with a partner, examine at least three collections and select three objects in total (one from each group) that they think have something in common with each other. They share with the rest of the group their items and the similarity between them.

Making a key

This works best with older children in the 3–7 age range. Children work in groups, each with a small collection of 5–10 objects and a large sheet of paper. They are asked to develop an identification key using 'yes'/'no' questions, maybe scribed by the teacher. Later other children try out the key, providing formative feedback on its effectiveness as a means of classifying the objects.

Label it

On post-it notes, write single words that describe a property of the object (e.g. shiny, hard, red). Stick the labels on appropriate objects. Can we move the labels to different objects in the room? Can we add more words?

Word bank

Using the word bank generated by the 'Label it' activity above, sort the words in a variety of ways, e.g. nouns, adjectives, those that can be both (e.g. glass), alphabetically.

Making a table

Chalk a table on the floor with two columns. Put a series of real objects down the side. Use the word bank again as headings for the table's columns. Use ticks or crosses to record the properties of the objects (see below).

	Shiny	Hard
Flower pot		✓
Box		
Tin	✓	✓

This can be developed into a Carroll diagram (2 x 2 grid) for sorting objects on the basis of two criteria:

	Shiny	Not shiny
Hard		
Not hard		

The actual objects can be placed into the appropriate cell of the diagram.

Learning story 9.2

Developing vocabulary

The first case study, taken from a small group of 5- and 6-year-olds playing with 'Gelli Baff', illustrates one way that new vocabulary can be introduced during structured exploration. Before introducing the new vocabulary the teacher pooled ideas together from the whole group. The children explained how adding pink crystals from the Gelli Baff kit had turned tap water into a 'gloop'. Then adding white crystals had changed the mixture back to tap water again.

Teacher: When did you put the white powder in? (*The teacher initiates discussion with one pair from the group that has pink gloop in their bowl, because so far they have only added pink crystals to the water.*)

Pair A: I didn't put any white powder in.

Teacher: You didn't put any white powder in. Ahh . . . do you hear what they're saying? They didn't put any white, they've only used the pink [crystals].

Pair A: We could throw a little bit of white in, we might . . . and if we mix it around it might get even darker. (*Pair A hypothesise that adding white crystals will make the solution 'darker'. They realise the mixture had changed colour by adding pink crystals and had described this change of property in terms of light and dark shades.*)

Teacher: Could you ask [another pair] what happened when they put the white powder in theirs? (*A pair that have added white crystals to their gloop is drawn into the discussion.*)

Pair B: When you put the white powder in there, it made it . . . umm . . . lighter and when . . . (*Pair B have adopted the language of pair A, i.e. 'lighter'.*)

Teacher: When you put pink in, and then put white in, yours has gone . . . yours is watery and theirs is nice and thick. It is like jelly. You put the pink powder in. More pink powder, started to make the jelly thicker.

Commentary

The teacher chooses to intervene at this point with language that more appropriately describes the property of the mixtures. She could have introduced viscous/not viscous (and may well do so at a later date) but for now 'watery' and 'thick' were developmentally appropriate terms to use with this group.

Teacher: What happened when you put the white in?

Pair B: It's . . .

Teacher: It's gone back to water so when you put the white powder in . . . what do you think the white powder did then, did it make your jelly bath thicker?

Pair B: It made it watery. (*Pair B have now adopted the language introduced to them by the teacher.*)

Learning story 9.3

Developing understanding

The second case study is taken from a plenary with a class of 6–8-year-olds. It illustrates how discussion can develop children's understanding of scientific concepts in response to practical work. Prior to the plenary the class had investigated the absorbency of a range of materials by testing which one was the best at mopping up a spillage on the floor. Initially the teacher sought to develop conceptual understanding by referring back to children's observations and measurements.

Teacher: Can somebody tell me why they think J Cloth and kitchen roll are the most absorbent? Oliver, what do you think?

Oliver: J Cloth because it's thick.

Teacher: Because it's thick. Molly?

Molly: Umm . . . because it umm . . . because it was umm . . . it has . . . umm . . . holes in it and it get . . . umm . . . if it has holes in it, it lets the water go down out into the . . . out into somewhere.

Teacher: Harry?

Harry: I thought the J Cloth just soaked up the most and . . . umm . . . was umm . . . and I . . . after I looked at the sheet and saw which one was the most longest and it was J Cloth, so . . .

Teacher: So your prediction was right.

Harry: Yes.

Teacher: Why do you think it was the most absorbent?

Harry: Umm . . . because . . . umm . . . it . . . I thought it because it went the longest.

Teacher: That showed it was the most absorbent.

Harry: Yes.

Teacher: Okay. Sarah, did you want to say something?

Sarah: J Cloth because it was hard to break.

Teacher: Okay, because it's quite strong.

Sarah: It was quite strong.

Teacher: It's strong. Hard to break. It's thick. That's what Oliver was saying.

Sarah: Yes.

Commentary

The teacher has used the plenary up to this point to elicit children's ideas. Harry has referred back to his results without providing an explanation for why the J Cloth soaked up liquids for the longest time. Oliver and Sarah believe the strength and thickness of the material are important factors. However it is Molly's explanation that the teacher wants to explore further. The teacher is aware that materials that are absorbent have many tiny holes in them meaning that they will soak up a liquid when they are in contact with it. It is Molly's explanation that is closest to the scientific view so warrants further probing.

Teacher: And, Molly, because it had lots of little holes in it and a sponge has got holes in it hasn't it, and you were saying why haven't we got sponge earlier, weren't you, Dylan?

Dylan: Yes.

Teacher: A sponge is really absorbent. What goes into those holes do you think?

Dylan: Air.

Teacher: Air. And when it's soaking the water up what goes into the holes?

Dylan: It's . . . umm . . . well it's air [that] pushes the water down so that the water goes down into it.

Teacher: Ah ah ah . . . sorry, sorry. There's lots of holes in sponge and perhaps there's holes in J Cloth, what might go into those holes?

Dylan: Umm . . . sometimes it's air that's . . . umm . . . there's air that pushes the water down. So it goes through the holes and it lets the . . . umm . . . cloth absorb.

Commentary

Dylan has attempted to explain why a material such as sponge absorbs water. He thinks air pushes water into the holes. Actually absorbency is related to the force of attraction between the solid material and the liquid that causes the liquid to be soaked up and held in place by the material. The teacher realises that Dylan's ideas may be confusing other children. At this stage she only wants children to understand that absorbent materials contain holes that can be filled with liquid. She decides it is now the right time to reinforce this message by returning to Molly's ideas.

Teacher: Okay, okay. I think things that are absorbent do tend to have holes in, like Molly said, she could see that little holes can fill up with water. They've got air in them but when the water comes it fills them with water. That makes it really absorbent.

ICT links

Computer programs such as FlexiTREE (see www.flexible.co.uk) can be used by children to construct branching databases, supporting their development of questioning skills, grouping and classification. This resource can be used in conjunction with the sorting games described earlier. For instance when 'making a key', children can list the objects or materials they want to sort and then type in a series of questions that group them. The programme enables children to evaluate each other's work (peer evaluation) by seeing if they derive the same answer as the authors of the branching database. If the database has been designed well, materials should be sorted in groups that match the authors' classification. It is important for teachers to consider the benefits of using ICT. It is possible for children to construct keys without using computer software so, how does using ICT help? In this instance, it enables databases to be displayed on an interactive whiteboard, which can be a motivating factor, and it also affords the opportunity for the database to be edited easily.

Another way that ICT can support children's learning is by enabling them to look closely at materials and objects. The Easi-Scope hand-held digital microscope (see www.tts-group.co.uk) is one example of a digital viewer that can be attached to a laptop. Observations can be made by traditional magnifying lenses or even pocket microscopes but the advantage of the digital viewer is that it enables a group to look all at once at the same object enabling them to see the same features and discuss their significance. For example, when studying soils it's possible for observations to be seen by the whole class (easily achieved by linking the device to the interactive whiteboard) so that the different fractions that constitute a soil can be highlighted – rock fragments, organic material, and the spaces between the solids occupied by air and moisture.

Related designing and making activities

Solid materials

There is a range of solid materials that children will encounter and use in design-and-make activities. These can be grouped together into three major divisions based on their properties – sheet materials, resistant materials and those materials that are mouldable (Collier et al. 2011). Each group of materials presents a range of possibilities for developing an understanding of the concept that the use to which a material is put is determined by its property.

Sheet materials

Sheet materials[1] can be either rigid or flexible but they lack strength because they are in the form of a thin sheet. Early Years children will encounter many examples of sheet materials – card, tin foil, cellophane and fabric – and often children will use sheet materials for aesthetic purposes. Layton (1992) considered the different values that shape design and technology endeavours. Aesthetic considerations are one such value; others include technical, economic, social, environmental, moral and spiritual. Set the challenge of designing an item of footwear, children's approach to their work may be influenced by these values:

■ Technical: children will want to choose the right material for the job. This value in design and technology has clear and obvious links to science. For example, outdoor shoes need to be made of waterproof materials.

1 There is a difference between the property of a *material* and property of an *object*. Strength is a property of the object because it is determined not only by the material from which the object is made but also by its shape and size. Hardness, for example, is a property of the material because it is an intrinsic quality that is unaffected by the object's shape/size. Sheet materials are weak because they have been formed into thin layers.

■ Aesthetic: children may question the aesthetic appeal of their product. Does the shoe look attractive?

■ Economic/environmental: children will need to consider using materials with minimal waste.

Resistant materials

Resistant materials may be flexible or rigid but unlike sheet materials they are strong. Early Years children will encounter wood, metal (e.g. stiff wire) and corrugated plastic from which they can build frames and structures. There may exist a feeling that cutting and joining sections of wood is the preserve of older primary or secondary children but with training in basic woodwork skills such as sawing, drilling and joining with Jinx Joints (see Collier et al. 2011 for more details), even young children are capable of making wooden structures.

Mouldable materials

These are solids that can be deformed into new shapes by hand, although tools can improve the level of detail of models produced. The material will retain its new shape because it is non-elastic. It is suggested by Siraj-Blatchford and MacLeod-Brudenell (1999) that children should be introduced to mouldable materials in the following order:

dry sand → damp sand → playdough → plastic/wet clay → bread dough → plasticine → papier mache

so that they are moving from materials requiring basic motor skills to those demanding a high degree of accuracy and coordination. Children will discover that this group of materials is particularly good for modelling organic objects.

Liquids and gases

Hydraulic and pneumatic systems controlled by liquids (probably water in the Early Years classroom) and gases (air) respectively are a way that young children can form an understanding of materials other than solids in a design-and-make context. Hydraulic systems can be made quite simply, although messily, by filling with water two syringes connected to each other by a length of flexible tubing. If the system is left unfilled by water it will be air-filled and therefore it will be a pneumatic system. Movement of one syringe is almost instantaneously transmitted to the other syringe by hydraulics, but there is a slight delay in the pneumatic system. This is because gases are more compressible than liquids. However, for young children it is enough for them to be aware of the material nature of air – 'stuff' is inside the tubing causing the movement to be transmitted from one syringe to another. Hydraulics and pneumatics can add movement, interest and amusement to models, e.g. inflating and deflating a balloon that serves as a nose on a face.

Summary

In this chapter we have described many different contexts in which young children may develop their understanding of everyday materials. Examples of how both child-initiated and adult-initiated exploration of collections of objects and materials can be planned and prepared for were given. Some suggestions for story books that provide an interesting starting point for teaching the topic of everyday materials were provided. Two learning stories illustrated how the language associated with materials and children's subject knowledge can be developed through discussion prompted by practical activity.

Discussion points

- How does a practitioner's understanding of the particulate nature of matter support teaching of everyday materials?
- What contexts for learning about everyday materials are most likely to generate a sense of awe and wonder in the learner?

A thematic approach to changing materials in Early Years settings

Sarah Earle and Christopher Collier

Purpose of this chapter

After reading this chapter you should have:

- appropriate scientific understanding of changing materials to support your interventions in young children's learning;
- an appreciation of a range of practical activities and contexts for learning about changing materials in science and D&T.

Introduction

Change is an exciting topic for young children. They begin to notice that the world around them changes and that their own actions can have an impact on it. They enjoy exploring the effect of their actions, beginning to develop their own investigations into changing materials. When one three-year-old exclaimed: 'Where is my ice cube?' (which he had placed in his nursery drawer to save for later) it was the start of a long-lasting interest in the effect of temperature on ice.

This chapter will consider contexts in which children can explore materials as they change shape and state, and observe materials over time. Children can change materials in a variety of ways including heating, cooling, drying or adding water to them, after which they can see if these changes can be reversed. It is essential that young children are involved in the 'doing' of these activities, that they are the ones causing the materials to change, so that they develop an understanding of cause and effect. Encouraging talk about the changing materials is also critical (Tunnicliffe 2013), developing observation, vocabulary and understanding.

Conceptual development at 3–7 years

Change and comparison are key themes in the Early Years Foundation Stage, with children developing an awareness of change using all of their senses. Exploring similarities and differences between materials, observing, explaining and talking about change are all detailed in the 'Understanding the world' Early Learning Goal (DfE 2012). The 'Expressive arts and design' Early Learning Goal also directs children to explore and experiment. Thus, there is a wide scope for exploring change through a variety of child-initiated contexts such as play with bubbles, creating 'potions', making jelly and cooking cakes.

In Key Stage 1 (DfE 2013) changing materials are explored in 'Everyday materials' (Year 1) where changing the shape of materials is specified and 'Uses of materials' (Year 2) where children could explore why different materials are suitable for a range of purposes. The concept of change is also explored in 'Seasonal changes' (Year 1) where children need to observe and describe weather, providing opportunities for exploring ice and puddles. In Key Stage 1 D&T pupils are required to use tools to manipulate materials by cutting, shaping, joining and finishing, increasing the accuracy of their use as they progress from Key Stage 1 to 2. They also use an increasing range of materials and ingredients, considering their properties such as their melting points when making selections.

Early Years themes and contexts for learning

The use of malleable materials is a good everyday context to begin the exploration of changing materials. Rolling and cutting out playdough shapes, making a plasticine person or a clay thumb pot are all activities in which you can 'see the science and D&T'. By asking 'How did you make that shape?' you are prompting the child to explain how they pushed or pulled, squashed or cut. They are exploring the effect of different tools and developing the fine motor control to be able to use them accurately. You can extend this by asking them to compare the feel of different materials such as playdough and plasticine, or yesterday's model compared to today's. This supports development of their vocabulary to describe materials, as discussed in the previous chapter, while also getting them to notice how the materials are changing over time. Children will be quick to spot if the playdough is becoming too dry or 'old'. Perhaps you could leave some out over night to prompt discussions about the causes of the crumbly feel and crusty edges.

TABLE 10.1 Conceptual understanding: changing materials

Key concepts in the Early Years curriculum	Subject knowledge for practitioners in the Early Years curriculum
Materials can be changed by being pushed or pulled	According to particle theory, all material is made up of bits that are too tiny to see. In the case of solid materials strong bonds exist between neighbouring particles holding them together. However it is possible to change the arrangement of the particles of materials by using force. Although squashing, cutting and stretching changes the form of the material, no new material is created. A lump of plasticine is still in essence plasticine after it has been pulled and pushed even though its shape may have changed.
Materials can be changed by heating and cooling	Although formal teaching of particle theory comes later in a child's education, it helps Early Years teachers with their teaching of changing materials if they appreciate the scientific explanation for changes of state caused by heating and cooling.
	In Table 9.1 the arrangement of particles in a solid, liquid and gas is explained. According to particle theory (sometimes called kinetic theory), particles making up a solid material are then tightly bound together and able to vibrate about a fixed point, but individual particles are unable to move from place to place. Heating a solid causes these bonds to weaken so that neighbouring particles are able to move relative to one and other – the solid has changed into a liquid. Further heating results in the particles moving about more freely. Bonds between neighbouring particles are broken – the liquid becomes a gas.
	On cooling, the particles of gas slow down and forge weak bonds with neighbouring particles to form liquid. Next the liquid particles slow down further and form strong bonds in a fixed structure, turning into a solid.
Freezing and melting, condensation and vaporation are reversible changes	At a young age children gain many experiences of materials changing from solid to liquid, liquid to gas and back again. Melting chocolate, making ice cream, puddles seemingly disappearing and water droplets forming on the classroom window on a cold day are all examples of materials changing through physical processes.
	These physical changes involve a change of state (e.g. solid to liquid) without new materials being formed. The appearance of the material changes but the particles that make up the material remain the same. Particles have simply been rearranged. The mass of the material remains the same too, although when water freezes its volume increases. As a result, ice floats on water. The names given to these reversible processes are freezing, melting, condensation and evaporation: solid $\rightarrow$ liquid = melting; liquid $\rightarrow$ gas = evaporation; gas $\rightarrow$ liquid = condensation; liquid $\rightarrow$ solid = freezing in the case of water or solidification more generally.
Materials can be changed by dissolving	Salt and sugar are examples of two materials young children may study that are soluble in water. Dissolving occurs when it is possible for a substance (such as sugar) to totally mix with a liquid. The solid material (solute) forms a solution when it and the liquid (solvent) have formed a uniform mixture. Two factors that affect the rate of dissolving are stirring the solution and the temperature of the solvent.

TABLE 10.1 continued

Key concepts in the Early Years curriculum	Subject knowledge for practitioners in the Early Years curriculum
	What happens at a particle level is quite complicated, but developing a mental model at this level does help explain why heat and stirring increase the rate of dissolution. Let's consider what happens when sugar dissolves in water. It is only at the boundary between the sugar face and water that mixing can occur. The sugar particles here will form loose bonds with the water particles. For further mixing to occur, the sugary mixture formed needs to be replaced by fresh water. Heating the water or stirring it enables this to happen more rapidly.
	Dissolving and melting are frequently confused but there are a number of differences. Dissolving requires two materials to be mixed together unlike melting which is the result of one material being heated. Dissolving cannot be reversed by cooling whereas melting can, and dissolving does not necessarily require heat but melting does.
	Dissolving is a reversible process – the solute can be recovered from the solution by evaporation, although it won't look exactly the same as it was at the start.
	Some solids don't dissolve in a liquid and are described as insoluble. For example, flour doesn't dissolve in water but instead forms a suspension. Eventually the flour will settle out if left undisturbed which won't happen in the case of a solution.
Sometimes new materials with different properties are formed	One of the most common ways that young children experience new materials being formed is through cookery. For example, boiling an egg fundamentally alters the egg's chemical structure. Baking dough in an oven does the same. Changes of this sort, which form new materials and are usually permanent, are termed chemical changes. They often result in the properties of the food (its density, rigidity, texture, colour etc.) being changed. During chemical changes a chemical reaction takes place in which particles undergo significant changes and a new material is created. No new matter is created, nor is matter destroyed, but the particles have been rearranged in such a way as to form new materials with different properties.
	Another form of permanent change is decay. It is brought about by the action of micro-organisms. Materials that are capable of decaying are called biodegradable.

Early Years activities that develop children's understanding of changing materials support their development towards the big idea in science that *all material is made of very small particles.*

Sources to develop background subject knowledge further:

Collier, C., Davies, D., Howe, A. and McMahon, K. (2011) *The Primary Science and Technology Encyclopedia*. London: David Fulton.

Harlen, W. (ed.) (2010) *Principles and Big Ideas of Science Education*. Hatfield: ASE

Howe, A., Davies, D., McMahon, K., Towler, L., Collier, C. and Scott, T. (2009) *Science 5–11: A Guide for Teachers*, 2nd edn. London: David Fulton (Chapter 3).

Peacock, G., Sharp, J., Johnsey, R. and Wright, D. (2012) *Primary Science: Knowledge and Understanding (Achieving QTS Series)*, 6th edn. Exeter: Learning Matters (Chapters 6 and 7).

Wenham, M. and Ovens, P. (2010) *Understanding Primary Science*, 3rd edn.) London: Sage (Chapters 6 and 8).

How materials change over time can also be explored within topics on the weather or seasons. What falls from the sky provides many opportunities for discussions and investigations. For example, you could support children to describe how cold it is when sleet or snow falls, or how rain soaked playgrounds on warm days dry quickly. Noticing the puddles drying or the ice melting is an important precursor to an understanding of physical and reversible changes.

Exploiting the weather as a context for learning requires some flexibility in planning so that the most is made of 'the snow day'. This spontaneity can be supported by some pre-prepared resources. For example, weather boxes can contain resources, activities and intervention cards, as described in Table 10.2.

Food is an important context for studying both physical and chemical changes to materials. Foods exhibit chemical changes when they decay over time. Examples include: cut apples turning brown, bananas ripening or strawberries turning mouldy. Leaving a packed lunch box (containing *sealed* transparent

TABLE 10.2 Pre-prepared weather box activities

Box	Example activities	Box contents
Rain	Make different shaped rain catchers from plastic bottles. Make shelters from the rain. Investigate what happens to waterproof and non-waterproof materials in the rain. Make a range of boats to play with in the puddles. Put pictures out in the rain: powder paint or chalk or felt tip pens on paper towels.	Plastic bottles, rain catchers, large plastic sheet, fabric squares, paper boats, paper towel strips, pens, chalk, powder paint
Wind	Play with kites, windsocks and balloons, investigating what makes them fly, turn and move. Wash dolls' clothes and peg out the washing. Watching bubbles move in the air. Feel the force of the wind on the parachute.	Kites, windsocks and balloons, pegs, washing line, dolls clothes, bubble making, parachute
Snow	Fill cups with snow and place them around the school, in the Sun and in the shade. Catch snowflakes on black card and observe them using a magnifier. Make different tracks in the snow, make or follow a trail around school. Investigate which movement keeps you warm outdoors, which are the best gloves? Build a snowman, snowdog . . .	Cups, black card, magnifiers, track makers, scarf, hats, gloves, stones for eyes/buttons/nose
Sun	Trace chalk shadows of people and objects. Draw and write with water and brushes on walls and playground, observing what happens to them after they have finished. Which are the best sunglasses (not looking directly at the Sun)? Make and try out a range of paper hats.	Chalk, brushes, buckets, sunglasses, hat instructions, paper

containers of food to allow observation without the risk of releasing clouds of fungal spores into the classroom) in the corner for a week could stimulate discussion of mould, decay, compost and hygiene.

Heating and cooling provide interesting examples of melting and solidifying (physical changes). Exploring the changing state of chocolate can stimulate discussion of properties of materials and the cause of any changes (as discussed in Learning story 10.1 below). Comparing cooked and uncooked food, such as eggs, rice or toast, can be used to develop an understanding that chemical changes are irreversible; you cannot get the raw egg back once it is cooked. Combining ingredients offers further opportunities for describing the properties of materials and explaining how they change when the wet ingredients are added to the dry. Placing these activities within a meaningful context can not only make learning feel purposeful, it is also more likely that the children will join in open discussion, rather than wait to be asked questions about the teacher's prompts. Making pizza, biscuits or cakes can be linked to parties, special events or story books (see 'Story books' section below).

When activities involve heat, planning must include consideration of risks, for example, ensuring sufficient adult supervision and knowing what should happen in the case of an accident. Risk assessment prior to the session should also take account of allergies and consider what instructions should be given to the children, for example, what they can touch or eat. Involving children in identifying and discussing risks supports them to understand and manage risks themselves. Measures can be taken to minimise risk, like using warm water for children to experience melting and placing candles in trays of sand. Further guidance can be found in the Association for Science Education's *Be Safe!* booklet (ASE 2010). Common sense and proportionate health and safety measures should help children to be safe but not stop them from 'doing'.

Scientific process skills

Observation is where science starts. Maybe it is quite easy to think of examples of visual observations such as noticing that the puddle has evaporated or the chocolate has melted, but other senses can also be engaged, e.g. hearing popcorn exploding in a saucepan. The practitioner can support the children's observation by drawing their attention to the salient features of a situation (see Learning story 10.1 below). When an adult exclaims at the sight of bubbles or steam, it helps the children to notice an important change.

Stimulating comparison is important, noting how the materials are similar or different, or how they have changed. For example, comparing a chocolate button that has been in the child's hand (e.g. while you read Michael Rosen's poem on chocolate) to one on the table provokes descriptive vocabulary and discussion of the causes of melting.

The next step could be to encourage children to raise their own questions. One way to do this is to model the asking of questions by 'wondering': I wonder why this chocolate is getting hard to pour? I wonder where the steam goes? I wonder where the best place to keep this chocolate would be? Such 'wonderings' could lead to a desire to explore (Davies 2011), and further question-raising by the children themselves. Children's questions can also be encouraged by purposefully praising the question rather than the answer in the form of question walls or verbal responses – 'That's a good question!' – praises the thinking skills, rather than knowledge recall. It also reassures children that it is alright not to know the answer, which is important in science since we want to ask questions for which we truly want to find out the answer, as well as acknowledging that this is sometimes not possible.

Prediction and explanation are also key skills that can be developed when examining changing materials. When presented with a range of powders or granules the children can be encouraged to think about what will happen if they are mixed with water. Predictions about what will happen to sand, bicarbonate of soda or sugar could be extended by asking the children to explain why they think the reactions happened. When asking for explanations, support can be provided by asking whether they have seen anything like this before. If children are able to link to a previous experience, of perhaps Granny putting sugar in her tea, then they are more likely to be forthcoming in their suggestions. Once they have mixed the materials and played with the sinking or fizzing or dissolving, there are further opportunities for discussion. For example, when a child explains that the sugar has 'disappeared' further probing could include: where is the sugar now? How do you know that? Can you taste the sugar? Why do you think we can't see it anymore? By providing such prompts to provoke their thinking, together with the resources to explore, you are supporting both concept and process skills development.

Story books

Many traditional tales could provide a context for changing materials. Stories that involve baking include: 'The Gingerbread Man' (biscuit), 'Goldilocks and the Three Bears' (porridge), 'The Magic Porridge Pot', 'The Little Red Hen' (bread) and 'The Big Pancake'. Such stories could lead onto designing and making the featured food. They could also be used as a stimulus for comparison: what was different about the three bears' porridge? How could you tell? The children could make the porridge, feel the bowls, explore the texture and how this changes as it cools. Observing and describing the changes of materials involved in making pancakes could involve an extensive vocabulary list, from dry flour to wet batter to solid pancake. Asking whether we can get the eggs or flour back is a good way of supporting the children to recognise that these changes are irreversible (de Boo 2000: 76). Exploring what would happen to the gingerbread man if he fell off the fox's back would be an interesting extension to the story and provide the stimulus for exploring what happens to different materials when they get wet.

Stories involving changes to the weather also provide an interesting starting point. For example, 'The Snowman' by Raymond Briggs is an excellent stimulus for work on weather and melting. Discussing why the snowman melted could lead on to testing out the children's ideas using snow (if you have it!) or ice cubes or ice lollies to explore where the 'snow' would last the longest. Naylor and Keogh (2000) ask in the form of a concept cartoon whether putting a coat on the snowman would help, with the intention of exploring the learner's understanding of thermal insulators. We return to this concept when discussing ice in the next section.

Intervening to develop young children's understanding

Providing children with novel materials stimulates interest and discussion, and 'surprises where children's experiences and ideas are challenged' (Feasey 2005: 23). A supplier of school resources like TTS is a good place to start when looking for something new. For example, 'Instant Snow' is a powder that just requires water to grow into some real looking snow. The fact that it does not feel like snow is a good thing since the children will notice that it is not the same and you can ask them to explain what is different. Another example of a material with a novel feel is moon sand, whose hydrophobic coating keeps it dry underwater.

However, everyday household items can also create a sense of wonder. For example, jelly crystals, wallpaper paste or cornflour all have interesting reactions when water is added. Children of any age are wowed by the non-Newtonian properties of cornflour, which will act as a solid under pressure (i.e. when hit/poked) and as a liquid when poured (when the pressure is taken off, the molecules move apart and flow like a liquid).

Water is an even cheaper resource for exploration. Play in the water trough where water is poured between different containers supports the children's developing understanding of the properties of a liquid. Noticing that it flows and takes the shape of its container could be developed by added wallpaper paste: how is it different now? Is it still a liquid? Pouring between containers can also be a context for exploring conservation, that there is the same amount of liquid even if it takes a different shape.

Using water is the simplest context for considering change of state. For example, using rollers or paintbrushes to investigate 'painting' on the wall or floor is an alternative to noticing puddles. A washing role-play area can also provide opportunities for discussing evaporation. Finding the best place to put the washing to dry could develop understanding of the role of the Sun and wind.

The SPACE project (Russell and Watt 1990) probed children's understanding of evaporation by asking them to consider the change in water level in a large container over a five-week period. Key Stage 1 children described how the water had 'dried up', while Key Stage 2 children were more likely to use the word 'evaporation'. However, few discussed water as a substance that could have different states or understood the transformation from liquid to gas. The foundations for these difficult concepts can be built by providing opportunities to explore such changes of state, perhaps using the more meaningful contexts discussed above.

Exploring ice is a fruitful activity. Playing with ice cubes can be extended to ice balloons or ice hands (balloons or rubber gloves filled with water and placed in the freezer (see Figure 10.1 and Learning story 10.2 below). Feeling and describing an ice hand can be followed by asking questions about it: 'Why does the little finger drop off first? Would the ice hand melt faster if it was chopped in half?' (Feasey 2005: 43). Another variant is to challenge the children to melt the ice to release the toy (freeze water in half of the container/ice cube tray, then add a small plastic animal and fill with water for freezing). These activities can develop children's understanding of melting and factors that could affect it, for example, by adding heat or salt, or placing in liquid water. If challenged to do the opposite and 'save the ice cube/snowman' then children can begin to explore thermal insulators. Understanding that a thermal insulator prevents heat transfer (thus keeping cold things cold and warm things warm) is a difficult concept for children to grasp, which is why it is in the Key Stage 2 curriculum. However, these early first-hand experiences build the foundations for such knowledge, which they will then be able to build on in later years.

FIGURE 10.1 What do ice balloons feel like?

Learning story 10.1

Melting chocolate

The following extract is an example of how an exciting context like melting chocolate can stimulate exploration of materials and develop the learners' vocabulary. The Reception children at St Martin's Garden in Bath were melting chocolate in a bowl above boiling water on a stove. Notice how the teacher supports their understanding by drawing attention to important features (e.g. boiling bubbles) and asks the children to explain what they mean.

Teacher: Now what happens to water when water boils?

Child 1: It gets burnt.

Teacher: You can burn yourself. Now if you have a look . . . you can see lots and lots of bubbles coming up and that tells us it's really boiling, and that tells us not to touch the black bit here. I'm going to put the chocolate inside the bowl and we're going to watch and see what happens. Now what do you think is going to happen?

Child 2: They will melt.

Teacher: You think they'll melt. What do you think's going to happen?

Child 3: They'll melt.

Teacher: Now what does that mean?

Child 3: It means it like goes . . . it goes all dribbly.

Teacher: It goes all dribbly. That's a good word. Please don't touch the black bit, okay, because it's going to get really hot. I'm going to turn it down a bit because it's getting very hot. What's this coming up in the air? Have a look.

Child 1: Smoke.

Teacher: Is it smoke?

Child 3: Steam.

Teacher: Steam, and that steam comes from the boiling hot water. Wow, now, if we move back a little bit, now can you see what's started to happen?

Child 2: It's melted.

Teacher: It's melted. It's starting to melt. I'm going to give this one a stir as well. This is all starting to melt here.

Commentary

The teacher goes on to explore mixing of different types of chocolate and what happens when marshmallows are added. After melting the chocolate, children were challenged to find a place where it turns back to an edible solid treat for their party, provoking the children to look around the room, with the teacher emphasising the temperature of the fridge as the key factor. Making chocolate treats is an attention-grabbing experience, the stirring and pouring is hands-on, and with the support of the teacher, the discussion is minds-on, developing their understanding and vocabulary of reversible changes.

Learning story 10.2

Child-led exploration

At Lypiatt Primary School and Children's Centre in Wiltshire, child-led learning is strong in the Foundation Stage, and science subject leader Katherine Laing is trying to develop this approach across the school. Lypiatt is a unique setting, it is the only school in the country serving forces families in transit. There is a mix of discrete and topic Science lessons, following the International Primary Curriculum. In addition, a local farmer teaches environmental studies and due to their small numbers (just three classes) they are able to offer children the opportunity to go on many trips to see science used in real life situations in the wider community.

Science in Early Years practice at Lypiatt is very much about hands-on exploration. The adult sometimes takes a facilitating role, extending children's understanding when required and verbalising their discoveries, or models curiosity through sustained shared interest in play. For example, when children are exploring ice balloons they are learning about many scientific concepts through play including: changing states of water, freezing points of water and density. This provides foundational scientific knowledge, which can be developed later on. They were fascinated by the way the ice moved in the water, how it felt to touch it, how it changed shape, and how the balloons sank lower in the water as it melted; some added salt to see what would happen and discovered how quickly ice melted (see Figure 10.2 and Figure 10.3).

The school was working towards the Primary Science Quality Mark (PSQM), an award that supports schools to evaluate, strengthen and celebrate their science provision (see www.psqm.org.uk). For her PSQM action plan Katherine needed to choose a focus for whole school development in science. After lesson observations, and questioning children and staff she identified the area of child-led investigation:

> Looking at our Science curriculum with an Early Years frame of mind, I felt it was too adult-led, children were working together as a class to carry out investigations with the teacher taking the lead role. I wanted to try and input the ideas and values of Early Years child-led learning throughout the school. My first step was to organise a series of child-led investigative science activities which involved all teachers.

Katherine uses the term 'child-led learning' as an umbrella term. She sees it as incorporating: children learning to **select their own resources** and materials they think they will need or would like to use in investigation. They begin to **ask their own questions** in science and have the opportunity to be allowed to **follow their own interests** including lines of enquiry and ideas in science. She sees the benefits of this child-led approach as: helping children to develop thinking skills; supporting them to be independent learners; encouraging questioning and interest; supporting choice in collaborative or individual learning; it is more open-ended therefore self-differentiating.

The first whole-school child-led activity was focused on children choosing their own resources. They were asked to design a tool that could make a big bubble using any resources. Children came up with a range of different methods of making bubbles, some made bubble blowers, some bubble wands, some children went further and made different shaped wands to see if this had any effect on the shape of the bubble. They thoroughly enjoyed the activity and there was a busy and purposeful atmosphere. The children shared and modified ideas although it took them a few minutes to settle into the activity indicating to Katherine that they needed training in using the child-led approach. Encouraging the older children and all teachers to adapt to a more child-led approach throughout the curriculum continues to be a focus for Katherine at Lypiatt.

FIGURE 10.2
Does ice float?

FIGURE 10.3
What happens when we add salt to ice?

ICT links

Digital images can provide a record of the material's appearance before it was changed, for example, the puddle before it evaporated or the chocolate before it melted. Many digital microscopes can be set up to take a photo every 30 seconds or so, enabling, for example, mould growth to be captured. Such time-lapse photography is also possible on a normal digital camera, as long as the photos are taken from the same position each time. Daily photos could be combined in a PowerPoint or slideshow to show seasonal change. The same principle applies to animation, with repeated photos of plasticine models combined to tell a story. For example, a plasticine gingerbread man could fall into a cellophane river and disintegrate, or a Humpty Dumpty egg could fall, split and be cooked by the Sun. Such modelling requires the children to sequence the events as the materials change and also consider the cause of those changes, for example, there needs to be water to dissolve the sugar in the gingerbread man and there needs to be heat to cook the egg.

Related designing and making activities

Providing a purpose for the design and making activities gives them meaning and raises the awareness of the need to design for an audience. For example, the children could be asked to design and make a boat to carry the gingerbread man safely across the river, castle-shaped biscuits for a medieval banquet, a coat for the snowman or a mud house for the fourth little pig.

Let us take bread as an example: children could explore a range of bread products. One way to do this is to play 'same but different': choose two types of bread and say how they are the same and how they are different (Kelly and Stead 2013: 77). Considering preferences within the group and suitability for a particular event will give children ownership of the task. Which bread do they think would be the most appropriate for a royal picnic, an end of term party or a parents' celebration afternoon? Children can explore the ingredients of different types of breads and what happens when ingredients are combined. Keeping back a small amount of dough at each stage supports the children to make comparisons (Kelly and Stead 2013: 83). Following bread recipes (e.g. www.grainchain.com) and exploring the raising agents provides further science and D&T opportunities.

Summary

Changing materials is so much a part of daily life that it is easy to overlook it, so we must support children to recognise and talk about the changes that they see

(Tunnicliffe 2013: 118). Noticing when something is different is the first step to describing or explaining the difference and considering the cause.

Changing materials is a very tactile topic; children want to touch and feel ice melting, flour combining into dough and bubbles popping. Your role as a teacher is to provide these opportunities and resources, together with extending their learning by asking them to describe and explain their experiences. In this way you are modelling the use of scientific vocabulary and developing their thinking about the changes and their causes.

Discussion points

- When is it appropriate to talk to children about particles?
- How would you ensure children experience melting and cooking safely?

A thematic approach to forces, magnets and electricity in Early Years settings

Dan Davies and Christopher Collier

Purpose of this chapter

After reading this chapter you should have:

- gained an understanding of progression in the main concept areas of forces, magnets and electricity from age 3–7;

- become aware of a variety of hands-on activities to engage children's curiosity and sense of wonder at the phenomena of forces, magnets and electricity;

- extended your repertoire of thematic approaches to developing children's understanding of key concepts related to forces, magnets and electricity, in tandem with their scientific skills.

Introduction

Forces, magnets and electricity are areas of children's experience of the world that can appear quite alien to many Early Years practitioners, for three reasons. The first is that the concepts associated with these physical phenomena may seem a bit abstract – we cannot see, hear or smell a force or a magnetic field. The second is that few practitioners come into Early Years professions with a background in physics, so they may lack confidence in their own understanding in these areas.

The final reason is that neither the Statutory Framework for the Early Years Foundation Stage (EYFS) (DfE 2012) nor the revised National Curriculum at Key Stage 1 in England (DfE 2013) make much reference to these areas, so practitioners could be forgiven for assuming that they are of little relevance. However, this is not the perspective of children, who will have lots of experiences of forces during their early years through playing in the bath or the play park; in fact in any situation where they are making themselves or objects move, float or fall. In their Early Years setting, some children may be developing more understanding of forces and movement through their epistemic play construction activities and wheeled toys in the outdoor area. A child playing with toy railway carriages with magnetic couplings will quickly discover that they 'magically' lock together when turned one way around, while pushing each other apart when reversed. Similarly, children's widespread experience of electrical appliances – from battery toys and games to tablet computers – will have got them thinking about the mysterious form of energy that makes these things work, even if they have not yet had the opportunity to play with batteries, bulbs and wire to make a simple circuit. Forces, magnets and electricity play important roles in young children's lives, so as practitioners we owe it to them to follow their curiosities and help them find out more.

Conceptual understanding from 3 to 7

In order to recognise the steps in understanding children are taking in forces, magnets and electricity – and therefore help scaffold their learning to the next level – it is important for practitioners to have a firm grasp of some fundamental contexts. These are laid out in Table 11.1.

Early Years themes and contexts for learning

The playground

Because the concept of a 'force' is quite abstract, it is particularly important to find meaningful contexts for children to explore forces in action. These contexts include water play, toys and PE. Activities such as construction play with vehicles, water play and play with mouldable materials will have given them appropriate first-hand knowledge of forces and their effects. Through a visit to a local playground children can experience different types of forces in a kinaesthetic 'whole body' way. Many settings have on-site play equipment, or are likely to be located near a play park with access to a slide, swings, a round-about, see-saw and climbing frame. A pre-visit discussion will help children to think in terms of pushes, pulls, starting, stopping, speeding up, slowing down

TABLE 11.1 Conceptual understanding: forces, magnets and electricity

Key concepts in the Early Years curriculum	Subject knowledge for practitioners in Early Years curriculum
A force is either a push or a pull	It is perhaps quite straightforward for young children to understand that the shape and movement of an object can be changed by them *directly* pushing or pulling it. Perhaps less obvious is that a range of other phenomena they will experience are related to forces and can also be described as either pushes or pulls. For example, friction is a push acting on a moving object, tending to slow it down. Air resistance is a type of friction, so is also a push, in this case between a moving object and air. Gravity, on the other hand, is always a pull, and is the result of an attraction that exists between two objects due to their mass. Upthrust is the push exerted by a liquid against an object that is placed in it.
	Magnetism is a force too. It can result in objects being pulled towards each other (the north pole of one magnet and the south pole of another are magnetically attracted to each other; a magnetic material is attracted to either pole of a magnet) or being pushed apart ('like' poles of magnets repel each other).
All movement begins and ends with a force	Whenever something starts moving, speeds up, slows down, stops or changes direction a force is involved. Take the example of a child rolling a ball across a flat surface. The child begins the movement by pushing the ball away from her.
Forces can alter an object's speed and direction of movement	Maybe more confusing is that after the ball has left her hand there is no forward force acting on the ball, only the backward force of friction slowing it down and eventually stopping it.
	There are many situations where forces act in pairs. As a falling object is pulled towards the Earth by gravity, air resistance pushes back against it. Objects pulled towards the bottom of a container holding water experience upthrust pushing back against them. Forces acting on the object are either in balance so that the object does not change its speed or direction of movement (remaining still or moving at a constant speed in a straight line), or they are out of balance so the object speeds up, slows down or changes direction.
	The forces acting on a parachute falling at a constant speed are in balance – the downward pull due to gravity is balanced by the push back of air resistance. The parachute is falling at its terminal velocity. If a boat is floating then the weight of the boat is balanced by the weight of water it displaces. Another way of expressing this is to say the pull on the boat due to gravity is balanced by the push back of the water.
Forces can change the shape of an object	When an object changes its shape forces are acting on it. A piece of clay can be squashed (pushed) or stretched (pulled) into a new shape. The ease with which an object deforms is related to its mechanical properties. Plasticine can be stiff at first and more flexible as it is worked. The elasticity of a material determines what it will do when the force is removed. Inelastic materials such as Blu-tak hold their shape, elastic materials (e.g. rubber bands) return to their original shape.
Forces are measurable and have a direction	For younger children it is enough for them to know that forces have a magnitude (they can be big or small) resulting in bigger or smaller effects, and that it is possible to measure them using non-standard units (maybe by constructing their own push and pull meters out of a piece of dowel, an elastic band and a cotton reel). Later children will learn that force is measured in Newtons (symbol N). An object with a mass of 100g exerts a force of about 1N at the Earth's surface. It is correct to describe its weight as 1N, although more commonly we express it in grams and kilograms, and in Early Years we are unlikely to make the distinction between mass (the amount of matter in an object) and weight (the force an object exerts due to gravity).
	Forces also act on objects in a direction although this is not always a good indicator of the direction of movement of the object (see description above of a ball rolling across a surface).
Mechanisms can change the size	A lever allows a small force over a large distance to exert a greater force over a short distance, or vice versa. Gears (toothed wheels that mesh to change the speed of rotary

TABLE 11.1 continued

Key concepts in the Early Years curriculum	Subject knowledge for practitioners in Early Years curriculum
and direction of a force	movement) and pulleys (grooved wheels over which a string or belt can run) do the same. On a bike we turn the large gear attached to the pedals, which turns (via a chain) a small gear attached to the rear wheel. A large force over a short distance in the front gear is changed to a smaller force over a longer distance in the rear gear.
	Wheels are a simple mechanism that can reduce friction. They replace a large friction force between the load and the ground with a smaller friction force between the wheel and the axle.
Magnetism is a force	The most visible property of a magnet is that it can exert a push or a pull on another magnet, or can pull on anything containing iron, steel, nickel and some other rare metals. When a magnet pulls on such an object it is said to be a force of 'attraction'. Magnets have two ends or poles: north and south (strictly speaking, north-seeking and south-seeking). These are so named because the Earth is a huge magnet (it contains a spinning iron core) and all permanent magnets tend to align with its magnetic poles. The only true test of a magnet is that it will push away or repel another magnet if the two like poles are aligned: like poles repel and opposites attract.
Electricity: a complete circuit is needed to make a bulb, buzzer or motor work	Electricity (current) involves the flow of billions of tiny particles (electrons) through conducting materials (e.g. metals). There needs to be a complete circuit for the electrons that are already in the battery, wire and component (lamp, buzzer or motor) to start moving – like a bicycle chain.
	Movement of electrons around the circuit is initiated by the battery which pushes electrons from the negative to the positive terminal. As electrons are already present in the wires and electrical component, the effect of adding a battery to the circuit is immediate, e.g. the bulb lights up instantaneously. We can stop this movement by breaking the circuit, by opening a switch for instance. The flow of electrons in the circuit is more correctly referred to as the electrical current.
	Electrical components in the circuit offer resistance to the flow of current. The lamp has two connections at the base and side so that electrons can flow through the filament, which heats up because it has a fairly high resistance causing the lamp to glow. Placing more than one lamp in an unbranched circuit (in series) increases the overall resistance of the circuit, lowering the current that flows through the lamps – each lamp appears dim.
Electricity is a form of energy	Electrical current can carry energy from one place to another – by definition this is in the form of electrical energy. In a simple circuit the battery converts chemical to electrical energy. Each electron in the circuit transfers some of this energy from the battery to an electrical component. A lamp transforms this electrical energy into light and heat, a buzzer into sound, a motor into kinetic energy. It is the energy that gets 'used' up (transformed into another type) not the electrons. There are still the same number of electrons in the circuit even once the chemical reaction in the battery is complete and it no longer has energy to drive electrons around the circuit (i.e. the battery is flat).

Early Years activities that develop children's understanding of forces, electricity and magnetism support their development towards the big idea in science that *objects can affect other objects at a distance (electromagnetism, gravity), changing the movement of an object requires a net force to act on it, energy can be transformed but the total amount of energy in the Universe remains the same.*

Sources to develop background subject knowledge further:

Collier, C., Davies, D., Howe, A. and McMahon, K. (2011) *The Primary Science and Technology Encyclopedia*. London: David Fulton.

Harlen, W. (ed.) (2010) *Principles and Big Ideas of Science Education*. Hatfield: ASE

Howe, A., Davies, D., McMahon, K., Towler, L., Collier, C. and Scott, T. (2009) *Science 5–11: A Guide for Teachers*, 2nd edn. London: David Fulton (Chapters 6 and 7).

Peacock, G., Sharp, J., Johnsey, R. and Wright, D. (2012) *Primary Science: Knowledge and Understanding (Achieving QTS Series)*, 6th edn. Exeter: Learning Matters (Chapters 8 and 10).

Wenham, M. and Ovens, P. (2010) *Understanding Primary Science*, 3rd edn. London: Sage (Chapters 10, 11 and 12).

and changing direction when they are on the equipment. One group could play while another group watches; encourage the children in the watching group to describe what is happening: 'Karla is pushing the roundabout', 'Drew is sliding down', 'Nathan will fall down when he lets go'. Take some digital photographs or movies of the children and discuss these afterwards. Ask questions such as: can we see anyone pushing? Why did the see-saw go up and down? What did it feel like on the swing? During dance and gymnastics activities children can cooperate to balance pushes or pulls – by leaning into each other or pulling away from each other to create body shapes and dance movements. When jumping and landing, the children can experience large and small pushes and their effects. There is even potential for talking about gripping (more friction) and slipping (less friction) in relation to appropriate shoes for gym, or when trying to hold on to a smooth bar.

Toys

Another productive theme for exploring forces, magnetism and electricity is 'toys'. Ask children to bring in toys from home – simple toys such as those for toddlers, or wind-up toys given away by burger bars with 'kids' meals' are ideal. The toys can be displayed and played with in the class and added to over a few days. How do we make the toy move? How do we make the toy stop? These questions can begin to elicit children's understanding. The collection can be sorted into toys that are pushed, pulled or both. Other categories might be toys that can move fast, toys that can only go slowly, toys that float, toys that fly. Provide a wide range of magnetic games and toys such as a fishing game, a racing game in which the racers are controlled by magnets under the board, fridge magnets, 'Antz' (in which players have to capture stacks of opponents magnetic 'ants', which disconcertingly flip over if the poles are similar), Brio trains with magnetic couplings, etc. Some of these could be made or brought in by children, demonstrating not only the huge range of applications for magnets but providing starting points for children to design their own toys or games using magnetic principles. A display of battery toys and other small mains appliances (not to be plugged in!) can be used for sorting activities. Talking to them and observing while they 'play' with electrical toys can tell us a lot about young children's understanding:

■ What electrical things do you need to plug in to a socket?

■ What things use a battery?

■ What are the smallest/biggest electrical things you can think of?

■ What is electricity like?

■ Where does it come from?

Water

Another great context for experiencing forces is water play. Ask children to bring in groups of three items; one that will float, one that will sink and one that can float or sink. Initially, allow children to play and explore: can they make 'floaters' sink or vice versa? Introduce some challenging items such as very light objects that sink (for example, paper clips); objects that are heavy but float (for example, a large off-cut or log of wood); objects that are obviously very light for their size (for example, a balloon); and objects that can be made to float or sink (for example, a foil tray or a lump of plasticine that can be made into a boat). Even non-directed, child-initiated activities need to be part of a carefully planned sequence, and the value of any experience we set up should be judged on the basis of its potential future pathways. For example, a water tray activity in which carefully chosen objects float at different levels may be more productive than one in which all have equal buoyancy, depending on the prior experience and observation skills of the children.

Story books

The story of 'The Enormous Turnip' – in which the farmer first tries to pull up the turnip, then one by one a series of other people and animals come to help – could be used to initiate a discussion with young children about forces. Why was it so hard to pull up? How did they make the pull bigger? What else do we pull? Which are big pulls and which are small pulls? This could lead into an investigation in which children explore the different strength of pull needed to move different objects. 'Mr Gumpy's Outing' by John Burningham (1970) can be a starting point for exploring how boats and other hollow objects float, and how many objects can be placed in them before they sink. 'Mr Gumpy's Motor Car' (Burningham 1973) gets stuck in the mud – a lot of pushing, pulling and problem-solving ensues. Roald Dahl's 'James and the Giant Peach' (1961) could prompt children to think about the peach rolling down a hill (how steep would it have to be?), floating on the sea (do potatoes, apples and peaches float?), being lifted by more and more seagulls until it lifts off the water (what force would be needed?) and finally getting stuck on top of the Empire State Building (how would it balance?). After their investigations they might wonder whether Mr Dahl chose the right fruit! What would happen if the book were 'James and the Giant . . . Turnip, Apple, Pear, Watermelon'? Finally, the classic tale of 'The Lighthouse Keeper's Lunch' (2007) by Ronda and David Armitage, and other books in the series, also provide good starting points for thinking and problem-solving around forces as the lighthouse keeper tries to transport his sandwiches safely to the lighthouse.

Scientific process skills

As they move from Reception into Key Stage 1, children will need support in developing a systematic approach to scientific enquiry, while recognising the need to continue with informal exploratory play. Within the context of the playground, this may involve sorting apparatus into those that can be pushed or pulled, those that go up and down, round and round, or back and forth. A physical activity in which children are using their own bodies can lend itself to a performance as the mode of communication for their findings. They might develop a dance or sequence that involves 'two pushes', 'a push and a pull', 'everything balanced', 'twists and rolls' or 'hard and soft pushes'. Children can then be introduced to the 'scientist game', including a set of 'rules' or steps to be followed. The rules are expressed in terms of questions that guide the process of scientific enquiry:

 What have we noticed?

 What are we going to find out?

 What do we think will happen?

 How did we do it?

 What did we find out?

The shapes used for each stage in the game are intended to convey something of what that particular step involves. Make a display or mobile of the shapes for the classroom, or even use giant versions on the floor for children to move between when playing the scientist game. 'I've moved to the think cloud so now I'm predicting what will happen' is a kinaesthetic way of remembering the process. An example of the 'scientist game' in practice is provided by Brunton and Thornton (2010), who advocate making a collection of rolling objects, including balls of different sizes and fruit/vegetables such as a potato, butternut squash, turnip, gourd, parsnip and carrot. They suggest a focus on predicting those that will be the best rollers and sorting them according to their different behaviours. So children could verbalise what they have noticed about the way the different objects role and decide on something they want to find out (which rolls the furthest or straightest?). They can be encouraged to talk about what they think will happen and how to go about 'testing' the rolling objects to make it 'fair', before describing what happened when they tried out their ideas.

Open-ended exploration activities are still appropriate for children nearing the end of Key Stage 1. For example, Feasey (2005: 31) reports on a class of six- and seven-year-olds who were given a selection of magnets and different materials; their open-ended instructions being to find out as much about the magnets as they could and also to think about what they would like to find out about them. Their result was a rich 'floor book' of ideas. Essentially, a floor book is a large format 'home-made' book of plain pages, made of sugar paper or flip-chart paper in which an adult or the children write and draw ideas, observations, predictions, questions and explanations. With young children the book is compiled on the floor so the group can all have a good view and opportunity to contribute. It can be completed during one session or revisited during a number of sessions (see Chapter 5). Similarly, many of children's early experiences of electrical components seem to fall under the general heading of 'exploration' – playing around to see what will happen. These can be structured as 'problem-solving' activities; for example, in Moorlands Infants School, Bath, Year 2 teacher Alison Stubbs set her class a set of challenges with a range of electrical components – batteries, wires, bulbs and buzzers. The challenges were to 'make a noise' (buzzers), 'light it up' (bulbs) and 'get in a spin' (motors). The children's demonstration of their achievement of each 'challenge' constituted the recording of the investigation.

EYFS and Key Stage 1 curriculum links

Although the specific topics of forces, magnets and electricity are not mentioned in either the Statutory Framework for the Early Years Foundation Stage or the revised National Curriculum at Key Stage 1 in England, both the processes by which children explore these phenomena and their technological applications are represented. For example, within the EYFS Specific Area of Learning 'Understanding the world', children are to: 'know about similarities and differences in relation to . . . objects . . . They make observations . . . and explain why some things occur, and talk about changes' (DfE 2012: 9). This goal could be met by describing how different objects behave when immersed in water and offering an explanation as to why some of them float. As children move into Key Stage 1 they are expected to:

> experience and observe phenomena . . . be curious and ask questions about what they notice. They should be helped to develop their understanding of scientific ideas by using different types of scientific enquiry to answer their own questions.
>
> (DfE 2013: 146)

This requirement could be met by 'playing the scientist game' (see above) in relation to collections of rolling objects, magnetic toys and electrical components; focusing upon specific skills during each enquiry activity, such as:

- asking simple questions and recognising that they can be answered in different ways;
- observing closely;
- using simple equipment;
- performing simple tests;
- identifying and classifying;
- using their observations and ideas to suggest answers to questions;
- gathering and recording data to help in answering questions.

(DfE 2013: 147)

This list of scientific process skills maps neatly onto the steps in the 'scientist game'. The curriculum documents also make reference to children's experience of using and creating technology, much of which makes extensive use of forces, magnets or electricity. For example, in the EYFS Specific Area of 'Understanding the world', children are to: 'recognise that a range of technology is used in places such as homes and schools. They select and use technology for particular purposes' (DfE 2012: 9). Such technology could include scissors (which use levers and forces), fridge magnets and torches. A more specific use of the term 'technology' to mean 'information communication technology' (ICT) can also be linked to these topics (for example, a laptop computer has a hinge (lever), an electrical power supply and magnets controlling the arrangement of liquid crystals on its screen).Through discussion, children can be encouraged to describe what each piece of technology is used for and how they think it works. The National Curriculum turns the focus towards the creation of technology:

> Through a variety of creative and practical activities, pupils should be taught the knowledge, understanding and skills needed to engage in an iterative process of designing and making. They should work in a range of relevant contexts, such as the home and school, gardens and playgrounds.

(DfE 2013: 181)

More specifically related to forces, the programme of study for design and technology goes on to require children to be taught to:

- build structures, exploring how they can be made stronger, stiffer and more stable;
- explore and use mechanisms, such as levers, sliders, wheels and axles, in their products.

(DfE 2013: 181)

Whether children are using construction kits or card, building strong structures and working mechanisms can involve discussion of force-related words (push, pull, turn, lift, slide, move, etc.).

Intervening to develop young children's understanding

The Effective Provision of Pre-School Education (EPPE) Project (Sylva et al. 2004) found that, in Early Years settings, freely chosen play activities often provided the best opportunities for adults to extend children's thinking. By engaging thoughtfully with children's play, skilful practitioners can extend its scope and involve the children in 'sustained shared thinking' (SST), which the team found was most likely to occur when children were interacting one-to-one with an adult or with a single peer partner. Achieving SST in play is hard – it requires an adult who is sensitive to the direction in which the child wishes to take the play, who listens carefully and waits for the ideal moment to join in (often when invited by the child). Clearly, dialogue is important here as it can help adult and child to arrive at shared meanings and provides access to the child's thinking for the adult to 'scaffold' their understanding (Bruner 1996). Siraj-Blatchford (2010: 156) quotes the following example of SST in relation to forces:

> Boy: (*He has been watching various items floating on water.*) Look at the fir cone. There's bubbles of air coming out.
> Nursery officer: It's spinning round.
> Boy: That's 'cause it's got air in it.
> Nursery officer: (*Picks up the fir-cone and shows the children how the scales go round the fir-cone in a spiral, turning the fir cone round with a winding action.*) When the air comes out in bubbles it makes the fir cone spin around.
> Girl: (*Uses a plastic tube to blow into the water.*) Look, bubbles.
> Nursery officer: What are you putting into the water to make bubbles? . . . What's coming out of the tube?
> Girl: Air.

Siraj-Blatchford goes on to claim that, on the basis of EPPE findings,

> almost half of all the child-initiated episodes which contained intellectual challenge included interventions from a staff member to extend the child's thinking. The evidence also suggested that adult 'modelling' often combined with sustained periods of shared thinking and open-ended questioning, was associated with better cognitive achievement.
>
> (Siraj-Blatchford 2010: 156)

However, Johnston (2011: 29) warns that 'adult intervention does not always move thinking forward, but combines with children's tacit ideas to create more complex alternative conceptions.' Glauert et al. (2007: 139) further caution that 'despite growing evidence of young children's capabilities, their skills and understandings can be fragile and fleeting. Performance may be inconsistent or ideas not generalised or applied across different contexts.' This suggests that children may feel the need to repeat experiences and have the opportunity to discuss their ideas on many occasions with adults.

For example, as practitioners we may need to plan a number of 'focus' activities around a particular concept area to give children the opportunity to develop their understanding. Drake (2009: 54) defines a 'focus' as 'an activity or experience that is planned with particular objectives in mind. Basic provision is often enhanced in a way that will enable children to develop certain skills, knowledge, concepts and attitudes and the role of the adult in supporting their learning is clearly defined.' Kallery et al. (2009) have examined young children's learning of the concept of floating and sinking through both play-based and more didactic approaches in Greek Early Years settings. They concluded that approaches that help children to make links between their exploratory (play-based) findings and scientific phenomena (in this case, the objects that were floating and sinking and the materials they were made of) were much more effective than formal teaching. Table 11.2 below offers some challenge questions practitioners can ask in response to children's ideas about floating and sinking as part of their water play:

At Key Stage 1 it is time to formalise some of this understanding and for children to begin to develop the big idea of 'forces' that brings all the earlier experiences together. For example, in order to start to develop the concept of 'upthrust' we can give children a ball or inflated balloon to press down into a tank of water, feeling the force of the water 'pushing back'. Another invisible force that children can begin to talk about in Key Stage 1 is friction. Younger children can begin to understand the concept of friction, though they do not need to name

TABLE 11.2 Intervening to develop young children's understanding of floating and sinking

Children's common ideas	Suggested questions and interventions
'It sinks because it's heavy/big'	*Do all heavy things sink?* *Can you find any big things that float?*
'It floats because it's small/light'	*Do all small/light things float?* *Can you find any small/light things that don't float?*
'It sinks because it's made of metal'	*Do all metal things sink?* (e.g. a cake tin)
'It floats because it's made of wood'	*Do all wooden things float?* (liquorice root and *lignum vitae* don't) *Can you find things that float that are not made of wood?*
'It floats because it's spread out'	*What happens if we spread this Plasticine out?* (it sinks) *What can you do to make this Plasticine float?* (make it into a boat shape with sides)
'It floats because it's got air inside'	*Will a sponge float if you squeeze it in the water?* *Do boats have air inside?*
	Try using a long Perspex tube filled with water to watch objects sink at different rates.

it; for example, a Year 1 child described friction as a 'naughty force', because it stops things from 'going'. However, friction can also be helpful: children will come to realise that there can be a 'grip' between two surfaces, such as shoes and a floor. They will notice that different surfaces might be 'grippy' or slippery. Bumpy soles may be grippy, but water will make a floor slippery. A child may get stuck on a slide because the interaction between their coat and the dirty slide produces a frictional force equal to their weight due to gravity, so the child stays still. You might let children put sand, water, talc, hand cream or cooking oil on their hands to experience the reduction of friction by lubricants.

The force of magnetism can be experienced and explored by children without any adult intervention; for example Brunton and Thornton (2010: 131) report the following episode in a nursery:

> Amy is playing with the trucks from the magnetic train set on the wooden floor. As she moves one of the trucks towards the stationary truck on the floor she notices that it spins round before the two trucks join together. Her shout of excitement alerts her friend Grace to the fact that something exciting is happening and she comes over to join her. The two children now move the trucks backwards and forwards across the floor looking at ways to repeat Amy's discovery. They continue to play with the trucks for another 20 minutes, moving them backwards and forwards and from side to side. Amy's key person observes what is happening and takes a series of photographs, but she does not interrupt the children's exploration. Later in the day she shares the photographs with the children and they talk again about what they saw happening.

In a Reception class, there is more of a role for the adult. For example, Angela had set up a display of magnets for the Reception class to explore in their first term at school. On one occasion she worked with groups of children to focus their attention on the display and assess their understanding. Angela played alongside the children while another adult made notes about the interactions in a 'floor book' using a different coloured pen to record each child's ideas, such as:

> The big magnets stick to each other.
> They are wobbly (two 'polo-mint' magnets on a dowel); they won't stick.
> When I stuck a magnet to another magnet they stuck really hard.
> What happens when you spin (the magnet)?
> What happens when you slide them on each other?

By the time they get to Year 1, children can be more directly challenged on their ideas about magnets and what is attracted to them, as demonstrated by the following exchange between Amy, a teacher at St Martin's Garden School, Bath, and a group of children investigating the strength of magnets:

Teacher: How about these things? Does it pick up any of these things?

Child: Wait, let me try on this one. No.

Teacher: But it does try . . . wait, wait, wait . . . it probably will pick up this, ready . . . Why do you think it'll pick that up, Evan?

Child: Because it's metal.

Child: It doesn't work.

Teacher: So it's . . . a clue is that how heavy it is, it doesn't get it.

Child: No, because it's not metal. Only silver. Only silver metal can work.

Teacher: This is silver, why won't it stick?

Child: Because it's plastic.

Teacher: Oh it's plastic is it? . . . Ooh, its picked up another magnet. Do you think . . . Ellie, do you think it will pick up this?

Child: No.

Teacher: Why not?

Child: It's not metal, it's wood.

Teacher: So do you think it will pick up all the metal things?

In this extract, Amy is investigating alongside the children and getting them to explain the reasons for their predictions and observations. She challenges their categorisation (all 'silver' things? All metals?) and introduces the idea of magnet strength.

Electricity is, in some senses, 'easy to do, hard to understand'. Children in Nursery classes can join electrical components together to make a complete circuit, yet to explain what is going on within that circuit requires understanding of some very abstract concepts. One of the common conceptual models young children hold in relation to electrical circuits is what Osborne et al. (1991) have termed the 'source–sink' model, in which the battery is seen as the 'source' of the electricity for the circuit, literally a store of electricity that is released down a wire and used up in the bulb (the 'sink' – think of electricity flowing down a plug hole). The usual indicator for this concept is a drawing showing one wire connecting the battery to the bulb (a 'circuit' which clearly does not work if you try it, even though the child may have had to use two wires to make their bulb light up – see Figure 11.1). One way to challenge this idea is to 'become' a circuit; a small group of say four children could hold a PE hoop loosely between them, with one (the 'battery') passing it through his or her hands to move the 'electricity' around the circuit. See Howe et al. (2009) for a fuller description of this use of analogy to support children's understanding of circuits.

FIGURE 11.1 Source–sink model

Learning story 11.1

Floating and sinking (Year 2)

Heidi Wood at Bathampton Primary School organised a circus of forces activities for her Year 2/3 class. One of the activities was to make boats from aluminium foil and plasticine. Here is an extract from a discussion between Heidi and the group of children carrying out this activity:

Teacher: Do they float by themselves (*referring to balls of foil*)?

Child 1: I don't know (*tries it out*).

Teacher: They float . . . why do they float by themselves do you think?

Child 1: Because they . . . when they're not . . . when they're not wrapped in anything, you can . . . umm . . . they have a lot of air, so when you don't have it, they have lots of air to stay up on the water.

Teacher: Where do you think the air is?

Child 1: In the water.

Teacher: Is it?

Child 1: Outside the water.

Child 2: I think . . . umm . . . the tin foil already floated because I think it had a less amount of air in so it could stay more on the water . . .

Teacher: So does foil always float?

Child 2: Uhh . . . if it's not got anything on it, yes. It does.

Child 1: Well, if it's crunched up, no it wouldn't.

Teacher: Ahh, now, why?

Child 1: It hasn't got any air in.

Teacher: Okay, so you're saying that if I . . .

Child 1: It's just got water in those little cracks.

Teacher: If I really scrunch it up and try and get rid of all the air, this might float, this might not, let's see. Ooh . . . it still floats actually. Why do you think it's floating?

Child 1: Because the water . . . because it's little and it doesn't have very much heavy, so the water's just pushing it up. But when . . . but we can watch . . .

Teacher: It's an interesting point, what is pushing it up? What do you think is pushing it up?

Child 1: Water doesn't store very much gravity but rocks are very heavy so they would sink, but some tin foil, if they're really scrunched up, then . . . uhh . . . the air would be out and umm . . . uhh . . .

Teacher: You're right, air does keep it afloat doesn't it?

Child 1: Yes.

Teacher: And water will push . . .

Child 1: No air can get into the stone and it's quite heavy and pushes against the water so it would just sink.

Commentary

In this example of SST, Child 1 is beginning to grapple with some of the tricky concepts underlying Archimedes' Principle, particularly the ideas of upthrust and balanced forces. There is evidence of some confusion about the role of air in floating (where does it come from? Does it push down or up?) but Heidi helps the children verbalise their ideas and gently challenges some of their explanations for observation, helping them to recognise any contradictions and clarify their thinking.

Learning story 11.2

Forces in air (Years 1–2)

A team of teachers at Red Beach Primary School near Auckland used plastic bottles, paper towels, water and umbrellas to start a whole-school topic on 'air'. The school has developed cross-age 'learning communities' and has adopted a philosophy of 'going deeper, doing less', which means that depth of understanding of fundamental scientific concepts is more important than curriculum coverage. Their learning model in science is based on three questions: 'what do we think?' (prediction, hypothesis); 'what do we notice?' (observation); and, perhaps most importantly 'what do we wonder?' (conjecture, possibility thinking, creativity). Sue, Cathy, Andrea and Fleur, the teachers of 'Archimedes community' at Red Beach, developed their topic on air around a series of 'immersion' challenges based on some of the fundamental concepts they wished to communicate: air is all around us, air takes up space, you can trap air, air can be squashed, air can be strong. These challenges were organised as a circus around the four classrooms and undertaken by children in small groups:

- Can you squash a plastic bottle? (*With the lid on or off.*)
- Can you run with an umbrella? (*Different sizes, pulled behind them for safety.*)
- Will the paper towel get wet? (*Stuffed into a glass, inverted into a tub of water.*)
- How quickly can you blow up the bag?

In response to the bottle-squashing activity, 'What do we think?' elicited the following responses:

- I think that when the lid is closed he won't be able to squash it because the air will be trapped.
- If you push it down hard enough the lid might come off.
- When the lid's on it will trap the air and it can't get out.

Once the children had tried squashing the bottle with and without its lid they responded to 'What do we notice' with the following observations:

- When you had the lid on you could squeeze it a tiny bit except a lot of that air went out to the sides.
- But with the lid off it's more squishy . . . the air blows out.
- Hold your hand there, you can feel the air can't you.

Asked to respond to 'What we wonder', one child came up with the following:

- I wonder – if it had a hole in it what would happen.

The paper towel challenge (Figure 11.2) produced the following predictions ('What we think'):

- The water will go up and the paper towel will get wet.
- I don't think the paper towel will get wet because when you put a glass over water it just goes round it.
- Tip it up the right way then it will get wet.

Their observations ('What we notice') also contained a high component of explanation and hypothesis:

– I think the glass is trapping the air in, so there's an air pocket that's keeping the paper dry.
– I also think the water is making a seal on the glass to stop the air getting out, so they're both like sealing it in and the water is pushing on the glass to seal it in there.
– And when we tipped it to the side all the air came out with bubbles and that meant the pocket had opened.

The activity itself had produced considerable wonder:

– We really, really wonder why the water is coming on the piece of paper but it still isn't getting wet!

Commentary
Sue, Cathy, Andrea and Fleur had used simple, everyday resources to produce challenges for children that invited them to think around the problem, conjecture and put forward alternative explanations for intriguing phenomena.

FIGURE 11.2 The paper towel challenge

Related designing and making activities

Designing and making moving toys provides a motivating context for learning about forces and mechanisms. If children start developing their ideas using construction kits there are also opportunities to develop their joining and fastening skills. Most kits commonly available in Early Years settings encourage accuracy in push-fitting, for which we suggest the following sequence to provide increasing challenge:

Sticklebricks → Mobilo → Lego Duplo → Lasy → First Gear → Polydron

In one Reception class in a Bath infant school, children had lots of experience of working with a variety of construction kits on a small scale. There was a class 'craze' for making ever-more elaborate wheeled vehicles. Katherine, the class teacher, wanted to capitalise and build on this enthusiasm. This led to her making formative assessments about what the children were able to do, their language development, their knowledge and understanding of the world and their interests. She had also identified a need to give the children opportunities to work on a larger scale and to develop the skills of cutting and joining wood. To begin the project, Katherine discussed with the class their recently made wheeled models, and introduced a new word – 'axle'. She showed them how an axle could be used to link pairs of wheels and allow them to turn. Some children were able to make free-hand labelled drawings of vehicles while others used the models as designs for the next stage. The children discovered how PVA glue and elastic bands might be used to join pieces of wood through this activity. They also learned about how wheels and axles can reduce friction. At a later stage, children could incorporate small magnets into their toys (e.g. to keep a door closed or join vehicles together), and even simple circuits to provide a light or siren for a fire engine.

Summary

In this chapter we have outlined the main scientific concepts children can learn through experiences that involve the phenomena of forces, magnets and electricity. We have recognised that, although they do not feature in current curriculum documentation for ages 3–7 in England, young children often experience them through play in the playground (pushes and pulls), with water (floating and sinking) and with toys and games featuring mechanical moving parts, magnetic attraction/repulsion and electronic working parts. We have explored ways of challenging children's ideas and moving their thinking forward through intervening in their play, and provided several examples of SST in relation to forces and magnets. Finally, we have highlighted the ways in which designing and making moving toys using construction kits and other media can enable children to apply their understanding of forces, magnets and electricity in practical ways.

Discussion points

- Should forces, magnets and electricity be explicitly mentioned in curriculum documentation for children aged 3–7?
- At what point should children be introduced to the formal procedures of scientific enquiry (the 'scientist game' – see above)?
- How should children be introduced to the safety aspects of electricity?

A thematic approach to sound, light and space in Early Years settings

Dan Davies and Christopher Collier

Purpose of this chapter

After reading this chapter you should have:

- gained an understanding of progression in the main concept areas of sound, light and space (the Earth and beyond) from age 3–7;

- become aware of a variety of hands-on activities to engage children's curiosity and sense of wonder at the phenomena of sound, light, day and night;

- extended your repertoire of thematic approaches to developing children's understanding of key concepts related to sound, light and space, in tandem with their scientific skills.

Introduction

Sound can be an enjoyable, hands-on (and 'ears-on'!) science topic to teach, particularly if you make the most of the extensive cross-curricular links that can be made with music. During their early years children will begin to notice similarities and differences between sounds and music and will learn to discern different sounds and their sources. They will enjoy making sounds and music with their own voices and bodies and with instruments. In the Foundation Stage the exploration of sound in a play context can be achieved through 'listening walks', identifying sounds with eyes closed, circle games such as 'keeper of the keys', and through using musical instruments such as drums, shakers and scrapers.

Each day, from the moment we open our eyes, we make use of light. When we read a book, look at a screen and enjoy works of art, the beauty of flowers or a view from the mountains we are sensing light that has reached our eyes. Light travels through space across distances that are unimaginable and so we can see stars that may not exist any more. Light from the Sun is the energy source that keeps our planet alive – plants photosynthesise and provide the basis for all other life on Earth. Lights that twinkle, sparkle, glitter and flicker will have intrigued children from an early age. Young children will know that lights can brighten a room, decorate a cake or light up the sky. They will have sung songs about colours, stars and rainbows and played games that involve hiding in the dark or covering their eyes and shutting out the light. The topic of light lends itself to 'awe and wonder' particularly well. Spectra or rainbows can be created in the classroom using a strong light source and a prism – a glass bowl of water can work as can water mist and some plastics.

Because the science topic of Space (the Earth and beyond) does not feature in the National Curriculum for England until Key Stage 2, we could be forgiven for thinking that this topic is not applicable to children younger than 7. However, do children only start gazing up into the sky as they leave Key Stage 1? Surely the concept of day and night is highly relevant to the youngest of Nursery children, who may count time to a waited-for event in 'sleeps'. Our whole notion of passing time is so closely related to the periods of rotation and orbit of the Earth around the Sun that no study of 'ourselves' or 'Autumn' is complete without some link to these concepts, however implicit.

Conceptual understanding

Table 12.1 outlines some of the key concepts in sound, light and space that young children will be encountering in their educational settings and daily lives, together with the knowledge that we as practitioners need to help them develop their understandings.

Early Years themes and contexts for learning

Music-making

There is so much potential for developing children's understanding of sound through music because it is possible to engage children of all ages and levels of attainment, and scope to return to this theme often by focusing on a different aspect of sound or music each time. There is a wide variety of instruments from

TABLE 12.1 Conceptual understanding: sound, light and space

Key concepts in the Early Years curriculum	Subject knowledge for practitioners in Early Years curriculum
There are many kinds of sounds	Sounds are made when objects vibrate. The size of the vibration (amplitude or volume) gives us loud and soft sounds. The frequency of vibrations – that is the number of movements back and forth per second – gives us high and low notes (pitch).
Sounds travel away from a source, getting fainter as they do	Sounds are transmitted outwards from their source in a longitudinal wave which can travel through solids, liquids and gases. Sound waves need a medium to travel through – they are unable to travel through a vacuum. The vibration from the source of sound causes particles (possibly air particles) surrounding it to move backwards and forwards rapidly. The back and forth movement is transmitted outwards from the source, a bit like ripples in a pond (although waves in a pond have an up and down motion rather than back and forth). As the sound wave travels away from its source, its energy is spread over a wider and wider area. Its amplitude diminishes and the sound becomes fainter.
We hear sounds when they enter our ears	Sound waves that enter our ears cause the eardrum to vibrate. This movement is transmitted via three small bones to the fluid-filled cochlea. Here thousands of small hair-like structures detect the movement of the fluid, sending nerve signals to the brain.
We see light with our eyes Without light (darkness) we cannot see	We only see something when light from it (either directly from the source of light, or reflected/scattered light) enters our eye. Light enters the eye through the pupil and is focused on the light-sensitive cells (retina) at the back of the eye by a lens. If there is no light (darkness), we cannot see since there is nothing to trigger the nerve cells in our retinas.
	White light is a mixture of coloured lights, all with a slightly different wavelength. It is possible to split white light into a rainbow of colours by using a prism – each colour of the spectrum is refracted (bent) a slightly different amount as it passes through the prism. When light falls on a green object, we see it as green because only that part of the spectrum is reflected back to our eyes. The other colours are absorbed by the object.
From Earth it is possible to see other objects in the Universe: the Sun, Moon and stars, and sometimes planets	Seven other planets as well as the Earth orbit the Sun (in order of distance from the Sun: Mercury, Venus, Earth, Mars, Jupiter, Saturn, Uranus, Neptune – but not Pluto, which is now classified as a 'dwarf planet'). These planets along with their moons make up the solar system. Venus, Mars and Jupiter are often visible in the night sky without the aid of a telescope. The solar system is only one star system (the Sun being its star) that makes up our galaxy, called the Milky Way. The Milky Way consists of about 500 billion stars – many other galaxies make up the Universe. In dark skies it is possible to see thousands of stars.
There are many different sources of light	Only true sources emit light (e.g. the Sun, other stars, the filament of a lamp, gas combusting in a flame). Other objects reflect or scatter light (e.g. the Moon, planets, shiny paper) but they don't emit their own light. Light travels from its source or a reflected surface in straight lines at 300,000,000 metres per second – nothing else travels faster.
The Sun is the only object in the solar system that is a large source of light	Light is a form of energy – our Sun is the source of nearly all the light around us. Most of the other sources of light (e.g. lamps powered by electricity generated by burning fossil fuels) ultimately are derived from the Sun's energy. Only light energy from other stars, nuclear power or volcanic activity has non-solar origins.
	We only spend roughly half the time in daylight, the time when our part of the Earth is facing the Sun. Day and night happen because the Earth spins on its axis – a period of one rotation takes 24 hours.

TABLE 12.1 continued

Key concepts in the Early Years curriculum	Subject knowledge for practitioners in Early Years curriculum
	We also experience variation in the intensity of light from Summer to Winter. This can be explained by the tilt of the Earth's orbit relative to the Sun. In a northern hemisphere Summer the northern hemisphere is tilting towards the Sun. Consequently, the Sun appears higher in the sky in comparison to Winter, and its energy is therefore concentrated in a relatively small area making it feel hotter in the Summer. The energy from the Winter Sun sitting low in the sky is spread out over a larger area, hence it feels colder.
Light can be reflected off surfaces	When light hits an object it can be absorbed, reflected or transmitted by the object. We usually use the term reflection to refer to the way light bounces off smooth surfaces in predictable ways. This kind of predictable reflection forms images because all reflected light rays maintain their position relative to one another from the time they left the object. Hence we can see our reflection in a mirror. However, reflection can also be used more generally to refer to light rebounding off an object in a random, scattered way. The light reflected from an object enables us to see it.
The Moon reflects light from the Sun	The Moon is not a source of light. We can only see it because it reflects light from the Sun. Half of the Moon is always illuminated by the Sun, but on Earth the proportion of the lit half we can see varies. Earth's gravitational field holds the Moon in orbit around the Earth and both are held in orbit around the Sun. It is the relative positions of Earth, the Moon and the Sun to one another that explain why different proportions of the lit half of the Moon are visible from the Earth over the course of a lunar month (roughly 29.5 days – the time it takes for the Moon to orbit the Earth). When the Sun and Moon are on opposite sides of the Earth we see the entire lit portion – the Moon is 'full'.
Some objects form shadows	Shadows occur because the path of light is blocked by an opaque object. Transparent objects let all light pass through them; translucent objects allow some light to pass through casting grey or coloured shadows.
The Sun, Moon and stars change their position giving the appearance from Earth that they move	The Sun only appears to move across the sky in an arc during the course of a day. It is the rotation of the Earth about its axis that explains this apparent movement. We can track the effect of this movement by recording the difference in position and length of shadows. The Moon and stars also appear to move across the night sky because of the Earth's spin. The fact that stars keep a fixed position relative to one another gives rise to the familiar constellations of stars that we are used to seeing in the night sky. Because the Earth orbits the Sun, we see different constellations at night in the Winter months than in the Summer.

Early Years activities that develop children's understanding of sound, light and space support their development towards the big idea in science that *Earth is part of the solar system which is one small part of the Universe, light and sound are examples of things that can be detected at a distance from their source.*

Sources to develop background subject knowledge further:

Collier, C., Davies, D., Howe, A. and McMahon, K. (2011) *The Primary Science and Technology Encyclopedia*. London: David Fulton.

Harlen, W. (ed.) (2010) *Principles and Big Ideas of Science Education*. Hatfield: ASE.

Howe, A., Davies, D., McMahon, K., Towler, L., Collier, C. and Scott, T. (2009) *Science 5–11: A Guide for Teachers*, 2nd edn. London: David Fulton (Chapter 4, 5 and 8).

Peacock, G., Sharp, J., Johnsey, R. and Wright, D. (2012) *Primary Science: Knowledge and Understanding (Achieving QTS Series)*, 6th edn. Exeter: Learning Matters (Chapters 11, 12 and 13).

Wenham, M. and Ovens, P. (2010) *Understanding Primary Science*, 3rd edn. London: Sage (Chapters 13 and 14).

all over the world that make sounds in different ways – usually through either beating (includes plucking and strumming), blowing (e.g. recorder), shaking (e.g. maracas) or scraping (e.g. violin). Children can explore ways to make sounds with instruments, feel the vibrations when sounds are being made and explore pitch and loudness. The theme of houses and homes provides a relevant and meaningful context for developing awareness of sources of sound, the variety of sounds in our environment and sound travelling through different materials. Children enjoy identifying a range of 'mystery' household sounds that have been pre-recorded, for example, filling a kettle, shutting a door and cleaning teeth.

Light and colour

Young children can be given opportunities for play that develops their experience of light through exploration of collections of shiny, transparent and translucent objects; mirrors, kaleidoscopes and torches; making shadows on a sunny day; making dark dens and looking at the world through different colour filters. They should be encouraged to communicate what they see and will begin to learn the vocabulary to enable them to describe their observations, e.g.: 'light, dark, shiny, dull, smooth, rough, mirror, shadow, reflection'. The topic of light enables us to link science with art and design. Activities such as colour mixing, making spinning colour wheels, and using paint colour charts to stimulate 'colour hunts' outside can stimulate children's imagination and promote a sense of 'awe and wonder' – a reminder of light's extensive links with religious education (RE). Celebrations such as birthdays, Christmas, Divali and Hanukkah are often used as topics in which to explore aspects of light. There are opportunities to explore reflective materials, shiny papers, stained-glass windows and various sources of light, for example, candles and Christmas tree lights.

In the dark

Although it is difficult to start a topic on space from an everyday context, young children's familiarity with day and night, sleeping and waking, the Moon and the stars can be used to initiate a discussion about why it gets dark at night. Although children are rarely in school when it is dark, they can be asked to talk about their experiences of going outside at night. Children as young as 5 or 6 are often asking the 'big questions' – Where did I come from? Has the universe always been here? – and a skilful teacher can turn these into open and thoughtful class or group discussions using a 'Philosophy for children' approach (Lipman 2003). This will involve adopting an 'interactive-dialogic' style of teaching (Mortimer and Scott 2003) in which every idea expressed is valued equally, rather than the teacher imposing an 'authoritative' version of scientific truth against which children's contributions are measured.

Story books

The story 'Peace at Last' by Jill Murphy (1995a) or the poem 'The Sound Collector' by Roger McGough are good starting points when working with young children on the topic of sound. Children can explore how far the sound of a clock, a telephone or an alarm will travel. You could discuss with the children when a sound becomes a 'noise' – is this just to do with whether we like the sound or not, or is it about loudness? Children enjoy exploring the qualities of sound to create a certain atmosphere or to describe the movement of an animal or character. A good starting point for this might be to listen to a recording of Prokofiev's 'Peter and the Wolf', in which every character has a different theme tune, or to watch an episode of 'Scooby Doo' in which sound effects are used to create atmospheres of fear or suspense.

Stories such as Jill Tomlinson's 'The Owl Who Was Afraid of the Dark' (1998) or Martin Waddell's 'Can't You Sleep Little Bear?' (2001) can be used to discuss children's fears and link the topic to that of light. For younger children, creating a dark area such as a cave can give children first-hand experience of darkness and how the introduction of light enables them to see objects. Stories such as 'Dark, Dark Tale' by Ruth Brown can be used to set the context for young children. The cave could have curtains to open and let in the light from the classroom or children could use torches to help them find objects in the cave. Plenty of children's stories (for example Jill Murphy's 'Whatever Next!', 1995b), comics and films feature space travel. Turning the role-play area into a space-ship to visit the Moon or other planets like the bear in 'Whatever Next!' can engage children in discussion about, for example, whether it would be possible to travel to the Sun, or whether the Moon is closer than the stars.

Scientific process skills

Children enjoy exploring different ways of making sounds: with their bodies, with instruments and with objects around them. They can sort them into different types of sound, such as banging sounds or tinkly sounds, or sort them according to how the sound is made, for example, by shaking, plucking, scraping or blowing. They can explore ways of changing sounds by using instruments to make quiet or loud sounds. An investigation that develops children's observation skills (using their sense of hearing rather than sight) involves seeing how many instruments children can recognise when blindfolded, or matching opaque shakers with transparent ones containing the same types of object (e.g. split peas, sand, paper clips). Another use of the blindfold is to stand a blindfolded child in the middle of a group and see whether they can point to the direction from which they can hear different children make sounds such as single claps.

In the topic of light, sorting a collection of shiny and dull objects is a good way to help children develop their classification skills while challenging some of their ideas about reflections and sources of light. The collection could include curved and flat surfaces such as spoons and mirrors, smooth and crumpled foils and different papers. Children can be encouraged to predict and hypothesise, using questions such as:

What happens when you shine the torch on the shiny objects?

Why can you see your reflection in some things and not in others?

Another aspect of the study of light that lends itself to practical enquiry is shadows. After some practical experience and exploratory activities, such as going for a 'shadow hunt' around the outdoor area of the setting, children can be asked to draw their own shadows and those formed by other objects such as football posts or fences.

The topic of space tends not to lend itself to 'fair test'-type investigations and is probably best taught through a series of illustrative activities or 'pattern-seeking' (Goldsworthy et al. 2000). Perhaps the most common pattern-seeking enquiry undertaken during this topic is an activity in which children place a stick in the playground on a sunny day, marking the position and length of the shadow every hour using either chalk directly onto the asphalt or marker pen on a large sheet of paper. Smyth (2007) advocates paired tutoring between older and younger pupils, and records and example of a ten-year-old child working with a 6-year-old to observe changes in shadow length in the playground over the course of a day.

EYFS and Key Stage 1 curriculum links

Sound, light and space are not specifically mentioned in the Statutory Framework for the Early Years Foundation Stage (DfE 2012). However, within the EYFS Specific Area of 'Expressive arts and design', children are to: 'sing songs, make music and dance, and experiment with ways of changing them. This could include using different instruments to create different textures of sound – made by plucking, banging, scraping or blowing – or using their voice and body to make sounds of different volumes and pitches, laying the foundations for the understanding of amplitude and frequency in later study.' The same Specific Area also requires children to: 'use and explore a variety of materials, tools and techniques, experimenting with colour ... Clearly colour is closely related to light, so children's experiences of mixing colours or applying different types of colour in their making will develop their intuitive understanding of how light reflects off surfaces.'

At Key Stage 1, the revised National Curriculum in England (2013) is more explicit in its reference to sound and light. For example, pupils should be taught to:

- observe and name a variety of sources of sound, noticing that we hear with our ears;
- recognise that sounds get fainter as the distance from the sound source increases.

Several of the activities referred to above under Contexts for Learning would address these statements. Similarly in relation to light, pupils should be taught to:

- observe and name a variety of sources of light, including electric lights, flames and the Sun;
- associate shadows with a light source being blocked by something.

By doing a 'light source' walk around the school and by experimenting with a shadow stick in the playground (see above), children will be able to develop their understanding of these areas. Interestingly, given that the physical science coverage within the revised National Curriculum at Key Stage 1 is generally lower than in the previous (1999) version, it is surprising to see some statements in the Programme of Study that could be seen as directly relevant to the study of the Earth and beyond (space). Pupils should be taught to:

- observe changes across the four seasons;
- observe and describe weather associated with the seasons and how day length varies.

Many of the changes children will notice when studying the topic of 'seasons' will relate to the natural world – leaves changing, plants growing, tadpoles hatching – but they may also notice how the period of daylight is longer in summer and the Sun appears higher in the sky (shorter shadows in the playground). This can then lay the foundations for the later understanding of how the tilt of the Earth's axis causes seasonal changes (a concept not currently covered until secondary school).

Intervening to develop young children's understanding

Listening walks, discussing sounds in the environment, listening to tapes and using musical instruments can provide children with lots of experience that will extend their awareness of sounds. Playing a version of 'Kim's game' (where a set of objects is displayed to be memorised, then one removed and the question asked 'Which object is now missing?') with sounds encourages listening skills and helps children to learn to identify sound when they cannot see the source. Twerton Infant School in Bath visited 'the egg' children's theatre to see 'Petrushka' as a puppet performance. Back at school, they worked together to create their own performance using puppets and musical instruments they had made. The scientific learning from the project included the production of sounds using different vibrating objects, altering the pitch by changing the length of vibration. Brunton and Thornton (2010) suggest making a musical washing line using a selection of kitchen tools made from different materials, such as wooden spoons, metal ladles, plastic tongs and small pans and cups. Children can choose which ones to suspend on the line and describe the differences in the sounds they make.

If the classroom can be darkened, children can observe that it is more difficult to see any object unless it emits its own light. Gradually increasing the light in the room can illustrate how we need light to see. Alternatively, objects can be placed in a box with a lid and a peephole on the side. Looking through the hole reveals darkness until the lid is lifted. When children are in the playground on a sunny day, asking probing questions about their observations can help extend their understanding of shadows:

> What can you tell me about your shadow?
>
> Where does the shadow begin?
>
> How can you change the shape of your shadow?
>
> How do you think it is made?

By illuminating translucent items from below on a 'light table' children can be encouraged to see the familiar differently. Giving them coloured light filters to look through or making their own 'colour telescopes' can further extend their experience. Children can be prompted into new patterns of play by presenting them with materials in new ways, for example, by changing the contents of the water tray to promote new thinking. A 'sparkly water tray' contains a range of objects small and large, some of which float, some sink, some reflect and some refract the light creating changing colours, leading to a range of questions and observations such as: what do these things do when they get wet? This wet mirror is a bit like the one in our bathroom that gets 'steamy'. Is this the same tinsel that was on the Christmas tree?

Young children will come up with a number of fascinating explanations for the difference between 'day' and 'night'. Here are a few examples, drawn from the SPACE research project (Osborne et al. 1993) and Year 1 children at Chandag Infants School, Keynsham, together with commentary:

> Night happens because we need to sleep. (*A typically 'egocentric' argument; external events are related to our needs.*)

The Sun goes down and down ... under the hills and you can't see the Sun and then the Sun pops back up when it's morning. (*An anthropomorphic idea of the Sun 'hiding' from us.*)

The Sun goes down and the Moon pops up on our world, the Earth. (*This common notion – that the Sun and Moon are in some way interchangeable – derives from the remarkable coincidence that, although the Sun and Moon are very different sizes and different distances from us, they appear exactly the same size in the sky. This idea can easily be challenged on a clear day when both Sun and Moon are visible simultaneously.*)

The Sun gets covered up by clouds. (*Based on very selective use of evidence!*)

It's morning in a different place when it's night-time here because it's a different country and the Sun can't go everywhere. (*This idea is moving towards a more scientific understanding by relating day and night to the apparent movement of the Sun. This child is probably ready to be introduced to the notion that it is the Earth that spins, giving the appearance that the Sun moves.*)

Modelling the Earth, Sun and Moon with plasticine is an effective strategy for eliciting children's ideas about the shapes of these bodies. The Earth may well be represented as a sphere, whereas some children may model the Sun as a flat disc (as it appears in the sky) or the Moon as a 'banana' shape (deriving from standardised depictions of a crescent Moon in story books). To help children relate day and night to the rotation of the Earth, we can seat them one at a time in a swivel chair while another child first walks clockwise around the chair shining a torch at its occupant. This simulates what appears to be happening from our Earth-centred view – that the Sun moves around us, and when it is behind us (on the other side of the Earth) we experience night. The seated child needs to keep their head still and describe what they observe (the light from the torch moving across their field of view, then disappearing). Next, the child in the chair rotates anti-clockwise while the torch-bearer stays still – this should produce a similar observation from the chair occupant.

Learning story 12.1

Exploring sounds

Brunton and Thornton (2010: 156) report the following learning story related to sound:

> Alex and Ben are playing outside. They pick up two sticks and use them to tap the side of the wooden shed. They create a banging noise which amuses them greatly. Their key person watches what they are doing and suggests they explore other places outside with their sticks to find out what sounds they can make. The boys find a metal bucket with a small volume of water in the bottom. When they hit the bucket it makes a loud ringing sound and the water in the bottom vibrates.

Learning story 12.2

Light and colour

Nursery worker Angela Millar at Oak Tree Day Nursery, Bath, works with 'John' (age 3.6) 'William' (3.5) and 'Simon' (2.10) on a guided exploration activity in the water tray. Through the new experience she has provided, she seeks to explore each child's understanding about light sources and colour, using a range of question-types:

- *attention-focusing:* drawing children's attention to a feature of the experience or phenomena they might have overlooked;
- *challenging:* inviting children to take a second look and rethink their initial statement.

The children take it in turns to fill the water tray from a jug:

Angela: If you watch, it's splashing as it hits the bottom of the tray. (*Attention-focusing question.*

As the tray begins to fill, the stream of water from the jug begins to make small bubbles.

John: Look.
Angela: What can you see? (*Responding to child's initiative.*)
John: Bubbles, little bubbles.

Angela invites each child in turn to choose a food colour and add a few drops to a jug of water. First Simon adds some blue colour to the jug. It forms a dense cloud of colour, beginning to diffuse throughout the water.

Angela: What's happening?
Simon: It's gone blue.
Angela: Is it all blue? (*Challenge, inviting a second look.*) What do we have to do to make it all blue? (*Prompt to action.*)
John: Mix it up.

Simon mixes the water in the jug, then carries it to the water tray.

Angela: What do you think will happen to the blue water when we tip it in? (*Person-centred question, inviting prediction.*)
Children: Don't know.

They pour it in, then add a jug of green water.

Angela: What colours can you see?
John: Green and blue.
Simon: There's a rainbow in it.
Angela: Is there? What colours can you see? (*Picking up on child's interest.*)

Simon: Blue and orange and red and yellow.
John: It's lots of colours.
Angela: What colours did we put in? What colour have we ended up with? (*Trying to get children to make the link between the component colours and the mixture.*)
John: Yellow.

Angela gives the children a torch each, and encourages them to shine it on to the surface of the water.

Angela: Have a go at shining it up from the bottom.

The children look at the light coming up through the water. Angela adds some more colour and it begins to swirl in the tray.

William: Ooo look at this one, it's got a swirly line all around here. (*See Figure 12.1.*)
Angela: See if you can follow the pattern with the torch. (*Encouragement to kinaesthetic learning.*)

John returns with a 'sparkler' he has made from silver paper (it is mid-November).

John: See if you can light this sparkler . . . (*Shines the torch on it.*) You can!

John starts to wave the sparkler over the water tray.

Angela: Can you see the sparkler in the water?
John: I can see the light in it. (*There was a dim reflection of the sparkler, but the torch was much brighter.*)
Angela: Can you see your sparkler underneath the water?

John puts the sparkler under the water tray. Children agree that it is hard to see.

Angela: Shine the torch on John's sparkler. Can you see it now? (*Challenging the idea that the 'shiny' paper sparkler might be a source of light; they can only see it when a true source of light shines on it.*)

Simon and John start to shine their torches onto the wall, bowl and other objects.

John: I can shine it on my head, on your head.
Angela: Can you shine it through the apron? (*Challenge, bringing out concept of translucency.*)
Angela: We're going to have a go outside in a minute. Then when it's dark later we're going to have another go. See if it's different.

Commentary
Although Angela initiated this activity, she was quick to pick up on the children's focus of attention and allow the exploration to move in an unanticipated direction. When John introduced the 'sparkler' she was aware that he was making the

connection between torches and fireworks, so used this opportunity to probe his understanding about sources of light. By inviting him to wave the sparkler underneath the water tray and then to illuminate it with a torch she was challenging his idea that the 'shiny' paper might itself be a source of light. Such interventions require careful observation of children to determine the direction of their focus; an awareness of children's 'alternative frameworks' (Driver 1983) in the concept area concerned; and a certain level of subject knowledge and understanding on the part of the practitioner.

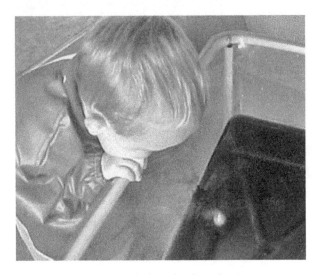

FIGURE 12.1 Shining a torch through coloured water

Learning story 12.3

The seasons

Joanne Hobson at Point Chevalier Primary School, Auckland, New Zealand, uses the story 'Nanny Mihi's Garden' by Melanie Drewery – set in a Maori context – to initiate a topic about the seasons with her Year 1 class. She starts by asking questions to help the children make links with their own experiences. 'Who has a vegetable garden? Where is the vegetable garden in the school? Who knows what's growing?' These questions help to establish the connection between plant growth and seasonal change. She then moves on to a card sorting activity involving a number of pictures of 'everyday' things such as woolly hats and ice creams, together with more 'scientific' links such as shadows, the Sun and night-time. Children are asked 'Does the card have anything to do with the seasons?' and to sort their cards collaboratively into 'yes', 'no', and 'maybe' piles. Next they walk round the room to look at other groups' choices and discuss their sorting decisions as a whole class. Finally, Joanne asks the children what they would like to find out about the seasons. Their questions revealed a real thirst for scientific knowledge that had been stimulated by both the story and card-sorting activity:

What do seeds need to grow? How do plants grow?
How come we have seasons?
Why do we have four seasons?
Why do we have months of the year?
Why do we have the Sun? Moon? stars?
Does every country in the world have seasons?
Why are lambs born in the Spring?
When does Spring come?
Why do we have a sun and a moon? How does day become night?

Joanne's creative approach to the beginning of this topic has generated enough questions to last the rest of the term!

Learning story 12.4

Day and night

Danieka Rivers at Point Chevalier Primary School, Auckland, uses a set of images from the Internet printed as A4 photographs for her 5–6-year-old children to examine as the starting point for a topic on 'day and night'. The photos include one

FIGURE 12.2 Modelling the movement of the Earth and Sun using a swivel chair and torch

of Auckland city at night, the Earth seen from space; sunrise over the sea; the Moon in the daytime; and the sun streaming through windows and casting shadows. These beautiful images immediately engage the children's attention as they discuss them, first in pairs, then in groups of four. They stimulate some very thoughtful responses:

Not everyone has night at the same time, because the world rotates round.
Sometimes it's a bit dark in the daytime, so it must be getting ready for the night.
Sometimes the Sun ain't out and it's raining so the Moon can shine.
In the morning time it's time for the Sun to come up, but the Moon needs to go down.
In the morning there might be nearly no Sun and then the Sun comes out and it gets brighter and then the evening then it starts all over again.

These statements vary in their degree of scientific accuracy, but all demonstrate the careful reasoning of which young children are capable. In order to probe their ideas further, Danieka asks them to draw 'a picture of how we get day and night,' and to explain their drawing to their partner. She follows this by seating the children in a large circle and inviting pairs to come and model the movement of the Earth and Sun using a swivel chair and torch, with other children taking it in turns to direct the 'movement of the spheres' and relate this to day and night (Figure 12.2). Finally, children are asked individually to come up and explain how day and night happen in different places on Earth using a globe and an overhead projector.

ICT links

Children in Key Stage 1 can use dataloggers to record sound and light levels. Connecting the datalogger to the computer allows simple visual representations of these real-time measurements, for example, a bar that goes up and down in response to sound levels, or a disc that becomes darker or lighter in colour in response to children putting their fingers over the light sensor. This will then give them a sense of an electronic measurement of a phenomenon they can also experience using their senses. ICT can offer additional possibilities for exploring seasonal changes in the outside world, for example, pictures taken by children before it rained, video of the class when they were playing outside, live links to web cams such as those provided by parks and zoos, simulations of day and night, summer and winter.

Related designing and making activities

Making musical instruments (shakers, elastic band 'guitars', sandpaper scrapers etc.) is a good way to reinforce children's understanding of the different ways in

FIGURE 12.3 Exploring a 'dark cave'

which sounds can be made. To help children understand how opaque materials block light, they can make simple shadow puppets. Adding some coloured cellophane can produce 'coloured shadows' enabling them to explore the concept of translucency. To experience darkness as the absence of light, building a dark cave in the classroom or setting is a lovely activity. For example, Reception teachers Di Rhodes and Margaret Harrison at Newbridge Primary School, Bath, based their science and technology topic around the book 'Can't You Sleep Little Bear?' by Martin Waddell. Di and the Reception team wanted to introduce children to the concept of darkness as the absence of light, and to allay some of their fears about the dark. They hoped that through building a class cave in the role-play area (Figure 12.3), children would realise that they need light to see (in the form of a torch or hole in the cave). These scientific concepts were reinforced through children designing dark caves in shoeboxes where Little Bear could sleep. The opportunity to engage children in talking about the caves they were designing and making enabled these teachers to probe understanding and relate the concept of darkness to other experiences, such as bonfire night. Selecting materials for the caves prompted discussion about whether colours could be seen in the dark, and the finished models enabled children to test their ideas about what they would be able to see.

Summary

In this chapter we have explored some of the themes and contexts available to practitioners when considering how to help children develop their awareness of sounds and light sources in their environments, such as playing with and making musical instruments, or looking at translucent objects on a light box. We have argued that the common Early Years topic of 'seasons' can be used to explore children's awareness of the Sun as a source of light and the way in which its position in the sky and the shadows it casts change over the year. We have seen how all three concept areas feature in the National Curriculum at Key Stage 1, while the EYFS area of Expressive Arts and Design includes the requirement for children to experiment with music and colour. We have looked at ways in which practitioners can challenge children's ideas about light sources and darkness through making 'dark caves' and how discussing photos and simple modelling activities can be used to explore concepts related to day and night. Overall, light, sound and space are exciting phenomena, which can produce a sense of wonder in children and lend themselves well to a thematic approach.

Discussion points

- Should discussion of the seasons in the Early Years classroom be limited to changes in the natural world, or should it begin to engage children in thinking about the relative movement of Earth and Sun, which causes seasonal changes?

- Why are shadows and reflections particularly difficult phenomena for young children to grasp and how would you help them develop a more scientific understanding of these concepts?

Moving on – transitions in Early Years science and technology

Alan Howe

Purpose of this chapter

After reading this chapter you should have an understanding of:

- the importance of considering the transition arrangements between Early Years settings and primary schools;
- the impact that moving from the foundation stage (EYFS) to Key Stage 1 can have on children's learning;
- the ways in which schools can manage transition effectively, in the context of science.

Introduction

Children experience many transitions in the ages 3–7: from home to a school environment, from play-based learning to more formal teaching, from 'areas of learning' to the subject-based National Curriculum. Widespread research evidence suggests that many young children might find the transition to primary school confusing as they move out of an environment of autonomy into one of conformity. Drawing upon research and new case studies, this chapter will consider the nature of progression in science through the 3 to 7 age range, explore the tensions faced by teachers in the light of sometimes conflicting requirements and will conclude with suggestions for practice to reduce children's experiences of discontinuities. This chapter will mostly focus on the transition between the end of the foundation stage and start of Key Stage 1 but will also consider the ways in which children can be supported in making a transition to Key Stage 2 ways of working in Year 2 (age 7).

The significance of 'transition'

There are a number of ways of exploring transition in education. Here we use the term to indicate a significant change in educational approach that is likely to impact on the child. In practice this might involve a change of teacher, environment, routine or a transfer to another school. It will always require that the child must *adapt* to new expectations and relationships.

We know that children go through many transitions in their lives and that most children cope well with them. Some children, particularly those who are vulnerable in some way, such as those with learning difficulties or who are 'summer born', will find coping more difficult. Alexander (2010: 370) suggests that 'effects of transition may be cumulative – that the legacy of a badly managed move early on could damage children's abilities to make successful transition throughout their school career'. For all these reasons, we need to consider carefully the ways in which transitional experiences can be managed so that negative impacts are minimised. This requires some thought and action by those on both sides of the transition.

You might have seen some examples of good practice in managing transitions, but there is evidence to indicate that transition from the EYFS into Key Stage 1 is not always well handled. Research from Sanders et al. (2005) suggests that there is a danger that the move to Year 1 may not be sufficiently recognised by school staff as a time of anxiety for children and their parents, while Ofsted (2007) reported that only two out of 10 local authorities they surveyed had clear guidance for schools on managing transition from the Reception class to Key Stage 1. Alexander (2010: 370) argues that concerns about transition have been 'glossed over'. Furthermore, Fisher (2010) notes that national data gleaned from Foundation Stage Profiles consistently show that significant numbers of children move into Year 1 without achieving all the Early Learning Goals, suggesting many children will need support to achieve within the framework of the National Curriculum.

In the next section we explore some of the factors that can contribute to a discontinuity at this point in children's education.

Exploring the differences

It is well documented that there have been differences between the practices seen in Early Years settings and those in schools (see Sanders et al. 2005 for a full review). It is not established in the literature, however, that a child's *needs* change between their 5th and 6th birthdays. Research into child development suggests the contrary – that five- and six-year-olds are likely to learn in very similar ways, and that there will be a similar range of cognitive abilities across any given group of five- or six-year-olds (Piaget 1929, Kuhn 2011).

There continues to be a vigorous debate about the extent to which pre-school education should be formal or informal, often typified by the assertion that an Early Years curriculum should be 'play' based. Educational practices are different because they are based on differing philosophies, which are often based on strongly held beliefs. In 2003, twenty-one eminent Early Years experts made this statement:

> In early childhood settings, by folklore and tradition, areas of knowledge are not normally taught in subjects; more often in themes, topics or areas of experience. Children and adults 'everyday' activities are used as the basis for planning. Practical 'experiential' learning is prioritised over abstract, disembedded knowledge. Sensory experiences are valued. Children are encouraged to make choices in what they learn at least for some part of each day ... Debates about the relative merits of subjects or 'developmentally appropriate practice' approaches to curricula for under-fives have been stronger on assertion than evidence.
>
> (British Educational Research Association Special
> Interest Group 2003: 21–2)

These experts seem to be suggesting that there is lack of empirical evidence to suggest children learn in one way rather than another. The major empirically-based Effective Provision of Pre-School Education Project (Sylva et al. 2004) found that effective pedagogy includes interaction traditionally associated with the term 'teaching', and identified that the most effective pedagogy combines both teaching and providing freely chosen yet potentially instructive play activities. Conversely, Fisher (2010) notes that there is no research evidence to suggest Year 1 children learn most effectively when sitting for long periods listening to teachers, watching them demonstrate concepts and carrying out exclusively adult planned activities.

To summarise this debate, it could be said that there is effective practice occurring on both sides of this transition, but teachers should look critically at their assumptions and beliefs about how four-, five- and six-year-olds learn. It cannot be denied however, that differences in practice exist across many settings. Sanders et al. (2005: 85) found the majority of Year 1 teachers they surveyed reported that there were 'considerable differences' between the learning environments in Reception and Year 1. The main differences reported by Year 1 teachers were that there was:

- less space;
- less play equipment/resources;
- less opportunity for outside play;
- less adult support;
- fewer child-initiated activities.

In the light of the debate outlined above it is not surprising that teachers report on feeling 'torn' between conflicting expectations (Fisher 2010) when teaching this age group.

Where teachers need to make decisions regarding pedagogy and assessment, tensions can be identified. The sorts of tensions teachers experience are outlined in Box 13.1. In the following case study, we discuss how two teachers identify and resolve tensions related to their practice around the transition 'zone' of EYFS and Key Stage 1. Jae is an Early Years teacher with a class of Reception and Year 1 children while Julia, who until recently taught Key Stage 2 children, now has a mixed Year 1 and 2 class. As participants in a professional development project 'See the science' (see Chapter 1) they had the opportunity to explore their science teaching and in particular focus on the ways in which they use questioning during science activities. They were supported by the project and talked to each other on many occasions about the ways in which they could develop their practice and learn from each other.

Both teachers agreed to recordings being made of their science teaching during the autumn term. They then reflected on their use of classroom talk, particularly their approach to questioning. A theoretical framework of communicative

Box 13.1

Possible tensions for the Early Years teacher

Teaching the child as a 'whole' person ↔ Teaching the child as a 'pupil'
Organising individual or small-group learning ↔ Organising whole-class learning
Child control of learning ↔ Teacher control of learning
Flexible/fluid groups ↔ Fixed groups (e.g. ability)
Observation-based assessment ↔ Assessment based on written evidence
Topic/integrated curriculum ↔ Subject/discrete curriculum
Immediate contexts for learning ↔ Distant contexts for learning
Learning from concrete experiences ↔ Learning from abstract experiences
Play-based learning ↔ Activity-based learning
Child-initiated curriculum ↔ Specified curriculum
Free flow days ↔ Timetabled lessons

approach (Mortimer and Scott 2003; see Box 3.4, p. 42) was used to analyse a number of interactions they had with children during science or 'science rich' classroom activity. The analysis highlighted that, as might be expected, the two teachers had somewhat different repertoires of questioning that had been developed from their prior teaching experience.

Jae, with a depth of experience in Early Years practice and strength in children's language development, tended to emphasise and value children's expressive language during recorded sessions. He would often praise children for introducing new vocabulary to a discussion and reiterate that vocabulary to demonstrate its use in context. He was happy to be led by children's ideas and interests during 'science rich' activities, even if that took them in an unintended and sometimes non-scientific direction. This approach is clearly addressing a central aim of an Early Years foundation curriculum, which requires that children learn to 'express themselves effectively' and 'develop their own narratives and explanations by connecting ideas or events' (DfE 2012). However, Jae was interested in extending his repertoire of classroom talk to make more use of 'dialogic-interactive' strategies; to explore science concepts, generate new meanings, and pose genuine questions (Mortimer and Scott 2003). He was also aware that there were subject-specific demands in the Year 1 curriculum that needed to be included, such as recognising and naming the leaf, flower, stem and root of flowering plants. This led Jae to consider carefully the ways in which he spoke to the children, the vocabulary he introduced and the questions he posed to facilitate science learning. He commented:

> The practitioner . . . [must] be ready to challenge children in their thinking. This is most effective in an interactive-dialogic approach which gives the children and the practitioner equal weighting in the discussions . . . however, [they]must always be ready to interject the correct vocabulary and scientific concepts when they arise, thus tilting the conversation towards a more interactive-authoritative slant as the children begin to gain a more scientific mind-set .
>
> (Jae Munroe, personal correspondence, 9 July 2013)

In a recorded session where children explored the plant life around the school playground, Jae focuses on plant structures:

> Shall we pull the flower up and see the roots? Can you see them? Have a look . . . careful look at those roots, what can you see when you look at those roots?
>
> Can you see [the roots], they're really long as well, look at this one here, look at this one. What can you tell me about this one?
>
> So what other parts of the plant can you see, apart from the roots, now?

Here Jae introduces and reiterates the word 'roots' while drawing children's attention to the features of the roots he wishes them to notice. It is a subtle shift from his approach earlier in the year where he was more inclined to be led by the children's interests and would build on their utterances.

Here are Jae's reflections on the practitioner's role during this phase of education:

> There is a definite cognitive transition as the children progress through the Early Years and Year 1 where practical science-rich activities, which are mainly exploratory in nature at the beginning of the year, become more formal as the children mature in their ideas and development. Here, more emphasis is placed upon the key scientific concepts and vocabulary so that they are able to assimilate the awe and wonder of finding out new things through exploring. The joy of lifting a plant from its pot and seeing the secret world of its underground parts is then built on, in a meaningful context, explaining that those 'stringy bits' which look like hairs, are actually called 'roots' and they have a fundamental role to play in the growing and development of the plant. In the same way, the metaphorical roots of the children's knowledge are nurtured, watered and fed so that they can grow into scientists with both the awe and wonder of discovering new things, coupled with the scientific knowledge and vocabulary to put meaningful factual contexts to their observations and findings.
>
> The practitioner, as an aide to the children's learning, must therefore be aware of this transition and adapt their repertoire of questioning skills to accommodate this. They must be sensitive to the excitement that the children have in discovering new things in the science-rich environment, which is ably created by the practitioner, but be ready to challenge children in their thinking.
>
> An experienced, sensitive practitioner must be able to judge the developmental ability of their cohort and be ready to adapt, assess and implement their repertoire of questioning according to the needs of the children. Bringing the correct terminology in too early may confuse the children and dampen their natural curiosity; interject too late and the key concepts and vocabulary will lose their impetus and the impact of putting a name to a concept or object will be lost. Thus an experienced practitioner will know when best to interject or stand back and always through this process, they must be aware of the language and questioning skills that they use.
>
> (Jae Munroe, personal correspondence, 9 July 2013)

In the class next door, Julia was working with her Year 1 and 2 class. Coming from five years of teaching in Key Stage 2, Julia was hoping to widen her repertoire of planning and teaching strategies to incorporate those considered appropriate to Early Years practice. After listening to a transcript of a recorded science lesson, which she felt was rather over-directed and focused on outcomes, in conversation, Julia resolved to:

build on children's responses, for example, one child had an idea that could have been investigated further but I was driven by the content or plan of the lesson. [I want] to take risks [and] to think about making the science curriculum more child-led . . . building on from their interests and questions/ thoughts. Allow children to explore, find other ways of recording.

(Julia Holder, 16 November 2012)

During the subsequent terms, Julia taught a number of activities that progressively gave children more control over the direction of their learning. In one lesson the children were sorting large pictures of living and non-living things. This provided a rich stimulus for a range of discussions, for example on gas exchange:

Child: I know how the trees, how . . . umm . . . plants help us to . . .
Julia: How do they help us?
Child: They produce oxygen.
Julia: They do, you're quite right. Well done, they do help us; they do help produce oxygen which we breathe, well done. What's oxygen?
Child: It's what . . . it's the air that we breathe in.
Julia: That's quite right, well done.
Child: We breathe umm . . . trees breathe . . . umm . . . us and trees are the opposite.
Julia: How are we the opposite?
Child: I can't remember the other one . . . umm . . . oxygen.
Julia: Are you thinking about another gas called carbon dioxide, is it carbon dioxide are you thinking about?
Child: Because we breathe out carbon dioxide and breathe in oxygen and that . . . and trees breathe out oxygen and breathe in . . .
Julia: Carbon dioxide. Do you know what they do with the carbon dioxide, with that special gas, do you know what they do?
Child: Does the oxygen come from the trees and the plants or does it just come . . . does it just come? Was it made or does it just come from the plants?
Julia: That's a good question isn't it?

It was interesting to note that although children were given more opportunity to develop their own thinking, this didn't lead to any less scientific talk. Other topics discussed during this lesson were photosynthesis, snail trails and predators, and the function of the human ribcage. It seems here that what Julia initially considered a more 'Early Years' approach to questioning actually led to more in-depth scientific learning as children drew on their own knowledge and articulated their thinking. In addition Julia achieved the objectives for the lesson (to distinguish between living and non-living things) although she didn't reach them by the route anticipated. After reflecting on her science teaching for the year Julia commented:

I recognised that I was focused on outcomes and I didn't always allow opportunities for building on from the responses or observations of the children. After some reflection, I realised I needed to make the science curriculum more child-led, to allow children to explore and to encourage dialogue and discussion. Through doing this, the children were heavily involved, engaged and they felt at ease to impart their knowledge or to ask questions. This classroom talk stimulated and extended their thinking and allowed for a wide range of scientific discussion . . . I feel I have discovered how classroom talk can lead to a greater level of engagement and how it can extend learning and depth of understanding.

(Julia Holder, personal correspondence, 14 July 2013)

In summary, the case studies show how two teachers with contrasting backgrounds in Primary education – coming from 'opposite directions' – have worked with each other and other colleagues to add to their repertoire of teaching approaches, one becoming more 'Early Years' and the other a little more 'formal'. Both teachers found that by paying attention to the kinds of talk going on during science activities they could to some degree resolve a tension at the heart of teaching during this phase of education – building on children's learning while at the same time moving them towards curricular objectives.

Curriculum (dis)continuity

There have been concerns expressed about the curriculum and pedagogical continuity between the EYFS and Key Stage 1 in England (Quick et al. 2002). Although these two curricula possess some common themes, it is questioned whether their commonalities are sufficient to enable them to be interwoven coherently (Ellis 2002; Quick et al. 2002). The National Curriculum documentation sets out a definition for the subject of science (DfE 2013: 144). With its emphatic reference to the 'disciplines' of biology, chemistry and physics it suggests that the authors have deposited into primary schools a traditional and arguably constraining notion of the subject, which fails to recognise, for those just starting formal school, the inter-disciplinary nature of much of their early learning, or reflect the ways in which children have acquired scientific knowledge to this point. There is clearly a considerable discontinuity between an Early Years approach and National Curriculum expectations, therefore demanding a good deal of interpretation on the part of the Key Stage 1 teacher if they are to ensure children don't find their Primary 'science' far beyond their current understanding. Discussed later in this chapter is the concept of 'bridging' across curricula and pedagogies. There is a recognition in both EYFS and Key Stage 1 documents that the best way for children to come to an understanding of the ways in which science is conducted is through 'practical activity', so ensuring a consistent pedagogy, one familiar to the five- year-old. The curriculum 'bridge' requires more careful construction.

There is scope for colleagues from the two phases to find common ground when planning activities. References in the EYFS to 'exploring', 'experienc[ing]', 'develop[ing] ideas', and 'developing strategies for doing things' can be equated with Key Stage 1 foci of 'experiencing and observing phenomena', being 'curious', 'ask[ing] questions about what they notice' and 'using different types of scientific enquiry'. The two curricula are enabling an investigative approach where children's questions and observations are a start point for enquiry. It was Johnston (1996) who first highlighted how exploration in Early Year's science is an essential developmental precursor to more formal understandings of scientific enquiry. The curricula are enabling that progression to occur by ensuring observation, talking and thinking remain central to both pedagogies.

Where the curricula outline concepts to be learned, continuities can again be acknowledged. The EYFS (DfE 2012: 7) identifies the need to 'know about similarities and differences' where Key Stage 1 formalises that into 'notic[ing] patterns and relationships' and develops learning in specific science-rich contexts such as the 'classification of common plants and animals' and 'compar[ing] and grouping together a variety of everyday materials on the basis of their simple physical properties' (DfE 2013: 148). Other examples of this continuity of conceptual development include the EYFS suggestion that there should be talk about 'how environments might vary' (DfE 2012: 7) where Key Stage 1 science requires the formal study of habitats, also the EYFS guidance that children should 'talk about change' is developed in Key Stage 1, where science concepts of night and day, growth, reproduction, change of shape etc. all offer specific opportunity to build on those initial conversations.

There are other aspects of the Key Stage 1 curriculum that offer considerable challenge to young children who may not have experienced ways of working demanded of them by the end of the Foundation stage. Such examples include 'identify and name a variety of common animals that are birds, fish, amphibians, reptiles, mammals and invertebrates', 'drawing diagrams showing the parts of different plants and trees' (DfE 2013: 148–50), 'observe changes across the four seasons' and 'observe and describe weather associated with the seasons and how day length varies' (DfE 2013: 150). Key Stage 1 teachers will need to be alert to the conceptual steps that such demands require – drawing diagrams is a considerable leap into abstract representation, identifying and naming animals suggests the need for a range of relevant experiences and good command of language, while observing change across seasons requires a relatively sophisticated conception of time passing. The previous chapters in this book should offer some guidance to teachers on how to develop these advanced concepts in specific contexts. The draft curriculum does offer comment on the importance of ensuring children are secure in their learning before moving on:

> Insecure, superficial understanding will not allow genuine progression:
> pupils may struggle at key points of transition . . . build up serious miscon-
> ceptions, and/or have significant difficulties in understanding higher-order
> content.
>
> (DfE 2013: 144)

Again, the broadly 'constructivist' approach of earlier chapters suggest pedagogies that would minimise the dangers of moving on without a secure
foundation.

Resolutions

Teachers are well used to resolving, or living with, tensions in their professional
lives. The reconciling of tensions can often lead to creative solutions. In this
chapter we have identified a number of tensions associated with changes to
curriculum and pedagogy. There are a number of ways in which schools and
settings can work together to ensure tensions are productive rather than
damaging to children's progress.

The consensus that emerges from research into transfer and transition is that,
in order to prevent problems arising, action needs to be taken at five levels. Barber
(1999) identifies these as five *bridges* that can serve to span the gap between two
schools. These bridges are:

- Administrative: involving formal liaison between schools at senior management level in order to establish and maintain common and complementary
  processes.
- Social and Personal: focusing on the development of links between pupils,
  parents and the adults around them.
- Curriculum: improving the continuity and progression across transition
  points.
- Pedagogy: considering how teachers teach, countering stereotypes of practice.
- Autonomy and management of learning: empowering the learner, seeing
  them as an active participant in the process.

Sanders et al. (2005) make a number of useful recommendations. Schools that
encourage staff to adopt similar routines, expectations and activities in Reception
and Year 1 will minimise the need for special transition arrangements. Practices
that can be brought into line can include common planning formats and the
allocation of resources to enable children in Year 1 to experience some play-based
activities that give access to opportunities such as sand and water, construction

materials and outdoor learning. Schools should particularly consider the needs of younger/less mature children, those who are less able, have special educational needs or a disability or speak English as an additional language. They should be ready to provide these children with additional support during the transition to Year 1.

Learning and Teaching Scotland (2010) recommend shared planning, for example by developing a shared theme/project from pre-school to primary, in order to enable dialogue and a shared understanding of roles and progression between practitioners. Settings are also encouraged to capitalise on the uses of technology including sharing of online resources; the use of email for dialogue across settings; sharing of digital profiles (such as that currently produced by 2simple (www.2simple.com). In contrast, Broström's (2002) study on transition practices in Denmark show some scepticism on the part of the participants regarding collaboration on curriculum and teaching methods. Of the participants, 40 per cent did not think practices that had to do with coordination of the curriculum or the teaching to be good ideas. Broström found that pre-school teachers were less positive about transition activities involving reading each other's documents, having shared meetings on educational practices, and coordination of the curriculum. However, they assigned a high priority to having shared meetings with pre-schools, kindergarten classes and parents before school started. It would seem that schools should proceed with caution on implementing transition arrangements.

Ofsted (2007) note that evaluation of practice is needed. In their survey, the majority of settings had 'no written policy about transition, many relying on custom and practice, and only a few evaluated their arrangements' (p. 22). Fabian and Dunlop (2006) recommend that schools evaluate the management of transitions and transfers from the perspective of *all* participants, which will in turn help to question the assumptions of the setting.

Further measures, perhaps appropriate where weaknesses in transitional arrangements have been identified, could include transitional processes identified within a school improvement plan and the designation of a transitions coordinator in pre-school and primary (ideally this could be two colleagues). Sanders et al. (2005) conclude that transition is best considered as a process, not an event and that the best outcomes are found when 'conditions are similar, communication is encouraged, and the process of change takes place gradually over time'.

A final consideration: while teachers might each year improve their practice and make children's transitions a more positive experience, the children will move on once again to another transition. At the end of the phase on which this book focuses, children reach, arguably, a more significant transition as they move from Key Stage 1 to 2. Fisher (2010; drawing on Robinson 2008) reminds us that around age seven, children go through significant cognitive developments. They:

- are more logical;
- can think in their heads/in an abstract way;
- understand opposites;
- take others point of view (although seeing things in black and white);
- cooperate and play games with rules;
- enjoy projects, collecting.

This clearly has implications for the Year 2 and Year 3 teachers as they prepare their pupils to build upon concepts that have been developed in a very practical way through play-based and activity-based learning. Now some children will be able to appreciate concepts such as energy, forces, evolution and growth, which all require a level of abstract thinking. They will also increasingly enjoy debate and discussion, to challenge conventional thinking and to question evidence. The challenge that poses for the teacher must be the subject of another book.

Summary

In this chapter we have seen that when making the transition between an Early Years setting and a Primary school, children can be faced with a number of challenges. In the context of their learning in science, schools can take a number of actions to resolve the tensions between accommodating children's previous experiences and moving them on to new ways of learning. Individual teachers can learn from their colleagues in the 'other' phase – pedagogies seen as 'Early Years' and 'primary school' can both support children's learning in the 4–6 age phase and teachers may wish to consider their own assumptions about the most effective ways of teaching young children. The concept of 'five bridges' is useful when evaluating the arrangements for transition and developing a more coherent educational experience for the child.

Discussion points

- Do you hold any stereotypical ideas about teaching that happens in the phase (Early Years or Primary) that you have little experience of?
- Is it reasonable to expect teachers of 4–6-year-olds to have a good understanding of both Early Years and primary curriculum requirements?
- Which of the 'five bridges' is the most important?

References

Addison, N., Burgess, L., Steers, J. and Trowell, J. (2010) *Understanding Art Education: Engaging Reflexively with Practice.* London: Routledge.

Adey, P. and Shayer, M. (2002) 'Cognitive acceleration comes of age'. In M. Shayer and P. Adey (eds) *Learning Intelligence: Cognitive Acceleration Across the Curriculum from 5 to 15 years.* Buckingham: Open University Press, 1–17.

Adey, P., Nagy, F., Robertson, A., Serret, N. and Wadsworth, P. (2003) *Let's Think Through Science!* London: NFER Nelson.

Alborough, J. (1999) *Duck in the Truck.* London: HarperCollins.

Alexander, R. (2000) *Culture and Pedagogy: International Comparisons in Primary Education.* Oxford: Blackwell.

Alexander, R. (2008) *Towards Dialogic Teaching: Rethinking Classroom Talk*, 4th edn. Osgoodby: Dialogos.

Alexander, R. (ed) (2010) *Children, their World, their Education.* London: Routledge.

Armitage, R. and Armitage, D. (2007) *The Lighthouse Keeper's Lunch.* New York: Scholastic.

ASE (Association of Science Education) (2010) *Be Safe!* Hatfield: ASE.

Athey, B. (2007) *Extending Thought in Young Children: A Parent–Teacher Partnership*, 2nd edn. London: Paul Chapman.

Barber, M. (1999) 'Taking the tide at the flood: transforming the middle years of schooling'. *Education Today, 49*(4): 3–17.

Baynes, K. (1992) *Children Designing: Learning Design.* Occasional Paper No. 1. Loughborough: Loughborough University of Technology.

Bell, B.F. (1981) 'When is an animal not an animal?' *Journal of Biological Education, 15*(3), 213–18.

Bell, B. and Barker, M. (1982) 'Towards a scientific concept of "animal"'. *Journal of Biological Education, 16*(3): 197–200.

Berg, C.A. (1992) 'Viewing intellectual development'. In R.J. Sterberg and C.A. Berg (eds) *Intellectual Development.* Cambridge: Cambridge University Press, 1–15.

Berger, A. (1997) *Narratives in Popular Culture, Media, and Everyday Life.* London: Sage.

Berk, L.E. (2003) *Child Development.* Boston, MA: Pearson Education.

Bianchi, L. and Feasey, R. (2011) *Science Beyond the Classroom Boundaries for 3–7 Year Olds.* Maidenhead: Open University Press.

Black, P. and Wiliam, D. (2009) 'Developing the theory of formative assessment'. *Educational Assessment, Evaluation and Accountability, 21*: 5–31.

Black, P., Harrison, C., Marshall, B. and Wiliam, D. (2002) *Inside the Black Box: Raising Standards Through Classroom Assessment.* London: King's College London, School of Education.

Blair, D. (2009) 'The child in the garden: an evaluative review of the benefits of school gardening'. *The Journal of Environmental Education, 40*(2): 15–40.

Briggs, R. (1978) *The Snowman*. London: Hamish Hamilton.

Briggs, R. (1997) *Jim and the Beanstalk*. St Louis, MO: Turtleback books.

Bristol Natural History Consortium (2013) 'Bioblitz: discover your local wildlife' [online]. Available at: www.bnhc.org.uk/home/bioblitz/ (accessed 17/09/2013).

British Educational Research Association Special Interest Group (2003) *Research: Pedagogy, Curriculum and Adult Roles, Training and Professionalism* [online]. Available at: www.bera.ac. uk/system/files/beraearlyyearsreview31may03.pdf (accessed 11/09/2013).

British Nutrition Foundation (2013) 'Healthy eating week' [online]. Available at: www.nutrition. org.uk/nutritioninthenews/pressreleases/healthyeatingweek (accessed 15/09/2013).

Brodie, K. (2013) *Observation, Assessment and Planning in the Early Years: Bringing it All Together*. Maidenhead: Open University Press.

Broström, S. (2002) 'Communication and continuity in the transition from kindergarten to school'. In H. Fabian and A.W. Dunlop (eds) *Transitions in the Early Years: Debating Continuity and Progression for Children in Early Education*. London: RoutledgeFalmer, 52–63.

Brown, R. (1992) *Dark, Dark Tale*. Harmondsworth: Picture Puffin.

Bruce, T. (1994) 'Play, the universe and everything!' In J. Moyles (ed.) *The Excellence of Play*. Buckingham: Open University Press, 189–98.

Bruce, T. (2011) *Early Childhood Education*, 4th edn. London: Hodder Education.

Bruner, J.S. (1963) *The Process of Education*. London: Random House.

Bruner, J.S. (1990) *Acts of Meaning*. Cambridge, MA: Harvard University Press.

Bruner, J.S. (1996) *The Culture of Education*. Cambridge, MA: Harvard University Press.

Bruner, J.S., Jolly, A. and Sylva, K. (eds) (1976) *Play: Its Role in Development and Evolution*. Harmondsworth: Penguin.

Brunton, P. and Thornton, L. (2010) *Science in the Early Years: Building Firm Foundations from Birth to Five*. London: Sage.

Burningham, J. (1970) *Mr Gumpy's Outing*. London: Jonathan Cape.

Burningham, J. (1973) *Mr Gumpy's Motor Car*. London: Jonathan Cape.

Carr, M. and Lee, W. (2012) *Learning Stories Constructing Learner Identities in Early Education*. London: Sage.

Child, L. (2006) *Snow Is My Favourite and My Best*. New York: Penguin Young Readers.

Clark, A., McQuail, S. and Moss, P. (2003) *Exploring the Field of Listening to and Consulting with Young Children*. Nottingham: DfES Publications.

Collier, C., Davies, D., Howe, A. and McMahon, K. (2011) *The Primary Science and Technology Encyclopedia*. Abingdon: David Fulton.

Dahl, R. (1961) *James and the Giant Peach*. New York: Alfred Knopf.

Davies, D. (1996) 'Professional design and primary children'. *International Journal of Technology and Design Education 6*: 45–59.

Davies, D. (2011) *Teaching Science Creatively*. London: Routledge.

Davies, D., Jindal-Snape, D., Collier, C., Digby, R., Hay, P. and Howe, A. (2012) 'Creative learning environments in education – a systematic literature review'. *Thinking Skills and Creativity, 8*: 80–91.

de Boo, M. (2000) *Science 3–6: Laying the Foundations in the Early Years*. Hatfield: Association for Science Education.

DfE (Department for Education) (1998) *Health and Safety of Pupils on Educational Visits*. London: DfE.

DfE (2011) *The Importance of Teaching: The Schools White Paper 2010*. London: DfE.

DfE (2012) *Statutory Framework for the Early Years Foundation Stage*. London: DfE.

DfE (2013) *The National Curriculum in England: Framework Document*. London: DfE.

Dityatev, A. and El Husseini, A. (eds) (2006) *Molecular Mechanisms of Synaptogenesis*. New York: Springer.

Donaldson, J. (1999) *The Gruffalo*. London: Macmillan.

Donaldson, J. (2004) *The Gruffalo's Child*. London: Macmillan.

Donaldson, J. (2008) *Stick Man*. New York: Scholastic.

Donaldson, M. (1978) *Children's Minds*. Glasgow: Fontana.

Drake, J. (2009) *Planning for Children's Play and Learning*, 3rd edn. London: David Fulton.

Driver, R. (1983) *The Pupil as Scientist?* Milton Keynes: Open University Press.

Durmas, A. (2013) 'The effects of a food project on children's categorization skills'. *Social Behavior and Personality: An International Journal*, 41(6): 939-46.

Early Education (2012) *Development Matters in the Early Years Foundation Stage (EYFS)*. London: Early Education.

Edelman, G.M. (1992) *Bright Air, Brilliant Fire: On the Matter of the Mind*. New York: Basic Books.

Edwards, A. (2001) 'Researching pedagogy: a socio-cultural agenda'. *Pedagogy, Culture and Society*, 9 (2): 161–86.

Edwards, G. and Rose, J. (1994) 'Promoting a quality curriculum in the early years through action research: a case study'. *Early Years*, 15(1): 42–7.

Ellis, N. (2002) *Firm Foundations? A Survey of ATL Members Working in the Foundation Stage*. London: ATL.

Fabian, H. and Dunlop, A.W. (2006) 'Strong foundations: early childhood care and education. Outcomes of good practice in transition processes for children entering primary school'. UNESCO [online]. Available at: www.unesdoc.unesco.org/images/0014/001474/147463e. pdf (accessed 12/09/2013).

Feasey, R. (2005) *Creative Science: Achieving the WOW factor with 5–11 Year Olds*. London: David Fulton.

Fisher, J. (2010) *Moving on to Key Stage 1*. Maidenhead: Open University Press.

Ganea, P.A., Ma, L. and DeLoache, J.S. (2011) 'Young children's learning and transfer of biological information from picture books to real animals'. *Child Development*, 82(5): 1421–33.

Gardner, H. (1987) *The Mind's New Science: A History of the Cognitive Revolution*. New York: Basic Books.

Gardner, P. (1994) 'Representations of the relationship between science and technology in the curriculum'. *Studies in Science Education* 24(1): 1–13.

Glauert, E., Heal, C. and Cook, J. (2007) 'Knowledge and understanding of the world'. In J. Riley (ed.) *Learning in the Early Years*, 2nd edn. London: Sage, 133–66.

Goldsworthy, A., Watson, R. and Wood-Robinson, V. (2000) *Developing Understanding (AKSIS Project)*. Hatfield: Association for Science Education (ASE).

Goswami, U. (2011) 'Cognitive neuroscience and learning and development'. In J. Moyles, J. Georgeson and J. Payler (eds) *Beginning Teaching Beginning Learning in Early Years and Primary Education*. Maidenhead: Open University Press, 21–31.

Goswami, U. and Bryant, P. (2007) *Children's Cognitive Development and Learning* (Primary Review Research Survey 2/1a). Cambridge: University of Cambridge.

Harlen, W. (2000) *The Teaching of Science in Primary Schools*, 3rd edn. London: Paul Chapman.

Harlen, W. and Qualter, A. (2004) *The Teaching of Science in Primary Schools*, 4th edn. London: David Fulton.

Harrington, D.M. (1990) 'The ecology of human creativity: a psychological perspective'. In M.A. Runco and R.S. Albert (eds) *Theories of Creativity*, London: Sage, pp. 143–69.

Hattingh, L. (2013) 'Symbolic Representations of Meaning: Three to Eight Year Olds Venture into Literacy'. Unpublished PhD thesis, Bath Spa University.

Howe, L. (1990) *Collins Primary Science, Key Stage I Set Two: Stories*. London: Collins Educational.

Howe, A., Davies, D. and Ritchie, R. (2001) *Primary Design and Technology for the Future: Creativity, Culture and Citizenship in the Curriculum*. London: David Fulton.

Howe, A., Davies, D., McMahon, K., Towler, L., Collier, C. and Scott, T. (2009) *Science 5–11: A Guide for Teachers*, 2nd edn. London: Routledge.

Hutt, C. (1979) 'Play in the under-fives: form, development and function'. In J.G. Howells (ed.) *Modern Perspectives in The Psychiatry of Infancy*. New York: Brunner/Mazel, 94–144.

Jarvis, T. and Rennie, L. (1996) 'Perceptions about technology held by primary teachers in England'. *Research in Science and Technology Education* 14(1): 43–55.

Jewitt, C. (2009a) 'Different approaches to multimodality'. In C. Jewitt (ed.) *The Routledge Handbook of Multimodal Analysis*. Abingdon: Routledge, 68–84.

Jewitt, C. (2009b) 'An introduction to multimodality'. In C. Jewitt (ed.) *The Routledge Handbook of Multimodal Analysis*. Abingdon: Routledge, 3–17.

Jewitt, C., Kress, G., Ogborn, J. and Tsatsarelis, C. (2001) *Multimodal Teaching and Learning: The Rhetorics of the Science Classroom*. London: Continuum.

Johnston, J. (1996) *Early Explorations in Science*. Buckingham: Open University Press.

Johnston, J. (2011) 'Learning in the Early Years'. In W. Harlen (ed.) *ASE Guide to Primary Science Education*. Hatfield: ASE, 25–33.

Johnston, J. and Hayed, M. (1995) 'Teachers' perceptions of science and science teaching'. *European Conference on Research in Science Education, Proceedings, Leeds 1995*. Leeds: University of Leeds.

Kallery, M., Psillos, D. and Tselfes, D. (2009) 'Typical didactical activities in the Greek Early Years Science classroom: do they promote learning?' *International Journal of Science Education*, 31(9), 1187–204.

Kelly, L. and Stead, D. (2013) *Enhancing Primary Science: Developing Effective Cross-Curricula Links*. Maidenhead: Open University Press.

Knight, S. (2011) *Risk and Adventure in Early Years Outdoor Play: Learning from Forest Schools*. London: Sage.

Kress, G. (1997) *Before Writing: Rethinking the Paths to Literacy*. London: Routledge.

Kress, G. (2000) 'Multimodality'. In B. Cope and M. Kalantzis (eds) *Multiliteracies: Literacy Learning and the Design of Social Futures*. London: Routledge, 179–200.

Kress, G. (2009) 'What is Mode?' In C. Jewitt (ed.) *The Routledge Handbook of Multimodal Analysis*. London: Routledge, 54–67.

Kress, G. (2010) *Multimodality: A Social Semiotic Approach to Contemporary Communication*. London: Routledge.

Kuhn, D. (2011) 'What is scientific thinking and how does it develop?' In U.C. Goswami (ed.) *The Wiley-Blackwell Handbook of Childhood Cognitive Development*, 2nd edn. Chichester: Wiley-Blackwell, 497–523.

Layton, D. (1992) 'Values in design and technology'. In C. Budgett-Meakin (ed.) *Make the Future Work*. London: Longman, 36–53.

Leach, J., Driver, R., Scott, P. and Wood-Robinson, C. (1992) *Progression in Conceptual Understanding of Ecological Concepts by Pupils Aged 5–16*. Leeds: Centre for Studies in Science and Mathematics Education, Leeds University.

Learning and Teaching Scotland (2010) 'Curriculum for excellence: preschool into primary transitions' [online]. Available at: www.educationscotland.gov.uk/Images/EYTransitions_tcm4-630848.pdf (accessed 12/09/2013).

Lemke, J. (1990) *Talking Science: Language, Learning and Values*. Norwood, NJ: Ablex Publishing Corporation.

Lepage, J.F. and Theoret, H. (2007) 'The mirror neuron system: grasping others' actions from birth?'. *Developmental Science*, 10(5): 513–29.

Lipman, M. (2003) *Thinking in Education*. Cambridge: Cambridge University Press.

Lobue, V., Bloom Pickard, M., Sherman, K., Axford, C. and Deloache, J.S. (2013) 'Young children's interest in live animals'. *British Journal of Developmental Psychology*, 31(1): 57–69.

MacNaughton, G. and Williams, G. (2004) *Teaching Young Children: Choices in Theory and Practice*. Maidenhead: Open University Press.

Matlin, M.W. (1998) *Cognition*, 4th edn. Fort Worth, TX: Harcourt Brace College.

McCormick, R., Davidson, M. and Levinson, R. (1995) 'Making connections: students' scientific understanding of electric currents in design and technology'. In J.S. Smith (ed.) *IDATER95*, 123–7. Loughborough: Loughborough University of Technology.

McGuiness, C. (1999) *From Thinking Skills to Thinking Classrooms: A Review and Evaluation of Approaches for Developing Pupils' Thinking*. Research Report RR115. London: DfEE.

Mercer, D. (1991) 'Accounting for what goes on in classrooms: what have neo-Vygotskians got to offer?'. *Education Section Review*, 15(2): 61–7.

Mercer, N. (2000) *Words and Minds*. London: Routledge.

Mercer, N. and Littleton, K. (2007) *Dialogue and the Development of Children's Thinking*. London: Routledge.

Millar, R. (2010) 'Practical work'. In Osbourne, J. and Dillon, J. (eds) *Good Practice in Science Teaching: What Research Has To Say*, 2nd edn. London: McGraw-Hill, 108–34.

Millar, R. and Osborne, J. (1998) *Beyond 2000: Science Education for the Future*. London: King's College London, School of Education.

Moon, N. (2010) *Lucy's Picture*. London: Orchard Books.

Mortimor, E.F. and Scott, P.H. (2003) *Meaning Making in Secondary Science Classrooms*. Buckingham: Open University Press.

Moyles, J. (1989) *Just Playing? The Role and Status of Play in Early Childhood Education*. Milton Keynes: Open University Press.

Murphy, J. (1995a) *Peace at Last*. Harmondsworth: Picture Puffin.

Murphy, J. (1995b) *Whatever Next!* Harmondsworth: Picture Puffin.

National Curriculum Design and Technology Working Group (1988) *Interim Report*. London: Department for Education and Science/Welsh Office.

Naylor, S. and Keogh, B. (1997) *Starting Points for Science*. Sandbach: Millgate House.

Naylor, S. and Keogh, B. (2000) *Concept Cartoons in Science Education*. Sandbach: Millgate House.

New Zealand Ministry of Education (1996) *Te Whàriki: Early Childhood Curriculum*. Wellington: Learning Media.

Nicholas, J. and Geers, A. (2007) 'Will they catch up? The role of age at cochlear implantation in the spoken language development of children with severe to profound hearing loss'. *Journal of Speech, Language and Hearing Research*, 50: 1048–62.

Novak, J.D. and Gowin, D.B. (1984) *Learning How to Learn*. Cambidge: Cambridge University Press.

Nutbrown, C. (2011) *Threads of Thinking*, 4th edn. London: Paul Chapman.

Ofsted (Office for Standards in Education) (2003) *The Education of Six Year Olds in England, Denmark and Finland. An International Comparative Study.* London: HMSO.

Ofsted (2007) *The Foundation Stage: A Survey of 144 Settings.* London: Ofsted [online]. Available at: www.ofsted.gov.uk/resources/foundation-stage (accessed 12/09/2013).

Ollerenshaw, C. and Ritchie, R. (1997) *Primary Science: Making It Work.* London: David Fulton.

Osborne, J., Wadsworth, P. and Black, P. (1991) *SPACE Research Report: Electricity.* Liverpool: Liverpool University Press.

Osborne, J., Wadsworth, P. and Black, P. (1992) *SPACE Research Report: Processes of Life.* Liverpool: Liverpool University Press.

Osborne, J.F., Wadsworth, P., Black, P.J. and Meadows, J. (1993) *SPACE Research Report: The Earth in Space.* Liverpool: Liverpool University Press.

Payler, J. (2009) 'Co-construction and scaffolding: guidance strategies and children's meaning-making'. In T. Papatheodorou and J. Moyles (eds) *Learning Together in the Early Years: Exploring Relational Pedagogy.* London: Routledge, 120–38.

Pearce, P. (1987) *The Tooth Ball.* Harmondsworth: Picture Puffins.

Penn, H. (2005) *Unequal Childhoods: Young Children's Lives in Poor Countries.* London: Routledge.

Piaget, J. (1929) *The Child's Conception of the World.* New York: Harcourt Brace.

Piaget, J. (1978) *The Development of Thought.* Oxford: Blackwell.

Pienkowski, J. (2005) *The Fairy Tales.* Harmondsworth: Puffin.

Prensky, M. (2001) 'Digital natives, digital immigrants'. *On the Horizon, 9*(5): 1–6.

Prince, C. (2010) 'Sowing the seeds: education for sustainability within the early years curriculum'. *European Early Childhood Education Research Journal, 18*(3): 423–34.

Quick, S., Lambley, C., Newcombe, E. and Aubrey, C. (2002) *Implementing the Foundation Stage in Reception Classes.* DfES Research Report 350. London: DfES.

Ralston, S. (2011) '"It takes a garden" project: Dewey and Pudup on the politics of school gardening'. *Ethics and Environment, 16*(2): 1–24.

Rice, C. (2011) *Mama, Let's Make a Moon.* Huntsville: Familias.

Riley, J. and Savage, J. (1994) 'Bulbs, buzzers and batteries: play and science'. In J. Moyles (ed.) *The Excellence of Play.* Buckingham: Open University Press, 136–44.

Rinaldi, C. (2006) *In Dialogue with Reggio Emilia: Listening, Researching and Learning.* London: Routledge.

Ritchie, R. (2001) *Primary Design and Technology. A Process for Learning,* 2nd edn. London: David Fulton.

Robinson, M. (2008) *Child Development from Birth to Eight: A Journey Through the Early Years.* Maidenhead: Open University Press.

Robson, S. (2006) *Developing Thinking and Understanding in Young Children: An Introduction for Students.* London: Routledge.

Rogoff, B. (1990) *Apprenticeship in Thinking: Cognitive Development in Social Context.* New York: Oxford University Press.

Rogoff, B. and Wertsch, J.V. (eds) (1984) *Children's Learning in the Zone of Proximal Development.* San Francisco, CA: Jossey-Bass.

Rose, J. (2006) *The Independent Review of the Teaching of Early Reading,* London: Department for Education and Skills.

Rose, J. and Rogers, S. (2012a) 'Principles under pressure: student teachers' perspectives on final teaching practice in early childhood classrooms'. *International Journal of Early Years Education, 20*(1): 43–58.

Rose, J. and Rogers, S. (2012b) *The Role of the Adult in Early Years Settings*. Maidenhead: Open University Press.

Rosen, M. and Oxenbury, H. (1989) *We're Going on a Bear Hunt*. London: Walker Books.

Roth, W., Goulart, M.I.M. and Plakitsi, K. (2013) *Science Education During Early Childhood: A Cultural-Historical Perspective*. London: Springer.

Rumelhart, D.E. (1980) 'Schemata: the building blocks of cognition'. In R.J. Spiro, B.C. Bruce and W.F. Brewer (eds) *Theoretical Issues in Reading Comprehension: Perspectives from Cognitive Psychology, Linguistics, Artificial Intelligence and Education*. Hillsdale, NJ: Erlbaum, 33–58.

Russell, T. and Watt, D. (1990) *Primary SPACE Science Processes and Concept Exploration Project Research Reports Growth*. Liverpool: Liverpool University Press.

Rye, J. Selmer, S., Pennington, S., Vanhorn, L., Fox, S. and Kane S. (2012) 'Elementary school garden programs enhance science education for all learners'. *Teaching Exceptional Children*, 44(6): 58–65.

Sanders, D., White, G., Burge, B., Sharp, C., Eames, A., McEuneand, R. and Grayson, H. (2005) *A Study of the Transition from the Foundation Stage to Key Stage 1*. Slough: NFER.

Schweinhart, L.J., Barnes, H.V. and Weikart, D.P. (1993) *Significant Benefits: The HighScope Perry Preschool Study Through Age 27*. Ypsilanti, MI: HighScope Press.

Seung, S. (2012) *Connectome – How the Brain's Wiring Makes Us Who We Are*. London: Allen Lane.

Shonkoff, J. (2010) 'Building a new biodevelopmental framework to guide the future of early childhood policy'. *Child Development*, 81(1): 357–67.

Siegler, R.S. (1998) *Children's Thinking*. Upper Saddle River, NJ: Prentice Hall.

Siraj-Blatchford, I. (2005) 'Quality interactions in the early years'. Paper presented at TACTYC annual conference Cardiff, Wales, 4–5 November.

Siraj-Blatchford, I. (2010) 'A focus on pedagogy: Case studies of effective practice'. In K.E. Sylva, E. Melhuish, P. Sammons, I. Siraj-Blatchford and B. Taggart (eds) *Early Childhood Matters: Evidence from the Effective Pre-school and Primary Education Project*. London: Routledge, 149–65.

Siraj-Blatchford, I. and Manni, L. (2008) ' "Would you like to tidy up now?" An analysis of adult questioning in the English Foundation Stage'. *Early Years*, 28(1): 5–22.

Siraj-Blatchford, I. and Sylva, K. (2004) 'Researching pedagogy in English Pre-schools'. *British Educational Research Journal*, 30(5): 713–30.

Siraj-Blatchford, I., Sylva, K., Muttock, S., Gilden, R. and Bell, D. (2002) *Researching Effective Pedagogy in the Early Years (REPEY)*. DfES Research Report 365. London: HMSO.

Siraj-Blatchford, J. and MacLeod-Brudenell, I. (1999) *Supporting Science, Design and Technology in the Early Years*. Buckingham: Open University Press.

Smyth, J. (2007) *Enhancing Early Years Science*. Stoke on Trent: Trentham Books.

Sternberg, R. (1985) *Beyond IQ: A Triarchic Theory of Human Intelligence*. Cambridge: Cambridge University Press.

Sutherland, P. (1992) *Cognitive Development Today: Piaget and his Critics*. London: Paul Chapman.

Sylva, K., Melhuish, E., Sammons P., Siraj-Blatchford, I. and Taggart, B.(2004) *The Effective Provision of Pre-School Education (EPPE) Project: Findings from Pre-school to end of Key Stage 1* [online]. Available at: www.ioe.ac.uk/RB_pre-school_to_end_of_KS1(1).pdf (accessed12/09/2013).

Thomas, M. and Knowland, V. (2009) 'Sensitive periods in brain development – implications for education policy'. *European Psychiatric Review*, 2(1): 17–20.

Tomlinson, J. (1998) *The Owl Who Was Afraid of the Dark*. New York: Egmont Books.

Tovey, H. (2007) *Playing Outdoors, Spaces and Places, Risk and Challenge*. Maidenhead: Open University Press.

Trevarthen, C. (1995) 'How children learn before school'. Lecture to BAECE, Newcastle University, 2 November.

Trivias, E. (1993) *The Three Little Wolves and the Big Bad Pig*. New York: Aladdin.

Tsekos, C., Tsekos, E. and Christoforidou, E. (2012) 'Ecology, literature and environmental education'. International Education Studies, 5(3): 187–92.

Tunnicliffe, S.D. (2013) *Talking and Doing Science in the Early Years: A Practical Guide for Ages 2–7*. London: Routledge.

Turner, T. and Krechevsky, M. (2003) 'Who are the teachers? Who are the learners?' *Educational Leadership, 60*(7): 40–43.

Turner, T., and Wilson, D. (2010) 'Reflections on documentation: a discussion with thought leaders from Reggio Emilia'. *Theory into Practice, 49*(1): 5–13.

Vecchi, V. (2010) *Art and Creativity in Reggio Emilia: Exploring the Role and Potential of Ateliers in Early Childhood Education*. London: Routledge.

von Glasersfeld, E. (1989) 'Learning as a constructive activity'. In P. Murphy and R. Moon (eds) *Developments in Learning and Assessment, 5–18*. Sevenoaks: Hodder & Stoughton, 135–46.

Vygotsky, L. (1978) *Mind in Society*. Cambridge, MA: Harvard University Press.

Waddell, M. (2001) *Can't You Sleep Little Bear?* London: Walker Books.

Watt, F. (2004a) *That's Not My Dolly*. London: Usborne.

Watt, F. (2004b) *That's Not My Dinosaur*. London: Usborne.

Welsh Assembly (2008) *Framework for Children's Learning for 3- to 7-Year-Olds in Wales*. Cardiff: Welsh Assembly.

Wertsh, J.V. (1998) *Mind as Action*. New York: Oxford University Press.

Whitebread, D. (ed.) (1996) *Teaching and Learning in the Early Years*. London: Routledge.

Whitehead, M. (2010) *Language and Literacy in the Early Years 0–7*, 4th edn. London: Sage.

Wild, M. (2011) 'Thinking together: exploring aspects of shared thinking between young children during a computer-based literacy task'. *International Journal of Early Years Education, 19*(3): 219–31.

Wood, D. and Wood, H. (1996) 'Vygotsky, tutoring and learning'. *Oxford Review of Education, 22*(1): 5–16.

Wood, D., Bruner, J. and Ross, G. (1976) 'The role of tutoring in problem-solving'. *Journal of Child Psychology and Psychiatry, 17*: 89–100.

Index